ONLY YESTERDAY

ONLY YESTERDAY

*An Informal History
of the Nineteen-Twenties*

by

FREDERICK LEWIS ALLEN

PERENNIAL LIBRARY
Harper & Row, Publishers
New York, Hagerstown, San Francisco, London

To the memory of D. P. A.

ONLY YESTERDAY *was originally published by Harper & Row, Publishers, in 1931.*

First PERENNIAL LIBRARY *edition published 1964 by Harper & Row, Publishers, Incorporated, New York.*

ISBN: 0-06-080004-6

78 79 80 81 82   30 29 28 27 26 25 24 23 22

Contents

Preface

This book is an attempt to tell, and in some measure to interpret, the story of what in the future may be considered a distinct era in American history: the eleven years between the end of the war with Germany (November 11, 1918) and the stock-market panic which culminated on November 13, 1929, hastening and dramatizing the destruction of what had been known as Coolidge (and Hoover) Prosperity.

Obviously the writing of a history so soon after the event has involved breaking much new ground. Professor Preston William Slosson, in *The Great Crusade and After*, has carried his story almost to the end of this period, but the scheme of his book is quite different from that of mine; and although many other books have dealt with one aspect of the period or another, I have been somewhat surprised to find how many of the events of those years have never before been chronicled in full. For example, the story of the Harding scandals (in so far as it is now known) has never been written before except in fragments, and although the Big Bull Market has been analyzed and discussed a thousand times, it has never been fully presented in narrative form as the extraordinary economic and social phenomenon which it was.

Further research will undoubtedly disclose errors and deficiencies in the book, and the passage of time will reveal the shortsightedness of many of my judgments and interpretations. A contemporary history is bound to be anything but definitive. Yet half the enjoyment of writing it has lain in the effort to reduce to some sort of logical and coherent order a mass of material untouched by any previous historian; and I have wondered whether some readers might not be interested and perhaps amused to find events and circumstances which they remember well—which seem to have happened only yesterday—woven into a pattern which at least masquerades as history. One advantage the book will have over most histories: hardly anyone old enough to read it can fail to remember the entire period with which it deals.

As for my emphasis upon the changing state of the public mind and upon the sometimes trivial happenings with which it was preoccupied, this has been deliberate. It has seemed to me that one who writes at such close range, while recollection is still fresh, has a special opportunity to record the fads and fashions and follies of the time, the things which millions of people thought about and talked about and became excited about and which at once touched their daily lives; and that he may prudently leave to subsequent historians certain events and policies, particularly in the field of foreign affairs, the effect of which upon the life of the ordinary citizen was less immediate and may not be fully measurable for a long time. (I am indebted to Mr. Mark Sullivan for what he has done in the successive volumes of *Our Own Times* to develop this method of writing contemporary history.) Naturally I have attempted to bring together the innumerable threads of the story so as to reveal the fundamental trends in our national life and national thought during the nineteen-twenties.

In an effort to eliminate footnotes and at the same time to express my numerous obligations, I have added an appendix listing my principal sources.

F. L. A.

I

Prelude: May, 1919

If time were suddenly to turn back to the earliest days of the Post-war Decade, and you were to look about you, what would seem strange to you? Since 1919 the circumstances of American life have been transformed—yes, but exactly how?

Let us refresh our memories by following a moderately well-to-do young couple of Cleveland or Boston or Seattle or Baltimore—it hardly matters which—through the routine of an ordinary day in May, 1919. (I select that particular date, six months after the Armistice of 1918, because by then the United States had largely succeeded in turning from the ways of war to those of peace, yet the profound alterations wrought by the Post-war Decade had hardly begun to take place.) There is no better way of suggesting what the passage of a few years has done to change you and me and the environment in which we live.

From the appearance of Mr. Smith as he comes to the breakfast table on this May morning in 1919, you would hardly know that you are not in the nineteen-thirties (though you might, perhaps, be struck by the narrowness of his trousers). The movement of men's fashions is glacial. It is different, however, with Mrs. Smith.

She comes to breakfast in a suit, the skirt of which—rather

tight at the ankles—hangs just six inches from the ground. She
has read in *Vogue* the alarming news that skirts may become
even shorter, and that "not since the days of the Bourbons has
the woman of fashion been visible so far above the ankle"; but
six inches is still the orthodox clearance. She wears low shoes
now, for spring has come; but all last winter she protected her
ankles either with spats or with high laced "walking-boots," or
with high patent-leather shoes with contrasting buckskin tops.
Her stockings are black (or tan, perhaps, if she wears tan
shoes); the idea of flesh-colored stockings would appall her. A
few minutes ago Mrs. Smith was surrounding herself with an
"envelope chemise" and a petticoat; and from the thick ruffles
on her undergarments it was apparent that she was not disposed to make herself more boyish in form than ample nature
intended.

Mrs. Smith may use powder, but she probably draws the line
at paint. Although the use of cosmetics is no longer, in 1919,
considered *prima facie* evidence of a scarlet career, and sophisticated young girls have already begun to apply them with
some bravado, most well-brought-up women still frown upon
rouge. The beauty-parlor industry is in its infancy; there are a
dozen hair-dressing parlors for every beauty parlor, and Mrs.
Smith has never heard of such dark arts as that of face-lifting.
When she puts on her hat to go shopping she will add a veil
pinned neatly together behind her head. In the shops she will
perhaps buy a bathing-suit for use in the summer; it will con-
sist of an outer tunic of silk or cretonne over a tight knitted
undergarment—worn, of course, with long stockings.

Her hair is long, and the idea of a woman ever frequenting a
barber shop would never occur to her. If you have forgotten
what the general public thought of short hair in those days,
listen to the remark of the manager of the Palm Garden in
New York when reporters asked him, one night in November,
1918, how he happened to rent his hall for a pro-Bolshevist
meeting which had led to a riot. Explaining that a well-dressed
woman had come in a fine automobile to make arrangements
for the use of the auditorium, he added, "Had we noticed then,
as we do now, that she had short hair, we would have refused
to rent the hall." In Mrs. Smith's mind, as in that of the manager of the Palm Garden, short-haired women, like long-haired
men, are associated with radicalism, if not with free love.

The breakfast to which Mr. and Mrs. Smith sit down may

have been arranged with a view to the provision of a sufficient number of calories—they need only to go to Childs' to learn about calories—but in all probability neither of them has ever heard of a vitamin.

As Mr. Smith eats, he opens the morning paper. It is almost certainly not a tabloid, no matter how rudimentary Mr. Smith's journalistic tastes may be: for although Mr. Hearst has already experimented with small-sized picture papers, the first conspicuously successful tabloid is yet to be born. Not until June 26, 1919, will the New York *Daily News* reach the newsstands, beginning a career that will bring its daily circulation in one year to nearly a quarter of a million, in five years to over four-fifths of a million, and in ten years to the amazing total of over one million three hundred thousand.

Strung across the front page of Mr. Smith's paper are headlines telling of the progress of the American Navy seaplane, the NC-4, on its flight across the Atlantic *via* the Azores. That flight is the most sensational news story of May, 1919. (Alcock and Brown have not yet crossed the ocean in a single hop; they will do it a few weeks hence, eight long years ahead of Lindbergh.) But there is other news, too: of the Peace Conference at Paris, where the Treaty is now in its later stages of preparation; of the successful oversubscription of the Victory Loan ("Sure, we'll finish the job!" the campaign posters have been shouting); of the arrival of another transport with soldiers from overseas; of the threat of a new strike; of a speech by Mayor Ole Hanson of Seattle denouncing that scourge of the times, the I. W. W.; of the prospects for the passage of the Suffrage Amendment, which it is predicted will enable women to take "a finer place in the national life"; and of Henry Ford's libel suit against the Chicago *Tribune*—in the course of which he will call Benedict Arnold a writer, and in reply to the question, "Have there been any revolutions in this country?" will answer, "Yes, in 1812."

If Mr. Smith attends closely to the sporting news, he may find obscure mention of a young pitcher and outfielder for the Boston Red Sox named Ruth. But he will hardly find the Babe's name in the headlines. (In April, 1919, Ruth made one home run; in May, two; but the season was much further advanced before sporting writers began to notice that he was running up a new record for swatting—twenty-nine home runs for the year; the season had closed before the New York Yankees, seeing gold in the hills, bought him for $125,000; and the summer of 1920 had arrived before a man died of excitement when he saw Ruth smash a ball into the bleachers, and it became clear that the mob had found a new idol. In 1919, the veteran Ty Cobb, not Ruth, led the American League in batting.)

The sporting pages inform Mr. Smith that Rickard has selected Toledo as the scene of a forthcoming encounter between the heavyweight champion, Jess Willard, and another future idol of the mob, Jack Dempsey. (They met, you may recall, on the Fourth of July, 1919, and sober citizens were horrified to read that 19,650 people were so depraved as to sit in a broiling sun to watch Dempsey knock out the six-foot-six-inch champion in the third round. How would the sober citizens have felt if they had known that eight years later a Dempsey-Tunney fight would bring in more than five times as much money in gate receipts as this battle of Toledo?) In the sporting pages there may be news of Bobby Jones, the seventeen-year-old Southern golf champion, or of William T. Tilden, Jr., who is winning tennis tournaments here and there, but neither of them is yet a national champion. And even if Jones were to win this year he would hardly become a great popular hero; for although golf is gaining every day in popularity, it has not yet become an inevitable part of the weekly ritual of the American business man. Mr. Smith very likely still scoffs at "grown men who spend their time knocking a little white ball along the ground"; it is quite certain that he has never heard of plus fours; and if he should happen to play golf he had better not show his knickerbockers in the city streets, or small boys will shout to him, "Hey, get some men's pants!"

Did I say that by May, 1919, the war was a thing of the past? There are still reminders of it in Mr. Smith's paper. Not only the news from the Peace Conference, not only the item about Sergeant Alvin York being on his way home; there is still that ugliest reminder of all, the daily casualty list.

Mr. and Mrs. Smith discuss a burning subject, the High Cost of Living. Mr. Smith is hoping for an increase in salary, but meanwhile the family income seems to be dwindling as prices rise. Everything is going up—food, rent, clothing, and taxes. These are the days when people remark that even the man without a dollar is fifty cents better off than he once was, and that if we coined seven-cent pieces for street-car fares, in another year we should have to discontinue them and begin to coin fourteen-cent pieces. Mrs. Smith, confronted with an appeal from Mr. Smith for economy, reminds him that milk has jumped since 1914 from nine to fifteen cents a quart, sirloin steak from twenty-seven to forty-two cents a pound, butter from thirty-two to sixty-one cents a pound, and fresh eggs from thirty-four to sixty-two cents a dozen. No wonder people on fixed salaries are suffering, and colleges are beginning to talk of applying the money-raising methods learned during the Liberty Loan campaigns to the increasing of college endowments. Rents are almost worse than food prices, for that matter; since the Armistice there has been an increasing shortage of houses and apartments, and the profiteering landlord has become an object of popular hate along with the profiteering middleman. Mr. Smith tells his wife that "these profiteers are about as bad as the I. W. W.'s." He could make no stronger statement.

Breakfast over, Mr. Smith gets into his automobile to drive to the office. The car is as likely to be a Lexington, a Maxwell, a Briscoe, or a Templar as to be a Dodge, Buick, Chevrolet, Cadillac, or Hudson, and it surely will not be a Chrysler; Mr. Chrysler has just been elected first vice-president of the General Motors Corporation. Whatever the make of the car, it stands higher than the cars of the nineteen-thirties; the passengers look down upon their surroundings from an imposing altitude. The chances are nine to one that Mr. Smith's automobile is open (only 10.3 per cent of the cars manufactured in 1919 were closed). The vogue of the sedan is just beginning. Closed cars are still associated in the public mind with wealth; the hated profiteer of the newspaper cartoon rides in a limousine.

If Mr. Smith's car is one of the high, hideous, but efficient model T Fords of the day, let us watch him for a minute. He climbs in by the right-hand door (for there is no left-hand door by the front seat), reaches over to the wheel, and sets the spark and throttle levers in a position like that of the hands of a clock at ten minutes to three. Then, unless he has paid extra for a self-starter, he gets out to crank. Seizing the crank in his right hand carefully, for a friend of his once broke his arm cranking), he slips his left forefinger through a loop of wire that controls the choke. He pulls the loop of wire, he revolves the crank mightily, and as the engine at last roars, he leaps to the trembling running-board, leans in, and moves the spark and throttle to twenty-five minutes of two. Perhaps he reaches the throttle before the engine falters into silence, but if it is a cold morning perhaps he does not. In that case, back to the crank again and the loop of wire. Mr. Smith wishes Mrs. Smith would come out and sit in the driver's seat and pull that spark lever down before the engine has time to die.

Finally he is at the wheel with the engine roaring as it should. He releases the emergency hand-brake, shoves his left foot against the low-speed pedal, and as the car sweeps loudly out into the street, he releases his left foot, lets the car into high gear, and is off. Now his only care is for that long hill down the street; yesterday he burned his brake on it, and this morning he must remember to brake with the reverse pedal, or the low-speed pedal, or both, or all three in alternation. (Jam your foot down on any of the three pedals and you slow the car.)

Mr. Smith is on the open road—a good deal more open than it will be a decade hence. On his way to work he passes hardly a third as many cars as he will pass in 1929; there are less than seven million passenger cars registered in the United States in 1919, as against over twenty-three million cars only ten years later. He is unlikely to find many concrete roads in his vicinity, and the lack of them is reflected in the speed regulations. A few states like California and New York permit a rate of thirty miles an hour in 1919, but the average limit is twenty (as against thirty-five or forty in 1931). The Illinois rate of 1919 is characteristic of the day; it limits the driver to fifteen miles in residential parts of cities, ten miles in built-up sections, and six miles on curves. The idea of making a hundred-mile trip in two and a half hours—as will constantly be done in the nineteen-thirties by drivers who consider themselves conservative—would seem to Mr. Smith perilous, and with the roads of 1919 to drive on he would be right.

In the course of his day at the office, Mr. Smith discusses business conditions. It appears that things are looking up. There was a period of uncertainty and falling stock prices after the Armistice, as huge government contracts were canceled and plants which had been running overtime on war work began to throw off men by the thousand, but since then conditions have been better. Everybody is talking about the bright prospects for international trade and American shipping. The shipyards are running full tilt. There are too many strikes going on, to be sure; it seems as if the demands of labor for higher and higher wages would never be satisfied, although Mr. Smith admits that in a way you can't blame the men, with prices still mounting week by week. But there is so much business activity that the men being turned out of army camps to look for jobs are being absorbed better than Mr. Smith ever thought they would be. It was back in the winter and early spring that there was so much talk about the ex-service men walking the streets without work; it was then that *Life* ran a cartoon which represented Uncle Sam saying to a soldier, "Nothing is too good for you, my boy! What would you like?" and the soldier answering, "A job." Now the boys seem to be sifting slowly but surely into the ranks of the employed, and the only clouds on the business horizon are strikes and Bolshevism and the dangerous wave of speculation in the stock market.

"Bull Market Taxes Nerves of Brokers," cry the headlines in the financial pages, and they speak of "Long Hours for Clerks." Is there a familiar ring to those phrases? Does it seem natural to you, remembering as you do the Big Bull Market of 1928 and 1929, that the decision to keep the Stock Exchange closed over the 31st of May, 1919, should elicit such newspaper comments as this: "The highly specialized machine which handles the purchase and sales of stocks and bonds in the New York market is fairly well exhausted and needs a rest"? Then listen; in May, 1919, it was a long series of *million-and-a-half-share* days which was causing financiers to worry and the Federal Reserve Board to consider issuing a warning against speculation. During that year a new record of six two-million-share days was set up, and on only 145 days did the trading amount to over a million shares. What would Mr. Smith and his associates think if they were to be told that within eleven years there would occur a sixteen-million-share day; and that they would see the time when three-million-share days would be referred to as "virtual stagnation" or as "listless trading by professionals only, with the general public refusing to become interested"? The price of a seat on the New York Stock Exchange in 1919 ranged between $60,000 and a new high record of $110,000; it would be hard for Mr. Smith to believe that before the end of the decade seats on the Exchange would fetch a half million.

In those days of May, 1919, the record of daily Stock Exchange transactions occupied hardly a newspaper column. The Curb Market record referred to trading on a real curb—to that extraordinary outdoor market in Broad Street, New York, where boys with telephone receivers clamped to their heads hung out of windows high above the street and grimaced and wigwagged through the din to traders clustered on the pavement below. And if there was anything Mrs. Smith was certain not to have on her mind as she went shopping, it was the price of stocks. Yet the "unprecedented bull market" of 1919 brought fat profits to those who participated in it. Between February 15th and May 14th, Baldwin Locomotive rose from 72 to 93, General Motors from 130 to 191, United States Steel from 90 to 104½, and International Mercantile Marine common (to which traders were attracted on account of the apparently boundless possibilities of shipping) from 23 to 47⅝.

When Mr. Smith goes out to luncheon, he has to proceed to his club in a roundabout way, for a regiment of soldiers just returned from Europe is on parade and the central thoroughfares of the city are blocked with crowds. It is a great season for parades, this spring of 1919. As the transports from Brest swing up New York Harbor, the men packed solid on the decks are greeted by Major Hylan's Committee of Welcome, represented sometimes by the Mayor's spruce young secretary, Grover Whalen, who in later years is to reduce welcoming to a science and raise it to an art. New York City has built in honor of the homecoming troops a huge plaster arch in Fifth Avenue at Madison Square, toward the design of which forty artists are said to have contributed. ("But the result," comments the New York *Tribune*, sadly, "suggests four hundred rather than forty. It holds everything that was ever on an arch anywhere, the lay mind suspects, not forgetting the horses on top of a certain justly celebrated Brandenburg Gate.") Farther up the Avenue, before the Public Library, there is a shrine of pylons and palms called the Court of the Heroic Dead, of whose decorative effect the *Tribune* says, curtly, "Add perils of death." A few blocks to the north an arch of jewels is suspended above the Avenue "like a net of precious stones, between two white pillars surmounted by stars"; on this arch colored searchlights play at night with superb effect. The Avenue is hung with flags from end to end; and as the Twenty-seventh Division parades under the arches the air is white with confetti and ticker tape, and the sidewalks are jammed with cheering crowds. Nor is New York alone in its enthusiasm for the returning soldiers; every other city has its victory parade, with the city elders on the reviewing stand and flags waving and the bayonets of the troops glistening in the spring sunlight and the bands playing "The Long, Long Trail." Not yet disillusioned, the nation welcomes its heroes—and the heroes only wish the fuss were all over and they could get into civilian clothes and sleep late in the mornings and do what they please, and try to forget.

Mr. and Mrs. Smith have been invited to a tea dance at one of the local hotels, and Mr. Smith hurries from his office to the scene of revelry. If the hotel is up to the latest wrinkles, it has a jazz-band instead of the traditional orchestra for dancing, but not yet does a saxophone player stand out in the foreground and contort from his instrument that piercing music, "endlessly sorrowful yet endlessly unsentimental, with no past, no memory, no future, no hope," which William Bolitho called the *Zeitgeist* of the Post-war Age. The jazz-band plays "I'm Always Chasing Rainbows," the tune which Harry Carroll wrote in wartime after Harrison Fisher persuaded him that Chopin's "Fantasie Impromptu" had the makings of a good ragtime tune. It plays, too, "Smiles" and "Dardanella" and "Hindustan" and "Japanese Sandman" and "I Love You Sunday," and that other song which is to give the Post-war Decade one of its most persistent and wearisome slang phrases, "I'll Say She Does." There are a good many military uniforms among the fox-trotting dancers. There is one French officer in blue; the days are not past when a foreign uniform adds the zest of war-time romance to any party. In the more dimly lighted palm-room there may be a juvenile petting party or two going on, but of this Mr. and Mrs. Smith are doubtless oblivious. F. Scott Fitzgerald has yet to confront a horrified republic with the Problem of the Younger Generation

After a few dances, Mr. Smith wanders out to the bar (if this is not a dry state). He finds there a group of men downing Bronxes and Scotch highballs, and discussing with dismay the

approach of prohibition. On the 1st of July the so-called
Wartime Prohibition Law is to take effect (designed as a war
measure, but not signed by the President until after the Armistice), and already the ratification of the Eighteenth
Amendment has made it certain that prohibition is to be permanent. Even now, distilling and brewing are forbidden. Liquor is therefore expensive, as the frequenters of midnight
cabarets are learning to their cost. Yet here is the bar, still
quite legally doing business. Of course there is not a woman
within eyeshot of it; drinking by women is unusual in 1919,
and drinking at a bar is an exclusively masculine prerogative.
Although Mr. and Mrs. Smith's hosts may perhaps serve cocktails before dinner this evening, Mr. and Mrs. Smith have never
heard of cocktail parties as a substitute for tea parties.

As Mr. Smith stands with his foot on the brass rail, he listens
to the comments on the coming of prohibition. There is some
indignant talk about it, but even here the indignation is by no
means unanimous. One man, as he tosses off his Bronx, says
that he'll miss his liquor for a time, he supposes, but he thinks
"his boys will be better off for living in a world where there is
no alcohol"; and two or three others agree with him. Prohibition has an overwhelming majority behind it throughout the United States; the Spartan fervor of war-time has not
yet cooled. Nor is there anything ironical in the expressed
assumption of these men that when the Eighteenth Amendment goes into effect, alcohol will be banished from the land.
They look forward vaguely to an endless era of actual drought.

At the dinner party to which Mr. and Mrs. Smith go that
evening, some of the younger women may be bold enough to
smoke, but they probably puff their cigarettes self-consciously,
even defiantly. (The national consumption of cigarettes in
1919, excluding the very large sizes, is less than half of what it
will be by 1930.)

After dinner the company may possibly go to the movies to
see Charlie Chaplin in "Shoulder Arms" or Douglas Fairbanks
in "The Knickerbocker Buckaroo" or Mary Pickford in
"Daddy Long Legs," or Theda Bara, or Pearl White, or
Griffith's much touted and much wept-at "Broken Blossoms."
Or they may play auction bridge (not contract, of course).
Mah Jong, which a few years hence will be almost obligatory,
is still over the horizon. They may discuss such best sellers of

the day as *The Four Horsemen of the Apocalypse*, Tarkington's *The Magnificent Ambersons*, Conrad's *Arrow of Gold*, Brand Whitlock's *Belgium*, and Wells's *The Undying Fire*. (The *Outline of History* is still unwritten.) They may go to the theater: the New York successes of May, 1919, include "Friendly Enemies," "Three Faces East," and "The Better 'Ole," which have been running ever since war-time and are still going strong, and also "Listen, Lester," Gillette in "Dear Brutus," Frances Starr in "Tiger! Tiger!" and—to satisfy a growing taste for bedroom farce—such tidbits as "Up in Mabel's Room." The Theater Guild is about to launch its first drama, Ervine's "John Ferguson." The members of the senior class at Princeton have just voted "Lightnin'" their favorite play (after "Macbeth" and "Hamlet," for which they cast the votes expected of educated men), and their favorite actresses, in order of preference, are Norma Talmadge, Elsie Ferguson, Marguerite Clark, Constance Talmadge, and Madge Kennedy.

One thing the Smiths certainly will not do this evening. They will not listen to the radio.

For there is no such thing as radio broadcasting. Here and there a mechanically inclined boy has a wireless set, with which, if he knows the Morse code, he may listen to messages from ships at sea and from land stations equipped with sending apparatus. The radiophone has been so far developed that men flying in an airplane over Manhattan have talked with other men in an office-building below. But the broadcasting of speeches and music—well, it was tried years ago by DeForest, and "nothing came of it." Not until the spring of 1920 will Frank Conrad of the Westinghouse Company of East Pittsburgh, who has been sending out phonograph music and baseball scores from the barn which he has rigged up as a spare-time research station, find that so many amateur wireless operators are listening to them that a Pittsburgh newspaper has had the bright idea of advertising radio equipment "which may be used by those who listen to Dr. Conrad's programs." And not until this advertisement appears will the Westinghouse officials decide to open the first broadcasting station in history in order to stimulate the sale of their supplies.

One more word about Mr. and Mrs. Smith and we may dismiss them for the night. Not only have they never heard of radio broadcasting; they have never heard of Coué, the Dayton Trial, cross-word puzzles, bathing-beauty contests, John J. Raskob, racketeers, Teapot Dome, Coral Gables, the *American Mercury*, Sacco and Vanzetti, companionate marriage, brokers' loan statistics, Michael Arlen, the Wall Street explosion, confession magazines, the Hall-Mills case, radio stock, speakeasies, Al Capone, automatic traffic lights, or Charles A. Lindbergh.

The Post-war Decade lies before them.

II

Back to Normalcy

Early on the morning of November 11, 1918, President Woodrow Wilson wrote in pencil, on an ordinary sheet of White House stationery, a message to the American people:

My Fellow Countrymen: The armistice was signed this morning. Everything for which America fought has been accomplished. It will now be our fortunate duty to assist by example, by sober, friendly counsel, and by material aid in the establishment of just democracy throughout the world.

Never was document more Wilsonian. In those three sentences spoke the Puritan schoolmaster, cool in a time of great emotions, calmly setting the lesson for the day; the moral idealist, intent on a peace of reconciliation rather than a peace of hate; and the dogmatic prophet of democracy, who could not dream that the sort of institutions in which he had believed all his life were not inevitably the best for all nations everywhere. Yet the spirit of the message suggests, at the same time, that of another war President. It was such a document as Lincoln might have written.

But if the man in the White House was thinking of Abraham Lincoln as he wrote those sentences—and no doubt he was— there was something which perhaps he overlooked. Counsels of idealism sometimes fail in the relaxation that comes with peace. Lincoln had not lived to see what happens to a policy of "sober, friendly counsel" in a post-war decade; he had been taken off in the moment of triumph.

Woodrow Wilson was not to be so fortunate.

[2]

What a day that 11th of November was! It was not quite three o'clock in the morning when the State Department gave out to the dozing newspaper men the news that the Armistice had really been signed. Four days before, a false report of the end of hostilities had thrown the whole United States into a delirium of joy. People had poured out of offices and shops and paraded the streets singing and shouting, ringing bells, blowing tin horns, smashing one another's hats, cheering soldiers in uniform, draping themselves in American flags, gathering in closely packed crowds before the newspaper bulletin boards, making a wild and hilarious holiday; in New York, Fifth Avenue had been closed to traffic and packed solid with surging men and women, while down from the windows of the city fluttered 155 tons of ticker tape and torn paper. It did not seem possible that such an outburst could be repeated. But it was.

By half-past four on the morning of the 11th, sirens, whistles, and bells were rousing the sleepers in a score of American cities, and newsboys were shouting up and down the dark streets. At first people were slow to credit the report; they had been fooled once and were not to be fooled again. Along an avenue in Washington, under the windows of the houses of government officials, a boy announced with painstaking articulation, "THE WAR IS OVAH! OFFICIAL GOVERNMENT ANNOUNCEMENT CONFIRMS THE NEWS!" He did not mumble as newsboys ordinarily do; he knew that this was a time to convince the skeptical by being intelligible and specific. The words brought incredible relief. A new era of peace and of hope was beginning—had already begun,

So the tidings spread throughout the country. In city after city mid-morning found offices half deserted, signs tacked up on shop doors reading "CLOSED FOR THE KAISER'S FUNERAL," people marching up and down the streets again as they had four days previously, pretty girls kissing every soldier they saw, automobiles slowly creeping through the crowds and intentionally backfiring to add to the noise of horns and rattles and every other sort of din-making device. Eight hundred Barnard College girls snake-danced on Morningside Heights in New York; and in Times Square, early in the morning, a girl mounted the platform of "Liberty Hall," a building set up for war-campaign purposes, and sang the "Doxology" before hushed crowds.

Yet as if to mock the Wilsonian statement about "sober, friendly counsel," there were contrasting celebrations in which the mood was not that of pious thanksgiving, but of triumphant hate. Crowds burned the Kaiser in effigy. In New York, a dummy of the Kaiser was washed down Wall Street with a firehose; men carried a coffin made of soapboxes up and down Fifth Avenue, shouting that the Kaiser was within it, "resting in pieces"; and on Broadway at Seventieth Street a boy drew pictures of the Kaiser over and over again on the sidewalk, to give the crowds the delight of trampling on them.

So the new era of peace began.

But a million men—to paraphrase Bryan—cannot spring from arms overnight. There were still over three million and a half Americans in the military service, over two million of them in Europe. Uniforms were everywhere. Even after the tumult and shouting of November 11th had died, the Expeditionary Forces were still in the trenches, making ready for the long, cautious march into Germany; civilians were still saving sugar and eating strange dark breads and saving coal: it was not until ten days had passed that the "lightless" edict of the Fuel Administration was withdrawn, and Broadway and a dozen lesser white ways in other cities blazed once more; the railroads were still operated by the government, and one bought one's tickets at United States Railroad Administration Consolidated Ticket Offices; the influenza epidemic, which had taken more American lives than had the Germans, and had caused thousands of men and women to go about fearfully with white cloth masks over their faces, was only just abating; the newspapers were packed with reports from the armies in Europe, news of the revolution in Germany, of Mr. Wilson's peace preparations, of the United War Work Campaign, to the exclusion of almost everything else; and day after day, week after week, month after month, the casualty lists went on, and from Maine to Oregon men and women searched them in daily apprehension.

November would normally have brought the climax of the football season, but now scratch college teams, made up mostly of boys who had been wearing the uniform of the Students' Army Training Corps, played benefit games "to put the War Work Fund over the top"; and further to strengthen the will to give, Charlie Brickley of Harvard drop-kicked a football across Wall Street into the arms of Jack Gates of Yale on the balcony of the Stock Exchange. Not only the news columns of the papers, but the advertisements also, showed the domination of war-time emotions. Next to an editorial on "The Right to Hate the Huns," ᐟor a letter suggesting that the appropriate punishment for the Kaiser would be to deport him from country to country, always as an "undesirable alien," the reader would find a huge United War Work Fund advertisement, urging him to GIVE—GIVE—GIVE! On another page, under the title of PREPARING AMERICA TO REBUILD THE WORLD, he would find a patriotic blast beginning, "Now that liberty has triumphed, now that the forces of Right have begun their reconstruction of humanity's morals, the world faces a material task of equal magnitude," and not until he had waded through several more sentences of sonorous rhetoric would he discover that this "material task" was to be accomplished through the use of Blank's Steel Windows.

And even as the process of demobilization got definitely under way, as the soldiers began to troop home from the camps, as censorship was done away with and lights were permitted to burn brightly again and women began to buy sugar with an easy conscience; even as this glorious peace began to seem a reality and not a dream, the nation went on thinking with the mind of people at war. They had learned during the preceding nineteen months to strike down the thing they hated; not to argue or hesitate, but to strike. Germany had been struck down, but it seemed that there was another danger on the horizon. Bolshevism was spreading from Russia through Europe; Bolshevism might spread to the United States. They struck at it—or at what they thought was it. A week after the Armistice, Mayor Hylan of New York forbade the display of the red flag in the streets and ordered the police to "disperse all unlawful assemblages." A few nights later, while the Socialists were holding a mass meeting in Madison Square Garden, five hundred soldiers and sailors gathered from the surrounding streets and tried to storm the doors. It took twenty-two mounted policemen to break up the milling mob and restore order. The next evening there was another riot before the doors of the Palm Garden, farther up town, where a meeting of sympathy for Revolutionary Russia was being held under the auspices of the Women's International League. Again soldiers and sailors were the chief offenders. They packed Fifty-eighth Street for a block, shouting and trying to break their way into the Palm Garden, and in the *mêlée* six persons were badly beaten up. One of the victims was a conservative stockbroker. He was walking up Lexington Avenue with a lady, and seeing the yelling crowd, he asked someone what all the excitement was about. A sailor called out, "Hey, fellows, here's another of the Bolsheviks," and in a moment a score of men had leaped upon him, ripped off his tie, and nearly knocked him unconscious. These demonstrations were to prove the first of a long series of post-war anti-Red riots.

The nation at war had formed the habit of summary action, and it was not soon unlearned. The circumstances and available methods had changed, that was all. Employers who had watched with resentment the rising scale of wages paid to labor, under the encouragement of a government that wanted no disaffection in the ranks of the workers, now felt that their chance had come. The Germans were beaten; the next thing to do was to teach labor a lesson. Labor agitators were a bunch of Bolsheviks, anyhow, and it was about time that a man had a chance to make a decent profit in his business. Meanwhile labor, facing a steadily mounting cost of living, and realizing that it was no longer unpatriotic to strike for higher wages, decided to teach the silk-stockinged profiteering employer a lesson in his turn. The result was a bitter series of strikes and lockouts.

There was a summary action with regard to liquor, too. During the war alcohol had been an obvious menace to the fighting efficiency of the nation. The country, already largely dry by state law and local option, had decided to banish the saloon once and for all. War-time psychology was dominant; no halfway measure would serve. The War-time Prohibition Act was already on the books and due to take effect July 1, 1919. But this was not enough. The Eighteenth Amendment, which would make prohibition permanent and (so it was thought) effective, had been passed by Congress late in 1917, and many of the states had ratified it before the war ended.

With the convening of the state legislatures in January, 1919, the movement for ratification went ahead with amazing speed. The New York *Tribune* said that it was "as if a sailing-ship on a windless ocean were sweeping ahead, propelled by some invisible force." "Prohibition seems to be the fashion, just as drinking once was," exclaimed the *Times* editorially. By January 16th—within nine weeks of the Armistice—the necessary thirty-six States had ratified the Amendment. Even New York State fell in line a few days later. Whisky and the "liquor ring" were struck at as venomously as were the Reds. There were some misgivings, to be sure; there were those who pointed out that three million men in uniform might not like the new dispensation; but the country was not in the mood to think twice. Prohibition went through on the tide of the war spirit of "no compromise."

Yet though the headlong temper of war-time persisted after the Armistice, in one respect the coming of peace brought about a profound change. During the war the nation had gone about its tasks in a mood of exaltation. Top sergeants might remark that the only good Hun was a dead one and that this stuff about making the world safe for democracy was all bunk; four-minute speakers might shout that the Kaiser ought to be boiled in oil; the fact remained that millions of Americans were convinced that they were fighting in a holy cause, for the rights of oppressed nations, for the end of all war forever, for all that the schoolmaster in Washington so eloquently preached. The singing of the "Doxology" by the girl in Times Square represented their true feeling as truly as the burning of the Kaiser in effigy. The moment the Armistice was signed, however, a subtle change began.

Now those who had never liked Wilson, who thought that he had stayed out of the war too long, that milk and water ran in his veins instead of blood, that he should never have been forgiven for his treatment of Roosevelt and Wood, that he was a dangerous radical at heart and a menace to the capitalistic system, that he should never have appealed to the country for the election of a Democratic Congress, or that his idea of going to Paris himself to the Peace Conference was a sign of egomania—these people began to speak out freely. There were others who were tired of applauding the French, or who had ideas of their own about the English and the English attitude toward Ireland, or who were sick of hearing about "our noble

Allies" in general, or who thought that we had really gone into the war to save our own skins and that the Wilsonian talk about making the world safe for democracy was dangerous and hypocritical nonsense. They, too, began to speak out freely. Now one could say with impunity, "We've licked the Germans and we're going to lick these damned Bolsheviki, and it's about time we got after Wilson and his crew of pacifists." The tension of the war was relaxing, the bubble of idealism was pricked. As the first weeks of peace slipped away, it began to appear doubtful whether the United States was quite as ready as Woodrow Wilson had thought "to assist in the establishment of just democracy throughout the world."

[3]

But the mind of Mr. Wilson, too, had been molded by the war. Since April, 1917, his will had been irresistible. In the United States open opposition to his leadership had been virtually stifled: it was unpatriotic to differ with the President. His message and speeches had set the tone of popular thought about American war aims and the terms of eventual peace. In Europe his eloquence had proved so effective that statesmen had followed his lead perforce and allowed the Armistice to be made upon his terms. All over the world there were millions upon millions of men and women to whom his words were as those of a Messiah. Now that he envisioned a new world order based upon a League of Nations, it seemed inevitable to him that he himself should go to Paris, exert this vast and beneficent power, and make the vision a reality. The splendid dream took full possession of him. Critics like Senator Lodge and even associates like Secretary Lansing might object that he ought to leave the negotiations to subordinates, or that peace should be made with Germany first, and discussion of the League postponed, in order to bring an unsettled world back to equilibrium without delay; but had he not silenced critics during the war and could he not silence them again? On the 4th of December—less than a month after the Armistice—the President sailed from New York on the *George Washington*. As the crowds along the waterfront shouted their tribute and the vessels in the harbor tooted their whistles and the guns roared in a presidential salute, Woodrow Wilson, standing on the bridge of the *George Washington,* eastward bound, must have felt that destiny was on his side.

The events of the next few weeks only confirmed him in this feeling. He toured France and England and Italy in incredible triumph. Never had such crowds greeted a foreigner on British soil. His progress through the streets of London could be likened only to a Coronation procession. In Italy the streets were black with people come to do him honor. "No one has ever had such cheers," wrote William Bolitho; "I, who heard them in the streets of Paris, can never forget them in my life. I saw Foch pass, Clemenceau pass, Lloyd George, generals, returning troops, banners, but Wilson heard from his carriage something different, inhuman—or superhuman." Seeing those overwhelming crowds and hearing their shouts of acclaim, how could Woodrow Wilson doubt that he was still invincible? If, when the Conference met, he could only speak so that they might hear, no diplomatists of the old order could withstand him. Destiny was taking him, and the whole world with him, toward a future bright with promise.

But, as it happened, destiny had other plans. In Europe, as well as in America, idealism was on the ebb. Lloyd George, that unfailing barometer of public opinion, was campaigning for reëlection on a "Hang the Kaiser" platform; and shout as the crowds might for Wilson and justice, they voted for Lloyd George and vengeance. Now that the Germans were beaten, a score of jealous European politicians were wondering what they could get out of the settlement at Paris for their own national ends and their own personal glory. They wanted to bring home the spoils of war. They heard the mob applaud Wilson, but they knew that mobs are fickle and would applaud annexations and punitive reparations with equal fervor. They went to Paris determined to make a peace which would give them plunder to take home.

And meanwhile in the Senate Chamber at Washington opposition to Wilson's League and Wilson's Fourteen Points increased in volume. As early as December 21, 1918, Henry Cabot Lodge, intellectual leader of the Republicans in the Senate, announced that the Senate had equal power with the President in treaty-making and should make its wishes known in advance of the negotiations. He said that there would be quite enough to do at Paris without raising the issue of the League. And he set forth his idea of the sort of peace which ought to be made—an idea radically different from President Wilson's. Lodge and a group of his associates wanted Germany to be disarmed, saddled with a terrific bill for reparations, and if possible dismembered. They were ready to give to the Allies large concessions in territory. And above all, they wanted nothing to be included in the peace settlement which would commit the United States to future intervention in European affairs. They prepared to examine carefully any plan for a League of Nations which might come out of the Conference and to resist it if it involved "entangling alliances." Thus to opposition from the diplomats of Europe was added opposition of another sort from the Senate and public opinion at home. Wilson was between two fires. He might not realize how they threatened him, but they were spreading.

The tide of events, had Wilson but known it, was turning against him. Human nature, the world over, was beginning to show a new side, as it has shown it at the end of every war in history. The compulsion for unity was gone, and division was taking its place. The compulsion for idealism was gone, and realism was in the ascendant.

Nor did destiny work only through the diplomats of the Old World and the senatorial patriots of the New. It worked also through the peculiar limitations in the mind and character of Woodrow Wilson himself. The very singleness of purpose, the very uncompromising quality of mind that had made him a great prophet, forced him to take upon his own shoulders at Paris an impossible burden of responsible negotiation. It prevented him from properly acquainting his colleagues with what he himself was doing at the sessions of the Council of Ten or the Council of Four, and from getting the full benefit of their suggestions and objections. It prevented him from taking the American correspondents at Paris into his confidence and thus gaining valuable support at home. It made him play a lone hand. Again, his intelligence was visual rather than oral. As Ray Stannard Baker has well put it, Wilson was "accustomed to getting his information, not from people, but out of books, documents, letters—the written word," and consequently "underestimated the value of . . . human contacts." At written negotiations he was a past master, but in the oral give and take about a small conference table he was at a disadvantage. When Clemenceau and Lloyd George and Orlando got him into the Council of Four behind closed doors, where they could play the game of treaty-making like a four-handed card game, they had already half defeated him. A superman might have gone to Paris and come home completely victorious, but Woodrow Wilson could not have been what he was and have carried the day.

This is no place to tell the long and bitter story of the President's fight for his ideals at Paris. Suffice it to say that he fought stubbornly and resourcefully, and succeeded to a creditable extent in moderating the terms of the Treaty. The European diplomats wanted to leave the discussion of the League until after the territorial and military settlements had been made, but he forced them to put the League first. Sitting as chairman of the commission appointed to draw up the League Covenant, he brought out a preliminary draft which met, as he supposed, the principal objections to it made by men at home like Taft and Root and Lodge. In Paris he confronted a practically unanimous sentiment for annexation of huge slices of German territory and of all the German colonies; even the British dominions, through their premiers, came out boldly for annexation and supported one another in their colonial claims; yet he succeeded in getting the Conference to accept the mandate principle. He forced Clemenceau to modify his demands for German territory, though he had to threaten to leave Paris to get his way. He forced Italy to accept less land than she wanted, though he had to venture a public appeal to the conscience of the world to do it. Again and again it was he, and he only, who prevented territories from being parceled out among the victors without regard to the desires of their inhabitants. To read the day-to-day story of the Conference is to realize that the settlement would have been far more threatening to the future peace of the world had Woodrow Wilson not struggled as he did to bring about an agreement fair to all. Yet the result, after all, was a compromise. The treaty followed in too many respects the provisions of the iniquitous secret treaties of war-time; and the League Covenant which Wilson had managed to imbed securely in it was too rigid and too full of possible military obligations to suit an American people tired of war and ready to get out of Europe once and for all.

The President must have been fully aware of the ugly imperfections in the Treaty of Versailles as he sailed back to America with it at the end of June, 1919, more than six months after his departure for France. He must have realized that, despite all his efforts, the men who had sat about the council table at Paris had been more swayed by fear and hate and greed and narrow nationalism than by the noble motives of which he had been the mouthpiece. No rational man with his eyes and ears open could have failed to sense the disillusionment which was slowly settling down upon the world, or the validity of many of the objections to the Treaty which were daily being made in the Senate at Washington. Yet what could Wilson do?

Could he come home to the Senate and the American people and say, in effect: "This Treaty is a pretty bad one in some respects. I shouldn't have accepted the Shantung clause or the Italian border clause or the failure to set a fixed German indemnity or the grabbing of a lot of German territory by France and others unless I had had to, but under the circumstances this is about the best we could do and I think the League will make up for the rest"? He could not; he had committed himself to each and every clause; he had signed the Treaty, and must defend it. Could he admit that the negotiators at Paris had failed to act in the unselfish spirit which he had proclaimed in advance that they would show? To do this would be to admit his own failure and kill his own prestige. Having proclaimed before the Conference that the settlement would be righteous and having insisted during the Conference that it was righteous, how could he admit afterward that it had not been righteous? The drift of events had caught him in a predicament from which there seemed to be but one outlet of escape. He must go home and vow that the Conference had been a love-feast, that every vital decision had been based on the Fourteen Points, that Clemenceau and Orlando and Lloyd George and the rest had been animated by an overpowering love for humanity, and that the salvation of the world depended on the complete acceptance of the Treaty as the charter of a new and idyllic world order.

That is what he did; and because the things he said about the Treaty were not true, and he must have known—sometimes, at least—that they were not, the story of Woodrow Wilson from this point on is sheer tragedy. He fell into the pit which is digged for every idealist. Having failed to embody his ideal in fact, he distorted the fact. He pictured the world, to himself and to others, not as it was, but as he wished it to be. The optimist became a sentimentalist. The story of the Conference which he told to the American people when he returned home was a very beautiful romance of good men and true laboring without thought of selfish advantage for the welfare of humanity. He said that if the United States did not come to the aid of mankind by indorsing all that had been done at Paris, the heart of the world would be broken. But the only heart which was broken was his own.

[4]

Henry Cabot Lodge was a gentleman, a scholar, and an elegant and persuasive figure in the United States Senate. As he strolled down the aisle of the Senate Chamber—slender, graceful, gray-haired, gray-bearded, the embodiment of all that was patrician—he caught and held the eye as might William Gillette on a crowded stage. He need not raise his voice, he need only turn for a moment and listen to a sentence or two of some colleague's florid speech and then walk indifferently on, to convince a visitor in the gallery that the speech was unworthy of attention. It was about Lodge that the opposition to Wilson gathered.

He believed in Americanism. He believed that the essence of American foreign policy should be to keep the country clear of foreign entanglements unless our honor was involved, to be ready to fight and fight hard the moment it became involved, and, when the fight was over, to disentangle ourselves once more, stand aloof, and mind our own business. (Our honor, as Lodge saw it, was involved if our prerogatives were threatened; to Woodrow Wilson, on the other hand, national honor was a moral matter: only by shameful conduct could a nation lose it.) As chairman of the Foreign Relations Committee, Lodge conceived it to be his duty to see that the United States was not drawn into any international agreement which would endanger this time-honored policy. He did not believe that the nations of the world could be trusted to spend the rest of their years behaving like so many Boy Scouts; he knew that, to be effective, a treaty must be serviceable in eras of bad feeling as well as good; and he saw in the present one many an invitation to trouble.

Senator Lodge was also a politician. Knowing that his Massachusetts constituents numbered among them hundreds of thousands of Irish, he asked the overworked peace delegates at Paris to give a hearing to Messrs. Frank P. Walsh, Edward F. Dunn, and Michael J. Ryan, the so-called American Commission for Irish Independence, though it was difficult for anyone but an Irishman to say what Irish independence had to do with the Treaty. Remembering, too, the size of the Italian vote, Lodge was willing to embarrass President Wilson, in the midst of the Italian crisis at the Conference, by saying in a speech to the Italians of Boston that Italy ought to have Fiume and control the Adriatic. Finally, Lodge had no love for Woodrow Wilson. So strongly did he feel that Wilson's assumption of the right to speak for American opinion was unwarranted and iniquitous, that when Henry White, the only Republican on the American Peace Commission, sailed for Europe, Lodge put into White's hands a secret memorandum containing his own extremely un-Wilsonian idea of what peace terms the American people would stand for, and suggested that White show it in strict confidence to Balfour, Clemenceau, and Nitti, adding, "This knowledge may in certain circumstances be very important to them in strengthening their position." No honorable man could have made such a suggestion unless he believed the defeat of the President's program to be essential to the country's welfare.

United with Lodge in skepticism about the Treaty, if in nothing else, was a curious combination of men and of influences. There were hard-shelled tories like Brandegee; there were Western idealists like Borah, who distrusted any association with foreign diplomats as the blond country boy of the old-fashioned melodrama distrusted association with the slick city man; there were chronic dissenters like La Follette and Jim Reed; there were Republicans who were not sorry to put the Democratic President into a hole, and particularly a President who had appealed in war-time for the election of a Democratic Congress; there were Senators anxious to show that nobody could make a treaty without the advice as well as the consent of the Senate, and get away with it; and there were not a few who, in addition to their other reasons for opposition, shared Lodge's personal distaste for Wilsonian rhetoric. Outside the Senate there was opposition of still other varieties. The Irish were easily inflamed against a League of Nations that gave "six seats to England." The Italians were ready to denounce a man who had refused to let Italy have Fiume. Many Germans, no matter how loyal to the United States they may have been during the war, had little enthusiasm for the hamstringing of the German Republic and the denial to Germany of a seat in the League. There were some people who thought that America had got too little out of the settlement. And there were a vast number who saw in the League Covenant, and especially in Article X, obligations with which they were not willing to have the nation saddled.

Aside from all these groups, furthermore, there was another factor to be reckoned with: the growing apathy of millions of Americans toward anything which reminded them of the war. They were fast becoming sick and tired of the whole European mess. They wanted to be done with it. They didn't want to be told of new sacrifices to be made—they had made plenty. Gone was the lift of the day when a girl singing the "Doxology" in Times Square could express their feelings about victory. This was all over now; the Willard-Dempsey fight and the arrival of the British dirigible R-34 at Long Island were much more interesting.

On the 10th of July, 1919, the President, back in Washington again, laid the Treaty of Versailles before the Senate, denying that the compromises which had been accepted as inevitable by the American negotiators "cut to the heart of any principle." In his words as he addressed the Senate was all the eloquence which only a few months ago had swayed the world. "The stage is set, the destiny disclosed. It has come about by no plan of our conceiving, but by the hand of God who led us into the way. We cannot turn back. We can only go forward, with lifted eyes and freshened spirit, to follow the vision. It was of this that we dreamed at our birth. America shall in truth show the way. The light streams upon the path ahead and nowhere else."

Fine words—but they brought no overwhelming appeal from the country for immediate ratification. The country was tired of going forward with lifted eyes, and Woodrow Wilson's prose style, now all too familiar, could no longer freshen its spirit. The Treaty—a document as long as a novel—was referred to Lodge's Committee on Foreign Relations, which settled down to study it at leisure. A month later Lodge rose in

the Senate to express his preference for national independence
and security, to insist that Articles X and XI of the League
Covenant gave "other powers" the right "to call out American
troops and American ships to any part of the world," and to
reply to Wilson: "We would not have our politics distracted
and embittered by the dissensions of other lands. We would not
have our country's vigor exhausted, or her moral force abated,
by everlasting meddling and muddling in every quarrel, great
and small, which afflicts the world." And within a fortnight
Lodge's committee began voting—although by a narrow margin in each case—to amend the Treaty; to give Shantung to
China, to relieve the United States of membership in international commissions, to give the United States the same vote as
Great Britain in the League, and to shut off the representatives
of the British dominions from voting on questions affecting the
British Empire. It began to look as if the process of making
amendments and reservations might go on indefinitely. Woodrow Wilson decided to play his last desperate card. He would
go to the people. He would win them to his cause, making a
speaking trip through the West.

His doctors advised against it, for physically the President
was almost at the end of his rope. Never robust, for months he
had been under a terrific strain. Again and again during the
Peace Conference, Ray Stannard Baker would find him, after a
long day of nerve-wracking sessions, looking "utterly beaten,
worn out, his face quite haggard and one side of it twitching
painfully." At one time he had broken down—had been taken
with a sudden attack of influenza, with violent paroxysms of
coughing and a fever of 103°—only to be up again and at his
labors within a few days. Now, in September, his nerves frayed
by continued overwork and by the thought of possible failure
of all he had given his heart and strength for, he was like a
man obsessed. He could think of nothing but the Treaty and
the League. He cared for nothing but to bring them through to
victory. And so, despite all that those about him could say, he
left Washington on September 3rd to undergo the even greater
strain of a speaking trip—the preparation and delivery of one
or even two speeches a day in huge sweltering auditoriums
(and without amplifiers to ease the strain on His voice); the
automobile processions through city after city (during which
he had to stand up in his car and continuously wave his hat to

the crowds); the swarms of reporters, the hand-shaking, the glare of publicity, and the restless sleep of one who travels night in and night out on a swaying train.

Again and again on that long trip of his, Woodrow Wilson painted the picture of the Treaty and the League that lived in his own mind, a picture which bore fainter and fainter resemblance to the reality. He spoke of the "generous, high-minded, statesman-like coöperation" which had been manifest at the Paris Conference; he said that "the hearts of men like Clemenceau and Lloyd George and Orlando beat with the people of the world," and that the heart of humanity beat in the document which they had produced. He represented America, and indeed every other country, as thrilling to a new ideal. "The whole world is now in a state where you can fancy that there are hot tears upon every cheek, and those hot tears are tears of sorrow. They are also tears of hope." He warned his audiences that if the Treaty were not ratified, disorder would shake the foundations of the world, and he envisioned "this great nation marching at the fore of a great procession" to "those heights upon which there rests nothing but the pure light of the justice of God." Every one of those forty speeches was different from every other, and each was perfectly ordered, beautifully phrased, and thrilling with passion. As an intellectual feat the delivery of them was remarkable. Yet each pictured a dream world and a dream Treaty, and instinctively the country knew it. (Perhaps, indeed, there were moments of terrible sanity when, as the President lay sleepless in his private car, he himself knew how far from the truth he had departed.) The expected surge of public opinion toward Wilson's cause failed to materialize. The Senate went right on discussing reservations. On September 24th, the first test vote went against the President 43 to 40.

On the night of the next day Wilson came to the end of his strength. For some time he had had indigestion and had slept little. After his long speech at Pueblo on the evening of September 25th he could not sleep at all. The train was stopped and Mr. and Mrs. Wilson took a walk together on a country road. When he returned to the train he was feverish and "as he slept under a narcotic, his mouth drooled. His body testified in many ways to an impending crash." The next morning when he tried to get up he could hardly stand. The train hurried on toward Washington and all future speaking engagements were canceled. Back to the White House the sick man went. A few days later a cerebral thrombosis partially paralyzed his left side. Another act of the tragedy had come to an end. He had given all he had to the cause, and it had not been enough.

[5]

There followed one of the most extraordinary periods in the whole history of the Presidency. For weeks Woodrow Wilson lay seriously ill, sometimes unable even to sign documents awaiting his signature. He could not sit up in a chair for over a month, or venture out for a ride in the White House automobile for five months. During all the rest of his term—which lasted until March 4, 1921, seventeen months after his breakdown—he remained in feeble and precarious health, a sick man lying in bed or sitting in an invalid's chair, his left side and left leg and left arm partially paralyzed. Within the White House he was immured as if in a hospital. He saw almost nobody, transacted only the most imperative business of his office. The only way of communicating with him was by letter, and as during most of this time all letters must pass through the hands of Mrs. Wilson or Admiral Grayson or others in the circle of attendants upon the invalid, and few were answered, there was often no way of knowing who was responsible for a failure to answer them or to act in accordance with the suggestions embodied in them. Sometimes, in fact, it was suspected that it was Mrs. Wilson who was responsible for many a White House decision—that the country was in effect being governed by a regency.

With the President virtually unable to function, the whole executive machine came almost to a stop. It could, to be sure, continue its routine tasks; and an aggressive member of the Cabinet like Attorney-General Palmer could go blithely ahead rounding up radicals and deporting them and getting out injunctions against strikers as if he had the full wisdom and power of the Presidency behind him; but most matters of policy waited upon the White House, and after a while it became clear that guidance from that quarter could hardly be expected. There were vital problems clamoring for the attention of the Executive: the high cost of living, the subsequent breakdown of business prosperity and increase of unemployment; the intense bitterness between capital and labor, culminating in the great steel and coal strikes; the reorganization of the government departments on a peace basis; the settlement of innumerable questions of foreign policy unconnected with the Treaty or the League. Yet upon most of these problems the sick man had no leadership to offer. Meanwhile his influence with Congress and the country, far from being increased by his martyrdom for the League, dwindled to almost nothing.

The effect of this strange state of affairs upon official Washington was well described a year or two later by Edward G. Lowry in *Washington Close-ups*:

"For a long time the social-political atmosphere of Washington had been one of bleak and chill austerity suffused and envenomed by hatred of a sick chief magistrate that seemed to poison and blight every human relationship. The White House was isolated. It had no relation with the Capitol or the local resident and official community. Its great iron gates were closed and chained and locked. Policemen guarded its approaches. It was in a void apart. . . . It all made for bleakness and bitterness and a general sense of frustration and unhappiness."

Mr. Wilson's mind remained clear. When the report went about that he was unable "to discharge the powers and duties" of his office and should, therefore, under the provisions of the Constitution, be supplanted by the Vice-President (and reports of this sort were frequent in those days) Senators Fall and Hitchcock visited him in behalf of the Senate to determine his mental condition. They found him keenly alive to the humor of their embarrassing mission; he laughed and joked with them and showed a complete grasp of the subjects under discussion. Nevertheless, something had gone out of him. His messages were lifeless, his mind was sterile of new ideas. He could not meet new situations in a new way: reading his public documents, one felt that his brain was still turning over old ideas, rearranging old phrases, that he was still living in that dream world which he had built about himself during the days of his fight for the League.

He had always been a lonely man; and now, as if pursued by some evil demon, he broke with one after another of those who still tried to serve him. For long years Colonel House had been his chief adviser as well as his affectionate friend. During the latter days of the Peace Conference a certain coolness had been noticed in Wilson's attitude toward House. This very conciliatory man had been perhaps a little too conciliatory in his negotiations during the President's absence from Paris; rightly or wrongly, the President felt that House had unwittingly played into the hands of the wily Clemenceau. Nevertheless, House hoped, on his return from Paris, to be able to effect a rapprochement between his broken chief and the defiant Senators. House wrote to suggest that Wilson accept certain reservations to the Treaty. There was no answer to the letter. House wrote again. No answer. There was never any explanation. The friendship and the political relationship, long so valuable to the President and so influential in the direction of policy, were both at an end—that was all one could say.

Robert Lansing had been at odds with the President over many things before and during the Peace Conference; yet he remained as Secretary of State and believed himself to be on good terms with his chief. During Wilson's illness, deciding that something must be done to enable the government to transact business, he called meetings of the Cabinet, which were held in the Cabinet Room at the White House offices. He was peremptorily dismissed. Last of all to go was the faithful Joe Tumulty, who had been Wilson's secretary through fair weather and foul, in the Governor's office at Trenton and for eight years at Washington. Although the break with Tumulty happened after Wilson left the White House, it deserves mention here because it so resembles the others and reveals what poison was working in the sick man's mind. In April, 1922, there was to be held in New York a Democratic dinner. Before the dinner Tumulty visited Wilson and got what he supposed to be an oral message to the effect that Wilson would "support any man [for the Presidency] who will stand for the salvation of America, and the salvation of America is justice to all classes." It seemed an innocuous message, and after ten years of association with Wilson, Tumulty had reason to suppose that he knew when Wilson might be quoted and when he might not. But as it happened, Governor Cox spoke at the Democratic dinner, and the message, when Tumulty gave it, was interpreted as an indorsement of Cox. Whereupon Wilson

wrote a curt letter to the *New York Times* denying that he had
authorized anybody to give a message from him. Tumulty at
once wrote to Wilson to explain that he had acted in good faith
and to apologize like a true friend for having caused the President embarrassment. His letter was "courteously answered by
Mrs. Wilson" (to use Tumulty's own subsequent words), but
Wilson himself said not a word more. Again Tumulty wrote
loyally, saying that he would always regard Mr. Wilson with
affection and would be "always around the corner when you
need me." There was no answer.

On the issue of the Treaty and the League Woodrow Wilson
remained adamant to the end. Call it unswerving loyalty to
principle or call it stubbornness, as you will—he would consent
to no reservations except (when it was too late) some innocuous "interpretive" ones, framed by Senator Hitchcock,
which went down to defeat. While the President lay critically
ill, the Senate went right on proposing reservation after
reservation, and on November 19, 1919, it defeated the Treaty.
Only a small majority of the Senators were at that time irreconcilable opponents of the pact; but they were enough to
carry the day. By combining forces with Wilson's Democratic
supporters who favored the passage of the Treaty without
change, they secured a majority against the long list of reservations proposed by Lodge's committee. Then by combining
forces with Lodge and the other reservationists, they defeated
the Treaty minus the reservations. It was an ironical result, but
it stood. A few months later the issue was raised again, and
once more the Treaty went down to defeat. Finally a resolution
for a separate peace with Germany was passed by both Houses
—and vetoed by Wilson as "an action which would place an
ineffaceable stain upon the gallantry and honor of the United
States." (A similar peace resolution was ultimately signed by
President Harding.) President Wilson's last hope was that the
election of 1920 would serve as a "great and solemn referendum" in which the masses of the people—those masses who,
he had always claimed, were on his side—would rise to vindi-
cate him and the country. They rose—and swamped the pro-
League candidate by a plurality of seven millions.

It is not pleasant to imagine the thoughts of the sick man in
the White House as defeat after defeat overwhelmed his cause
and mocked the great sacrifice he had made for it. How soon

the realization came upon him that everything was lost we do not know. After his breakdown, as he lay ill in the White House, did he still hope? It seems likely. All news from the outside world was filtered to him through those about him. With his life hanging in the balance, it would have been quite natural—if not inevitable—for them to wish to protect him from shock, to tell him that all was going well on the Hill, that the tide had swung back again, that this token and that showed that the American people would not fail him. On such a theory one might explain the break with Colonel House. Possibly any suggestion for compromise with the Lodge forces seemed to the President simply a craven proposal for putting up the white flag in the moment of victory. But whether or not this theory is justified, sooner or later the knowledge must have come, as vote after vote turned against the Treaty, and must have turned the taste of life to bitterness. Wilson's icy repudiation of faithful Joe Tumulty was the act of a man who has lost his faith in humankind.

[6]

Back in the early spring of 1919, while Wilson was still at Paris, Samuel G. Blythe, an experienced observer of the political scene, had written in the *Saturday Evening Post* of the temper of the leaders of the Republican Party as they faced the issues of peace:

"You cannot teach an Old Guard new tricks. . . . The Old Guard surrenders but it never dies. Right at this minute, the ancient and archaic Republicans who think they control the destinies of the Republican Party—think they do!—are operating after the manner and style of 1896. The war hasn't made a dent in them. . . . The only way they look is backward."

The analysis was sound; but the Republican bosses, however open to criticism they may have been as statesmen, were at least good politicians. They had their ears where a good politician's should be—to the ground—and what they heard there was a rumble of discontent with Wilson and all that he represented. They determined that at the election of 1920 they would choose as the Republican standard-bearer somebody who would present, both to themselves and to the country, a complete contrast with the idealist whom they detested. As the year rolled round and the date for the Republican Convention approached, they surveyed the field. The leading candidate was General Leonard Wood, a blunt soldier, an inheritor of Theodore Roosevelt's creed of fearing God and keeping your powder dry; he made a fairly good contrast with Wilson, but he promised to be almost as unmanageable. Then there was Governor Lowden of Illinois—but he, too, did not quite fulfill the ideal. Herbert Hoover, the reliever of Belgium and war-time Food Administrator, was conducting a highly amateur campaign for the nomination; the politicians dismissed him with a sour laugh. Why, this man Hoover hadn't known whether he was a Republican or Democrat until the campaign began! Hiram Johnson was in the field, but he also might prove stiff-necked, although it was to his advantage that he was a Senator. The bosses' inspired choice was none of these men: it was Warren Gamaliel Harding, a commonplace and unpretentious Senator from Ohio.

Consider how perfectly Harding met the requirements. Wilson was a visionary who liked to identify himself with "forward-looking men"; Harding, as Mr. Lowry put it, was as old-fashioned as those wooden Indians which used to stand in front of cigar stores, "a flower of the period before safety razors." Harding believed that statesmanship had come to its apogee in the days of McKinley and Foraker. Wilson was cold; Harding was an affable small-town man, at ease with "folks"; an ideal companion, as one of his friends expressed it, "to play poker with all Saturday night." Wilson had always been difficult of access; Harding was accessible to the last degree. Wilson favored labor, distrusted business men as a class, and talked of "industrial democracy"; Harding looked back with longing eyes to the good old days when the government didn't bother business men with unnecessary regulations, but provided them with fat tariffs and instructed the Department of Justice not to have them on its mind. Wilson was at logger-heads with Congress, and particularly with the Senate; Harding was not only a Senator, but a highly amenable Senator. Wilson had been adept at making enemies; Harding hadn't an enemy in the world. He was genuinely genial. "He had no knobs, he was the same size and smoothness all the way round," wrote Charles Willis Thompson. Wilson thought in terms of the whole world; Harding was for America first. And finally, whereas Wilson wanted America to exert itself nobly, Harding wanted to give it a rest. At Boston, a few weeks before the Convention, he had correctly expressed the growing desire of the people of the country and at the same time had unwittingly added a new word to the language, when he said, "America's present need is not heroics but healing; not nostrums but normalcy; not revolution but restoration; . . . not surgery but serenity." Here was a man whom a country wearied of moral obligations and the hope of the world could take to its heart.

It is credibly reported that the decision in favor of Harding was made by the Republican bosses as early as February, 1920, four months before the Convention. But it was not until four ballots had been taken at the Convention itself—with Wood leading, Lowden second, and Harding fifth—and the wilted delegates had dispersed for the night, that the leaders finally concluded to put Harding over. Harding's political manager, an Ohio boss named Harry M. Daugherty, had predicted that the Convention would be deadlocked and that the nomination would be decided upon by twelve or thirteen men "at two o'clock in the morning, in a smoke-filled room." He was precisely right. The room was Colonel George Harvey's, in the Hotel Blackstone. Boies Penrose, lying mortally ill in Philadelphia, had given his instructions by private wire to John T. Adams. The word was passed round, and the next afternoon Harding was nominated.

The Democrats, relieved that Wilson's illness had disqualified him, duly nominated another equally undistinguished Ohio politician, Governor James M. Cox. This nominee had to swallow the League of Nations and did. He swung manfully around the circle, shouting himself hoarse, pointing with pride. But he hadn't a chance in the world. Senator Harding remained in his average small town and conducted a McKinley-esque front-porch campaign; he pitched horseshoes behind the house with his Republican advisers like an average small-town man and wore a McKinley carnation; he said just enough in behalf of "an association of nations" to permit inveterate Republicans who favored the League to vote for him without twinges of conscience, and just enough against Wilson's League to convince the majority that with him in the White House they would not be called upon to march to the aid of suffering Czechoslovakia; and the men and women of the United States

woke up on the morning of November 3rd to find that they
had swept him into the Presidency by a margin of sixteen
millions to nine millions. Governor Cox, the sacrificial victim,
faded rapidly into the mists of obscurity.

The United States had rendered its considered judgment on
"our fortunate duty to assist by example, by sober, friendly
counsel, and by material aid in the establishment of just democracy throughout the world." It had preferred normalcy.

[7]

Woodrow Wilson lived on in Washington—in a large and
comfortable house on S Street—for over three years after this
final crushing defeat. Those who came to call upon him toward
the end found a man prematurely old, huddled in a big chair
by the fireplace in a sunny south room. He sat with his hands
in his lap, his head a little on one side. His face and body were
heavier than they had been in his days of power; his hair, now
quite gray, was brushed back over an almost bald head. As he
talked he did not move his head—only his eyes followed his
visitor, and his right arm swung back and forth and occasionally struck the arm of the chair for emphasis as he
made his points. The old-time urbanity was in his manner as he
said, "You must excuse my not rising; I'm really quite lame."
But as he talked of the foreign policy of the United States and
of his enemies, his tone was full of hatred. This was no time to
sprinkle rose-water round, he said; it was a time for fighting—
there must be a party fight, "not in a partisan spirit, but on
party lines." Still he clung to the last shred of hope that his
party might follow the gleam. Of the men who had made the
fulfillment of his great project impossible he spoke in unspar-
ing terms. "I've got to get well, and then I'm going out to get a
few scalps." So he nursed his grievance; an old man, helpless
and bitter.

On Armistice Day, five years after the triumphant close of
the war, he stood on the steps of his house—supported so that
he should not fall—and spoke to a crowd that had gathered to
do him honor. "I am not," said he, "one of those that have the
least anxiety about the triumph of the principles I have stood
for. I have seen fools resist Providence before and I have seen

their destruction, as will come upon these again—utter destruction and contempt. That we shall prevail is as sure as that God reigns."

Three months later he was dead.

III

The Big Red Scare

If the American people turned a deaf ear to Woodrow Wilson's plea for the League of Nations during the early years of the Post-war Decade, it was not simply because they were too weary of foreign entanglements and noble efforts' to heed him. They were listening to something else. They were listening to ugly rumors of a huge radical conspiracy against the government and institutions of the United States. They had their ears cocked for the detonation of bombs and the tramp of Bolshevist armies. They seriously thought—or at least millions of them did, millions of otherwise reasonable citizens—that a Red revolution might begin in the United States the next month or next week, and they were less concerned with making the world safe for democracy than with making America safe for themselves.

Those were the days when column after column of the front pages of the newspapers shouted the news of strikes and anti-Bolshevist riots; when radicals shot down Armistice Day paraders in the streets of Centralia, Washington, and in revenge the patriotic citizenry took out of the jail a member of the I. W. W.—a white American, be it noted—and lynched him by tying a rope around his neck and throwing him off a bridge; when properly elected members of the Assembly of New York State were expelled (and their constituents thereby disfranchised) simply because they had been elected as members of the venerable Socialist Party; when a jury in Indiana took two minutes to acquit a man for shooting and killing an alien because he had shouted, "To hell with the United States"; and when the Vice-President of the nation cited as a dangerous manifestation of radicalism in the women's colleges the fact that the girl debaters of Radcliffe had upheld the affirmative in an intercollegiate debate on the subject: "Resolved, that the recognition of labor unions by employers is essential to successful collective bargaining." It was an era of lawless and disorderly defense of law and order, of unconstitutional defense of the Constitution, of suspicion and civil conflict—in a very literal sense, a reign of terror.

For this national panic there was a degree of justification. During the war the labor movement had been steadily gaining in momentum and prestige. There had been hundreds of strikes, induced chiefly by the rising prices of everything that the laboring-man needed in order to live, but also by his new consciousness of his power. The government, in order to keep up production and maintain industrial peace, had encouraged collective bargaining, elevated Samuel Gompers to one of the seats of the mighty in the war councils at Washington, and given the workers some reason to hope that with the coming of peace new benefits would be showered upon them. Peace came, and hope was deferred. Prices still rose, employers resisted wage increases with a new solidarity and continued to insist on long hours of work, Woodrow Wilson went off to Europe in quest of universal peace and forgot all about the laboring-men; and in anger and despair, they took up the only weapon ready to their hand—the strike. All over the country they struck. There were strikes in the building trades, among the longshoremen, the stockyard workers, the shipyard men, the subway men, the shoe-workers, the carpenters, the telephone operators, and so on *ad infinitum*, until by November, 1919, the total number of men and women on strike in the industrial states was estimated by Alvin Johnson to be at least a million, with enough more in the non-industrial states, or voluntarily abstaining from work though not engaged in recognized strikes, to bring the grand total to something like two million.

Nor were all of these men striking merely for recognition of their unions or for increases in pay or shorter hours—the traditional causes. Some of them were demanding a new industrial order, the displacement of capitalistic control of industry (or at least of their own industry) by government control: in short, something approaching a social régime. The hitherto conservative railroad workers came out for the Plumb Plan, by which the government would continue to direct the railroads and labor would have a voice in the management. When in September, 1919, the United Mine Workers voted to strike, they boldly advocated the nationalization of the mines; and a delegate who began his speech before the crowded convention with the words, "Nationalization is impossible," was drowned out by boos and jeers and cries of "Coal operator! Throw him out!" In the Northwest the I. W. W. was fighting to get the whip hand over capital through One Big Union. In North Dakota and the adjoining grain states, two hundred thousand farmers joined Townley's Non-Partisan League, described by its enemies—with some truth—as an agrarian soviet. (Townley's candidate for governor of Minnesota in 1916, by the way, had been a Swedish-American named Charles A. Lindbergh, who would have been amazed to hear that his family was destined to be allied by marriage to that of a Morgan partner.) There was an unmistakable trend toward socialistic ideas both in the ranks of labor and among liberal intellectuals. The Socialist party, watching the success of the Russian Revolution, was flirting with the idea of violent mass-action. And there was, too, a rag-tag-and-bobtail collection of communists and anarchists, many of them former Socialists, nearly all of them foreign-born, most of them Russian, who talked of going still further, who took their gospel direct from Moscow and, presumably with the aid of Russian funds, preached it aggressively among the slum and factory-town population.

This latter group of communists and anarchists constituted a very narrow minority of the radical movement—absurdly narrow when we consider all the to-do that was made about them. Late in 1919 Professor Gordon S. Watkins of the University of Illinois, writing in the *Atlantic Monthly*, set the membership of the Socialist party at 39,000, of the Communist Labor party at from 10,000 to 30,000, and of the Communist party at from 30,000 to 60,000. In other words, according to this estimate, the Communists could muster at the most hardly more than one-tenth of one per cent of the adult population of the country; and the three parties together—the majority of whose members were probably content to work for their ends by lawful means—brought the proportion to hardly more than two-tenths of one per cent, a rather slender nucleus, it would seem, for a revolutionary mass movement.

But the American business man was in no mood to consider whether it was a slender nucleus or not. He, too, had come out of the war with his fighting blood up, ready to lick the next thing that stood in his way. He wanted to get back to business and enjoy his profits. Labor stood in his way and threatened his profits. He had come out of the war with a militant patriotism; and mingling his idealistic with his selfish motives, after the manner of all men at all times, he developed a fervent belief that 100-per-cent Americanism and the Welfare of God's Own Country and Loyalty to the Teachings of the Founding Fathers implied the right of the business man to kick the union organizer out of his workshop. He had come to distrust anything and everything that was foreign, and this radicalism he saw as the spawn of long-haired Slavs and unwashed East-Side Jews. And, finally, he had been nourished during the war years upon stories of spies and plotters and international intrigue. He had been convinced that German sympathizers signaled to one another with lights from mountain-tops and put ground glass into surgical dressings, and he had formed the habit of expecting tennis courts to conceal gun-emplacements. His credulity had thus been stretched until he was quite ready to believe that a struggle of American laboring-men for better wages was the beginning of an armed rebellion directed by Lenin and Trotsky, and that behind every innocent professor who taught that there were arguments for as well as against socialism there was a bearded rascal from eastern Europe with a money bag in one hand and a smoking bomb in the other.

[2]

The events of 1919 did much to feed this fear. On the 28th of April—while Wilson was negotiating the Peace Treaty at Paris, and homecoming troops were parading under Victory Arches—an infernal machine "big enough to blow out the entire side of the County-City Building" was found in Mayor Ole Hanson's mail at Seattle. Mayor Hanson had been stumping the country to arouse it to the Red Menace. The following afternoon a colored servant opened a package addressed to

Senator Thomas R. Hardwick at his home in Atlanta, Georgia, and a bomb in the package blew off her hands. Senator Hardwick, as chairman of the Immigration Committee of the Senate, had proposed restricting immigration as a means of keeping out Bolshevism.

At two o'clock the next morning Charles Caplan, a clerk in the parcel post division of the New York Post Office, was on his way home to Harlem when he read in a newspaper about the Hardwick bomb. The package was described in this news story as being about six inches long and three inches wide; as being done up in brown paper and, like the Hanson bomb, marked with the (false, of course) return address of Gimbel Brothers in New York. There was something familiar to Mr. Caplan about this description. He thought he remembered having seen some packages like that. He racked his brain, and suddenly it all came back to him. He hurried back to the Post Office—and found, neatly laid away on a shelf where he had put them because of insufficient postage, sixteen little brown-paper packages with the Gimbel return address on them. They were addressed to Attorney-General Palmer, Postmaster-General Burleson, Judge Landis of Chicago, Justice Holmes of the Supreme Court, Secretary of Labor Wilson, Commissioner of Immigration Caminetti, J. P. Morgan, John D. Rockefeller, and a number of other government officials and capitalists. The packages were examined by the police in a neighboring fire-house, and found to contain bombs. Others had started on their way through the mails; the total number ultimately accounted for reached thirty-six. (None of the other packages were carelessly opened, it is hardly necessary to say; for the next few days people in high station were very circumspect about undoing brown-paper packages.) The list of intended recipients was strong evidence that the bombs had been sent by an alien radical.

Hardly more than a month later there was a series of bomb explosions, the most successful of which damaged the front of Attorney-General Palmer's house in Washington. It came in the evening; Mr. Palmer had just left the library on the ground floor and turned out the lights and gone up to bed when there was a bang as of something hitting the front door, followed by the crash of the explosion. The limbs of a man blown to pieces were found outside, and close by, according to the newspaper reports, lay a copy of *Plain Words,* a radical publication.

The American public read the big headlines about these outrages and savagely resolved to get back at "these radicals."

How some of them did so may be illustrated by two incidents out of dozens which took place during those days. Both of them occurred on May Day of 1919—just after Mr. Caplan had found the brown-paper packages on the Post Office shelf. On the afternoon of May Day the owners and staff of the *New York Call*, a Socialist paper, were holding a reception to celebrate the opening of their new office. There were hundreds of men, women, and children gathered in the building for innocent palaver. A mob of soldiers and sailors stormed in and demanded that the "Bolshevist" posters be torn down. When the demand was refused, they destroyed the literature on the tables, smashed up the offices, drove the crowd out into the street, and clubbed them so vigorously—standing in a semicircle outside the front door and belaboring them as they emerged—that seven members of the *Call* staff went to the hospital.

In Cleveland, on the same day, there was a Socialist parade headed by a red flag. An army lieutenant demanded that the flag be lowered, and thereupon with a group of soldiers leaped into the ranks of the procession and precipitated a free-for-all fight. The police came and charged into the *mêlée*—and from that moment a series of riots began which spread through the city. Scores of people were injured, one man was killed, and the Socialist headquarters were utterly demolished by a gang that defended American institutions by throwing typewriters and office furniture out into the street.

The summer of 1919 passed. The Senate debated the Peace Treaty. The House passed the Volstead Act. The Suffrage Amendment passed Congress and went to the States. The R-34 made the first transatlantic dirigible flight from England to Mineola, Long Island, and returned safely. People laughed over *The Young Visiters* and wondered whether Daisy Ashford was really James M. Barrie. The newspapers denounced sugar-hoarders and food profiteers as the cost of living kept on climbing. The first funeral by airplane was held. Ministers lamented the increasing laxity of morals among the young. But still the fear and hatred of Bolshevism gripped the American mind as new strikes broke out and labor became more aggressive and revolution spread like a scourge through Europe. And then, in September, came the Boston police strike, and the fear was redoubled.

[3]

The Boston police had a grievance: their pay was based on a minimum of $1,100, out of which uniforms had to be bought, and $1,100 would buy mighty little at 1919 prices. They succumbed to the epidemic of unionism, formed a union, and affiliated with the American Federation of Labor. Police Commissioner Curtis, a stiff-necked martinet, had forbidden them to affiliate with any outside organization, and he straightway brought charges against nineteen officers and members of the union for having violated his orders, found them guilty, and suspended them. The Irish blood of the police was heated, and they threatened to strike. A committee appointed by the mayor to adjust the dispute proposed a compromise, but to Mr. Curtis this looked like surrender. He refused to budge. Thereupon, on September 9, 1919, a large proportion of the police walked out at the time of the evening roll call.

With the city left defenseless, hoodlums proceeded to enjoy themselves. That night they smashed windows and looted stores. Mayor Peters called for State troops. The next day the Governor called out the State Guard, and a volunteer police force began to try to cope with the situation. The Guardsmen and volunteer police—ex-service men, Harvard students, cotton brokers from the Back Bay—were inexperienced, and the hoodlums knew it. Guardsmen were goaded into firing on a mob in South Boston and killed two people. For days there was intermittent violence, especially when Guardsmen upheld the majesty of the law by breaking up crap games in that garden of sober Puritanism, Boston Common. The casualty list grew, and the country looked on with dismay as the Central Labor Union, representing the organized trade unionists of the city, debated holding a general strike on behalf of the policemen. Perhaps, people thought, the dreaded revolution was beginning here and now.

But presently it began to appear that public opinion in Boston, as everywhere else, was overwhelmingly against the police and that theirs was a lost cause. The Central Labor Union prudently decided not to call a general strike. Mr. Curtis discharged the nineteen men whom he had previously suspended and began to recruit a new force.

Realizing that the game was nearly up, old Samuel Gompers, down in Washington, tried to intervene. He wired to the Governor of Massachusetts that the action of the Police Commissioner was unwarranted and autocratic.

The Governor of Massachusetts was an inconspicuous, sour-faced man with a reputation for saying as little as possible and never jeopardizing his political position by being betrayed into a false move. He made the right move now. He replied to Gompers that there was "no right to strike against the public safety by anybody, anywhere, any time"—and overnight he became a national hero. If there had been any doubt that the strike was collapsing, it vanished when the press of the whole country applauded Calvin Coolidge. For many a week to come, amateur policemen, pressed into emergency service, would come home at night to the water side of Beacon Street to complain that directing traffic was even more arduous than a whole day of golf at the Country Club; it took time to recruit a new force. But recruited it was, and Boston breathed again.

Organized labor, however, was in striking mood. A few days later, several hundred thousand steel-workers walked out of the mills—after Judge Gary had shown as stiff a neck as Commissioner Curtis and had refused to deal with their union representatives.

Now there was little radicalism among the steel strikers. Their strike was a protest against low wages and long hours. A considerable proportion of them worked a twelve-hour day, and they had a potentially strong case. But the steel magnates had learned something from the Boston Police Strike. The public was jumpy and would condemn any cause on which the Bolshevist label could be pinned. The steel magnates found little difficulty in pinning a Bolshevist label on the strikers. William Z. Foster, the most energetic and intelligent of the strike organizers, had been a syndicalist (and later, although even Judge Gary didn't know it then, was to become a Communist). Copies of a syndicalist pamphlet by Foster appeared in newspaper offices and were seized upon avidly to show what a revolutionary fellow he was. Foster was trying to substitute unions organized by industries for the ineffective craft unions, which were at the mercy of a huge concern like the Steel Corporation; therefore, according to the newspapers, Foster was a "borer from within" and the strike was part of a radical conspiracy. The public was sufficiently frightened to prove more interested in defeating borers from within than in mitigating the lot of obscure Slavs who spent twelve hours a day in the steel mills.

The great steel strike had been in progress only a few weeks when a great coal strike impended. In this case nobody needed to point out to the public the Red specter lurking behind the striking miners. The miners had already succeeded in pinning the Bolshevist label on themselves by their enthusiastic vote for nationalization; and to the undiscriminating newspaper reader, public control of the mining industry was all of a piece with communism, anarchism, bomb-throwing, and general Red ruin. Here was a new threat to the Republic. Something must be done. The Government must act.

It acted. A. Mitchell Palmer, Attorney-General of the United States, who enjoyed being called the "Fighting Quaker," saw his shining opportunity and came to the rescue of the Constitution.

[4]

There is a certain grim humor in the fact that what Mr. Palmer did during the next three months was done by him as the chief legal officer of an Administration which had come into power to bring about the New Freedom. Woodrow Wilson was ill in the White House, out of touch with affairs, and dreaming only of his lamented League: that is the only explanation.

On the day before the coal strike was due to begin, the Attorney-General secured from a Federal Judge in Indianapolis an order enjoining the leaders of the strike from doing anything whatever to further it. He did this under the provisions of a food-and-fuel-control Act which forbade restriction of coal production during the war. In actual fact the war was not only over, it had been over for nearly a year: but legally it was not over—the Peace Treaty still languished in the Senate. This food-and-fuel-control law, in further actual fact, had been passed by the Senate after Senator Husting had explicitly declared that he was "authorized by the Secretary of Labor, Mr. Wilson, to say that the Administration does not construe this bill as prohibiting strikes and peaceful picketing and will not so construe it." But Mr. Palmer either had never heard of this assurance or cared nothing about it or decided that unforeseen conditions had arisen. He got his injunction, and the coal strike was doomed, although the next day something like four hundred thousand coal miners, now leaderless by decree of the Federal Government, walked out of the mines.

The public knew nothing of the broken pledge, of course; it would have been a bold newspaper proprietor who would have published Senator Husting's statement, even had he known about it. It took genuine courage for a paper even to say, as did the *New York World* at that time, that there was "no Bolshevist menace in the United States and no I. W. W. menace that an ordinarily capable police force is not competent to deal with." The press applauded the injunction as it had applauded Calvin Coolidge. The Fighting Quaker took heart. His next move was to direct a series of raids in which Communist leaders were rounded up for deportation to Russia, *via* Finland, on the ship *Buford*, jocosely known as the "Soviet Ark." Again there was enthusiasm—and apparently there was little concern over the right of the Administration to tear from their families men who had as yet committed no crime. Mr. Palmer decided to give the American public more of the same; and thereupon he carried through a new series of raids which set a new record in American history for executive transgression of individual constitutional rights.

Under the drastic war-time Sedition Act, the Secretary of Labor had the power to deport aliens who were anarchists, or believed in or advocated the overthrow of the government by violence, or were affiliated with any organization that so believed or advocated. Mr. Palmer now decided to "cooperate" with the Secretary of Labor by rounding up the alien membership of the Communist party for wholesale deportation. His under-cover agents had already worked their way into the organization; one of them, indeed, was said to have become a leader in his district (which raised the philosophical question whether government agents in such positions would have imperiled their jobs by counseling moderation among the comrades).

In scores of cities all over the United States, when the Communists were simultaneously meeting at their various headquarters on New Year's Day of 1920, Mr. Palmer's agents and police and voluntary aides fell upon them—fell upon everybody, in fact, who was in the hall, regardless of whether he was a Communist or not (how could one tell?)—and bundled them off to jail, with or without warrant. Every conceivable bit of evidence—literature, membership lists, books, papers, pictures on the wall, everything—was seized, with or without a search warrant. On this and succeeding nights other Communists and suspected Communists were seized in their homes. Over six thousand men were arrested in all, and thrust summarily behind the bars for days or weeks—often without any chance to learn what was the explicit charge against them. At least one American citizen, not a Communist, was jailed for days through some mistake—probably a confusion of names— and barely escaped deportation. In Detroit, over a hundred men were herded into a bull-pen measuring twenty-four by thirty feet and kept there for a week under conditions which the mayor of the city called intolerable. In Hartford, while the suspects were in jail the authorities took the further precaution of arresting and incarcerating all visitors who came to see them, a friendly call being regarded as *prima facie* evidence of affiliation with the Communist party.

Ultimately a considerable proportion of the prisoners were released for want of sufficient evidence that they were Communists. Ultimately, too, it was divulged that in the whole country-wide raid upon these dangerous men—supposedly armed to the teeth—exactly three pistols were found, and no explosives at all. But at the time the newspapers were full of reports from Mr. Palmer's office that new evidence of a gigantic plot against the safety of the country had been unearthed; and although the steel strike was failing, the coal strike was failing, and any danger of a socialistic régime, to say nothing of a revolution, was daily fading, nevertheless to the great mass of the American people the Bolshevist bogey became more terrifying than ever.

Mr. Palmer was in full cry. In public statements he was reminding the twenty million owners of Liberty bonds and the nine million farm-owners and the eleven million owners of savings accounts, that the Reds proposed to take away all they had. He was distributing boiler-plate propaganda to the press, containing pictures of horrid-looking Bolsheviks with bristling beards, and asking if such as these should rule over America. Politicians were quoting the suggestion of Guy Empey that the proper implements for dealing with the Reds could be "found in any hardware store," or proclaiming, "My motto for the

Reds is S. O. S.—ship or shoot. I believe we should place them all on a ship of stone, with sails of lead, and that their first stopping-place should be hell." College graduates were calling for the dismissal of professors suspected of radicalism; school-teachers were being made to sign oaths of allegiance; business men with unorthodox political or economic ideas were learning to hold their tongues if they wanted to hold their jobs. Hysteria had reached its height.

[5]

Nor did it quickly subside. For the professional super-patriot (and assorted special propagandists disguised as super-patriots) had only begun to fight. Innumerable patriotic societies had sprung up, each with its executive secretary, and executive secretaries must live, and therefore must conjure up new and ever greater menaces. Innumerable other gentlemen now discovered that they could defeat whatever they wanted to defeat by tarring it conspicuously with the Bolshevist brush. Big-navy men, believers in compulsory military service, drys, anti-cigarette campaigners, anti-evolution Fundamentalists, defenders of the moral order, book censors, Jew-haters, Negro-haters, landlords, manufacturers, utility executives, upholders of every sort of cause, good, bad, and indifferent, all wrapped themselves in Old Glory and the mantle of the Founding Fathers and allied their opponents with Lenin. The open shop, for example, became the "American plan." For years a pestilence of speakers and writers continued to afflict the country with tales of "sinister and subversive agitators." Elderly ladies in gilt chairs in ornate drawing-rooms heard from executive secretaries that the agents of the government had unearthed new radical conspiracies too fiendish to be divulged before the proper time. Their husbands were told at luncheon clubs that the colleges were honeycombed with Bolshevism. A cloud of suspicion hung in the air, and intolerance became an American virtue.

William J. Burns put the number of resident Communists at 422,000, and S. Stanwood Menken of the National Security League made it 600,000—figures at least ten times as large as those of Professor Watkins. Dwight Braman, president of the Allied Patriotic Societies, told Governor Smith of New York that the Reds were holding 10,000 meetings in the country every week and that 350 radical newspapers had been established in the preceding six months.

But not only the Communists were dangerous; they had, it seemed, well-disguised or unwitting allies in more respectable circles. The Russian Famine Fund Committee, according to Ralph Easley of the National Civic Federation, included sixty pronounced Bolshevist sympathizers. Frederick J. Libby of the National Council for the Reduction of Armaments was said by one of the loudest of the super-patriots to be a Communist educated in Russia who visited Russia for instructions (although as a matter of fact the pacifist churchman had never been in Russia, had no affiliations with Russia, and had on his board only American citizens). *The Nation, The New Republic,* and *The Freeman* were classed as "revolutionary" by the executive secretary of the American Defense Society. Even *The Survey* was denounced by the writers of the Lusk Report as having "the endorsement of revolutionary groups." Ralph Easley pointed with alarm to the National League of Women Voters, the Federal Council of Churches, and the Foreign Policy Association. There was hardly a liberal civic organization in the land at which these protectors of the nation did not bid the citizenry to shudder. Even the National Information Bureau, which investigated charities and was headed by no less a pillar of New York respectability than Robert W. DeForest, fell under suspicion. Mr. DeForest, it was claimed, must be too busy to pay attention to what was going on; for along with him were people like Rabbi Wise and Norman Thomas and Oswald Villard and Jane Addams and Scott Nearing and Paul U. Kellogg, many of whom were tainted by radical associations.

There was danger lurking in the theater and the movies. The Moscow Art Theater, the Chauve Souris, and Fyodor Chaliapin were viewed by Mr. Braman of the Allied Patriotic Societies as propagandizing agencies of the Soviets; and according to Mr. Whitney of the American Defense Society, not only Norma Talmadge but—yes—Charlie Chaplin and Will Rogers were mentioned in "Communist files."

Books, too, must be carefully scanned for the all-pervasive evil. Miss Hermine Schwed, speaking for the Better America Federation, a band of California patriots, disapproved of *Main Street* because it "created a distaste for the conventional good life of the American," and called John Dewey and James Harvey Robinson "most dangerous to young people." And as for the schools and colleges, here the danger was more insidious and far-reaching still. According to Mr. Whitney, Professors Felix Frankfurter and Zacharia Chafee (*sic*) of Harvard and Frederick Wells Williams and Max Solomon Mandell of Yale were "too wise not to know that their words, publicly uttered and even used in classrooms, are, to put it conservatively, decidedly encouraging to the Communists." The schools must be firmly taken in hand: text-books must be combed for slights to heroes of American history, none but conservative speakers must be allowed within the precincts of school or college, and courses teaching reverence for the Constitution must be universal and compulsory.

The effect of these admonitions was oppressive. The fear of the radicals was accompanied and followed by a fear of being thought radical. If you wanted to get on in business, to be received in the best circles of Gopher Prairie or Middletown, you must appear to conform. Any deviation from the opinions of Judge Gary and Mr. Palmer was viewed askance. A liberal journalist, visiting a formerly outspoken Hoosier in his office, was not permitted to talk politics until his frightened host had closed and locked the door and closed the window (which gave on an airshaft perhaps fifty feet wide, with offices on the other side where there might be ears to hear the words of heresy). Said a former resident of a Middle Western city, returning to it after a long absence: "These people are all afraid of something. What is it?" The authors of *Middletown* quoted a lonely political dissenter forced into conformity by the iron pressure of public opinion as saying, bitterly, "I just run away from it all to my books." He dared not utter his economic opinions openly; to deviate ever so little from those of the Legion and the Rotary Club would be to brand himself as a Bolshevist.

"America," wrote Katharine Fullerton Gerould in *Harper's Magazine* as late as 1922, "is no longer a free country, in the old sense; and liberty is, increasingly, a mere rhetorical figure. . . . No thinking citizen, I venture to say, can express in freedom more than a part of his honest convictions. I do not of course refer to convictions that are frankly criminal. I do mean that everywhere, on every hand, free speech is choked off in one direction or another. The only way in which an American citizen who is really interested in all the social and political problems of his country can preserve any freedom of expression, is to choose the mob that is most sympathetic to him, and abide under the shadow of that mob."

Sentiments such as these were expressed so frequently and so vehemently in later years that it is astonishing to recall that in 1922 it required some temerity to put them in print. When Mrs. Gerould's article was published, hundreds of letters poured into the Harper office and into her house—letters denouncing her in scurrilous terms as subversive and a Bolshevist, letters rejoicing that at last some one had stood up and told the truth. To such a point had the country been carried by the shoutings of the super-patriots.

[6]

The intolerance of those days took many forms. Almost inevitably it took the form of an ugly flare-up of feeling against the Negro, the Jew, and the Roman Catholic. The emotions of group loyalty and of hatred, expanded during war-time and then suddenly denied their intended expression, found a perverted release in the persecution not only of supposed radicals, but also of other elements which to the dominant American group—the white Protestants—seemed alien or "un-American."

Negroes had migrated during the war by the hundreds of thousands into the industrial North, drawn thither by high wages and by the openings in mill and factory occasioned by the draft. Wherever their numbers increased they had no choice but to move into districts previously reserved for the whites, there to jostle with the whites in street cars and public places, and in a hundred other ways to upset the delicate equilibrium of racial adjustment. In the South as well as in the North the Negroes had felt the stirrings of a new sense of independence; had they not been called to the colors just as the whites had been, and had they not been fighting for democracy and oppressed minorities? When peace came, and they found they were to be put in their place once more, some of them showed their resentment; and in the uneasy atmosphere of the day this was enough to kindle the violent racial passions which smoulder under the surface of human nature. Bolshevism was bad enough, thought the whites, but if the niggers ever got beyond control . . .

One sultry afternoon in the summer of 1919 a seventeen-year-old colored boy was swimming in Lake Michigan by a Chicago bathing-beach. Part of the shore had been set aside by mutual understanding for the use of the whites, another part for the Negroes. The boy took hold of a railroad tie floating in the water and drifted across the invisible line. Stones were thrown at him; a white boy started to swim toward him. The colored boy let go of the railroad tie, swam a few strokes, and sank. He was drowned. Whether he had been hit by any of the stones was uncertain, but the Negroes on the shore accused the whites of stoning him to death, and a fight began. This small incident struck the match that set off a bonfire of race hatred. The Negro population of Chicago had doubled in a decade, the blacks had crowded into white neighborhoods, and nerves were raw. The disorder spread to other parts of the city—and the final result was that for nearly a week Chicago was virtually in a state of civil war; there were mobbings of Negroes, beatings, stabbings, gang raids through the Negro district, shootings by Negroes in defense, and wanton destruction of houses and property; when order was finally restored it was found that fifteen whites and twenty-three Negroes had been killed, five hundred and thirty-seven people had been injured, and a thousand had been left homeless and destitute.

Less than a year later there was another riot of major proportions in Tulsa. Wherever the colored population had spread, there was a new tension in the relations between the races. It was not alleviated by the gospel of white supremacy preached by speakers and writers such as Lothrop Stoddard, whose *Rising Tide of Color* proclaimed that the dark-skinned races constituted a worse threat to Western civilization than the Germans or the Bolsheviks.

The Jews, too, fell under the suspicion of a majority bent upon an undiluted Americanism. Here was a group of inevitably divided loyalty, many of whose members were undeniably prominent among the Bolsheviki in Russia and among the radical immigrants in America. Henry Ford discovered the menace of the "International Jew," and his *Dearborn Independent* accused the unhappy race of plotting the subjugation of the whole world and (for good measure) of being the source of almost every American affliction, including high rents, the shortage of farm labor, jazz, gambling, drunkenness, loose morals, and even short skirts. The Ford attack, absurd as it was, was merely an exaggerated manifestation of a widespread anti-Semitism. Prejudice became as pervasive as the air. Landlords grew less disposed to rent to Jewish tenants, and schools to admit Jewish boys and girls; there was a public scandal at Annapolis over the hazing of a Jewish boy; Harvard College seriously debated limiting the number of Jewish students; and all over the country Jews felt that a barrier had fallen between them and the Gentiles. Nor did the Roman Catholics escape censure in the regions in which they were in a minority. Did not the members of this Church take their orders from a foreign pope, and did not the pope claim temporal power, and did not Catholics insist upon teaching their children in their own way rather than in the American public schools, and was not all this un-American and treasonable?

It was in such an atmosphere that the Ku-Klux Klan blossomed into power.

The Klan had been founded as far back as 1915 by a Georgian named Colonel William Joseph Simmons, but its first five years had been lean. When 1920 arrived, Colonel Simmons had only a few hundred members in his amiable patriotic and fraternal order, which drew its inspiration from the Ku-Klux Klan of Reconstruction days and stood for white supremacy and sentimental Southern idealism in general. But in 1920 Simmons put the task of organizing the Order into the hands of one Edward Y. Clarke of the Southern Publicity Association. Clarke's gifts of salesmanship, hitherto expended on such blameless causes as the Roosevelt Memorial Association and the Near East Relief, were prodigious. The time was ripe for the Klan, and he knew it. Not only could it be represented to potential members as the defender of the white against the black, of Gentile against Jew, and of Protestant against Catholic, and thus trade on all the newly inflamed fears of the credulous small-towner, but its white robe and hood, its flaming cross, its secrecy, and the preposterous vocabulary of its ritual could be made the vehicle for all that infantile love of hocuspocus and mummery, that lust for secret adventure, which survives in the adult whose lot is cast in drab places. Here was a chance to dress up the village bigot and let him be a Knight of the Invisible Empire. The formula was perfect. And there was another inviting fact to be borne in mind. Well organized, such an Order could be made a paying proposition.

The salesmen of memberships were given the entrancing title

of Kleagles; the country was divided into Realms headed by King Kleagles, and the Realms into Domains headed by Grand Goblins; Clarke himself, as chief organizer, became Imperial Kleagle, and the art of nomenclature reached its fantastic pinnacle in the title bestowed upon Colonel Simmons: he became the Imperial Wizard. A membership cost ten dollars; and as four of this went into the pocket of the Kleagle who made the sale, it was soon apparent that a diligent Kleagle need not fear the wolf at the door. Kleagling became one of the profitable industries of the decade. The King Kleagle of the Realm and Grand Goblin of the Domain took a small rake-off from the remaining six dollars of the membership fee, and the balance poured into the Imperial Treasury at Atlanta.

An inconvenient congressional investigation in 1921—brought about largely by sundry reports of tarrings and featherings and floggings, and by the disclosure of many of the Klan's secrets by the *New York World*—led ultimately to the banishment of Imperial Kleagle Clarke, and Colonel Simmons was succeeded as Imperial Wizard by a Texas dentist named Hiram Wesley Evans, who referred to himself, perhaps with some justice, as "the most average man in America"; but a humming sales organization had been built up and the Klan continued to grow. It grew, in fact, with such inordinate rapidity that early in 1924 its membership had reached—according to the careful estimates of Stanley Frost—the staggering figure of nearly four and a half millions. It came to wield great political power, dominating for a time the seven states of Oregon, Oklahoma, Texas, Arkansas, Indiana, Ohio, and California. Its chief strongholds were the New South, the Middle West, and the Pacific coast, but it had invaded almost every part of the country and had even reached the gates of that stronghold of Jewry, Catholicism, and sophistication, New York City. So far had Clarke's genius and the hospitable temper of the times carried it.

The objects of the Order as stated in its Constitution were "to unite white male persons, native-born Gentile citizens of the United States of America, who owe no allegiance of any nature to any foreign government, nation, institution, sect, ruler, person, or people; whose morals are good, whose reputations and vocations are exemplary . . . to cultivate and promote patriotism toward our Civil Government; to practice an honorable Klanishess toward each other; to exemplify a practical benevolence; to shield the sanctity of the home and the chastity of womanhood; to maintain forever white supremacy, to reach and faithfully inculcate a high spiritual philosophy through an exalted ritualism, and by a practical devotion to conserve, protect, and maintain the distinctive institutions, rights, privileges, principles, traditions and ideals of a pure Americanism."

Thus the theory. In practice the "pure Americanism" varied with the locality. At first, in the South, white supremacy was the Klan's chief objective, but as time went on and the organization grew and spread, opposition to the Jew and above all to the Catholic proved the best talking point for Kleagles in most localities. Nor did the methods of the local Klan organizations usually suggest the possession of a "high spiritual philosophy." These local organizations were largely autonomous and beyond control from Atlanta. They were drawn, as a rule, mostly from the less educated and less disciplined elements of the white Protestant community. ("You think the influential men belong here?" commented an outspoken observer in an Indiana city. "Then look at their shoes when they march in parade. The sheet doesn't cover the shoes.") Though Imperial Wizard Evans inveighed against lawlessness, the members of the local Klans were not always content with voting against allowing children to attend parochial schools, or voting against Catholic candidates for office, or burning fiery crosses on the hilltop back of the town to show the niggers that the whites meant business. The secrecy of the Klan was an invitation to more direct action.

If a white girl reported that a colored man had made improper advances to her—even if the charge were unsupported and based on nothing more than a neurotic imagination—a white-sheeted band might spirit the Negro off to the woods and "teach him a lesson" with tar and feathers or with the whip. If a white man stood up for a Negro in a race quarrel, he might be kidnapped and beaten up. If a colored woman refused to sell her land at an arbitrary price which she considered too low, and a Klansman wanted the land, she might receive the K. K. K. ultimatum—sell or be thrown out. Klan members would boycott Jewish merchants, refuse to hire Catholic boys, refuse to rent their houses to Catholics. A hideous tragedy in Louisiana, where five men were kidnapped and later found bound with wire and drowned in a lake, was laid to Klansmen. R. A.

Patton, writing in *Current History*, reported a grim series of brutalities from Alabama: "A lad whipped with branches until his back was ribboned flesh; a Negress beaten and left helpless to contract pneumonia from exposure and die; a white girl, divorcée, beaten into unconsciousness in her own home; a naturalized foreigner flogged until his back was a pulp because he married an American woman; a Negro lashed until he sold his land to a white man for a fraction of its value."

Even where there were no such outrages, there was at least the threat of them. The white-robed army paraded, the burning cross glowed across the valley, people whispered to one another in the darkness and wondered "who they were after this time," and fear and suspicion ran from house to house. Furthermore, criminals and gangs of hoodlums quickly learned to take advantage of the Klan's existence: if they wanted to burn someone's barn or raid the slums beyond the railroad tracks, they could do it with impunity now: would not the Klan be held responsible? Anyone could chalk the letters K. K. K. on a fence and be sure that the sheriff would move warily. Thus, as in the case of the Red hysteria, a movement conceived in fear perpetuated fear and brought with it all manner of cruelties and crimes.

Slowly, as the years passed and the war-time emotions ebbed, the power of the Klan waned, until in many districts it was dead and in others it had become merely a political faction dominated by spoilsmen: but not until it had become a thing of terror to millions of men and women.

[7]

After the Palmer raids at the beginning of 1920 the hunt for radicals went on. In April the five Socialist members of the New York State Assembly were expelled on the ground that (as the report of the Judiciary Committee put it) they were members of "a disloyal organization composed exclusively of perpetual traitors." When Young Theodore Roosevelt spoke against the motion to expel, he was solemnly rebuked by Speaker Sweet, who mounted the rostrum and read aloud passages from the writings of T. R. senior, in order that the Americanism of the father might be painfully contrasted with the un-Americanism of the son. When Assemblyman Cuvillier, in the midst of a speech, spied two of the Socialist members actually

occupying the seats to which they had been elected, he cried:
"These two men who sit there with a smile and a smirk on their
faces are just as much representatives of the Russian Soviet
Government as if they were Lenin and Trotsky themselves.
They are little Lenins, little Trotskys in our midst." The little
Lenins and Trotskys were thrown out by an overwhelming
vote, and the *New York Times* announced the next day that "It
was an American vote altogether, a patriotic and conservative
vote. An immense majority of the American people will ap-
prove and sanction the Assembly's action." That statement,
coming from the discreet *Times,* is a measure of the temper of
the day.

Nevertheless, the tide was almost ready to turn. Charles
Evans Hughes protested against the Assembly's action, thereby
almost causing apoplexy among some of his sedate fellow-
members of the Union League Club, who wondered if such a
good Republican could be becoming a parlor pink. May Day
of 1920 arrived in due course, and although Mr. Palmer
dutifully informed the world in advance that May Day had
been selected by the radicals as the date for a general strike
and for assassinations, nothing happened. The police, fully
mobilized, waited for a revolutionary onslaught that never
arrived. The political conventions rolled round, and although
Calvin Coolidge was swept into the Republican nomination for
Vice-President on his record as the man who broke the Boston
police strike, it was noteworthy that the Democratic Convention did not sweep the Fighting Quaker into anything at
all, and that there was a certain unseemly levity among his
opponents, who insisted upon referring to him as the quaking
fighter, the faking fighter, and the quaking quitter. It began to
look as if the country were beginning to regain its sense of
humor.

Strikes and riots and legislative enactments and judicial
rulings against radicals continued, but with the coming of the
summer of 1920 there were at least other things to compete for
the attention of the country. There was the presidential campaign; the affable Mr. Harding was mouthing orotund
generalizations from his front porch, and the desperate Mr.
Cox was steaming about the country, trying to pull Woodrow
Wilson's chestnuts out of the fire. There was the ticklish
business situation: people had been revolting against high
prices for months, and overall parades had been held, and the

Rev. George M. Elsbree of Philadelphia had preached a sermon in overalls, and there had been an overall wedding in New York (parson, bride, and groom all photographed for the rotogravure section in overalls), and the department stores had been driven to reduce prices, and now it was apparent that business was riding for a fall, strikes or no strikes, radicals or no radicals.

There was the hue and cry over the discovery of the bogus get-rich-quick schemes of Charles Ponzi of Boston. There was Woman Suffrage, now at last a fact, with ratification of the Amendment by the States completed on August 18th. Finally, there was Prohibition, also at last a fact, and an absorbing topic at dinner tables. In those days people sat with bated breath to hear how So-and-so had made very good gin right in his own cellar, and just what formula would fulfill the higher destiny of raisins, and how bootleggers brought liquor down from Canada. It was all new and exciting. That the Big Red Scare was already perceptibly abating by the end of the summer of 1920 was shown by the fact that the nation managed to keep its head surprisingly well when a real disaster, probably attributable to an anarchist gang, took place on the 16th of September.

If there was one geographical spot in the United States that could justly be called the financial center of the country, it was the junction of Broad and Wall Streets in New York. Here, on the north side of Wall Street, stood the Sub-Treasury Building, and next to it the United States Assay Office; opposite them, on the southeast corner, an ostentatiously unostentatious three-story limestone building housed the firm of J. P. Morgan & Company, the most powerful nexus of capitalism in the world; on the southwest corner yawned the excavation where the New York Stock Exchange was presently to build its annex, and next to this, on Broad Street, rose the Corinthian pillars of the Exchange itself. Government finance, private finance, the passage of private control of industry from capitalistic hand to hand: here stood their respective citadels cheek by jowl, as if to symbolize the union into one system of the government and the money power and the direction of business—that system which the radicals so bitterly decried.

Almost at this precise spot, a moment before noon on September 16th, just as the clerks of the neighborhood were getting ready to go out for luncheon, there was a sudden blinding

flash of bluish-white light and a terrific crashing roar, followed
by the clatter of falling glass from innumerable windows and
by the screams of men and women. A huge bomb had gone off
in the street in front of the Assay Office and directly opposite
the House of Morgan—gone off with such appalling violence
that it killed thirty people outright and injured hundreds,
wrecked the interior of the Morgan offices, smashed windows
for blocks around, and drove an iron slug through the window
of the Bankers' Club on the thirty-fourth floor of the Equitable
Building.

A great mushroom-shaped cloud of yellowish-green smoke
rose slowly into the upper air between the skyscrapers. Below
it, the air was filled with dust pouring out of the Morgan windows and the windows of other buildings—dust from shrapnel-
bitten plaster walls. And below that, the street ran red with the
blood of the dead and dying. Those who by blind chance had
escaped the hail of steel picked themselves up and ran in terror
as glass and fragments of stone showered down from the buildings above; then there was a surge of people back to the horror
again, a vast crowd milling about and trying to help the victims
and not knowing what to do first and bumping into one another and shouting; then fire engines and ambulances clanged
to the scene and police and hospital orderlies fought their way
through the mob and brought it at last to order.

In the House of Morgan, one man had been killed, the chief
clerk; dozens were hurt, seventeen had to be taken to hospitals.
But only one partner had been cut in the hand by flying glass;
the rest were in conference on the other side of the building or
out of town. Mr. Morgan was abroad. The victims of the
explosion were not the financial powers of the country, but
bank clerks, brokers' men, Wall Street runners, stenographers.

In the Stock Exchange, hardly two hundred feet away,
trading had been proceeding at what in those days was considered "good volume"—at the rate of half a million shares or so
for the day. Prices had been rising. Reading was being bid up
2⅛ points to 93¾, Baldwin Locomotive was going strong at
110¾, there was heavy trading in Middle States Oil, Steel was
doing well at 89⅜. The crash came, the building shook, and
the big windows smashed down in a shower of glass; those on
the Broad Street side had their heavy silk curtains drawn, or
dozens of men would have been injured. For a moment the

brokers, not knowing what had happened, scampered for anything that looked like shelter. Those in the middle of the floor, where an instant before the largest crowd of traders had been gathered around the Reading post, made for the edges of the room lest the dome should fall. But William H. Remick, president of the Exchange, who had been standing with the "money crowd" at the side of the room, kept his head. Remarking to a friend, "I guess it's about time to ring the gong," he mounted the rostrum, rang the gong, and thereby immediately ended trading for the day. (The next day prices continued to rise as if nothing had happened.)

Out in the middle of Wall Street lay the carcass of a horse blown to pieces by the force of the explosion, and here and there were assembled bits of steel and wood and canvas which, with the horse's shoes and the harness, enabled the police to decide that a TNT bomb had gone off in a horse-drawn wagon, presumably left unattended as its driver escaped from the scene. For days and months and years detectives and Federal agents followed up every possible clue. Every wagon in the city, to say nothing of powder wagons, was traced. The slugs which had imbedded themselves in the surrounding buildings were examined and found to be window sash-weights cut in two—but this, despite endless further investigation, led to nothing more than the conclusion that the explosion was a premeditated crime. The horse's shoes were identified and a man was found who had put them on the horse a few days before; he described the driver as a Sicilian, but the clue led no further. Bits of steel and tin found in the neighborhood were studied, manufacturers consulted, records of sale run through. One fragment of iron proved to be the knob of a safe, and the safe was identified; a detective followed the history of the safe from its manufacture through various hands until it went to France with the Army during the war and returned to Hoboken—but there its trail was lost. Every eye-witness's story was tested and analyzed. Reports of warnings of disaster received by business men were run down but yielded nothing of real value. Suspected radicals were rounded up without result. One bit of evidence remained, but how important it was one could not be sure. At almost the exact minute of the explosion, a letter-carrier was said to have found in a post-box two or three blocks from the scene—a box which had been emptied only half an hour before—five sheets of paper on which was crudely printed, with varying misspellings,

> Rememer
> We will not tolerate
> any longer
> Free the politiCal
> prisoniers or it will be
> sure death to all oF you
> American   Anarchists
>   Fighters

A prominent coal operator who was sitting in the Morgan offices when the explosion took place promptly declared that there was no question in his mind that it was the work of Bolshevists. After years of fruitless investigation, there was still a question in the minds of those who tried to solve the mystery. But in the loose sense in which the coal operator used the term, he was probably right.

The country followed the early stages of the investigation with absorbed interest. Yet no marked increase in anti-Bolshevist riots took place. If the explosion had occurred a few months earlier, it might have had indirect consequences as ugly as the damage which it did directly. But by this time the American people were coming to their senses sufficiently to realize that no such insane and frightful plot could ever command the support of more than a handful of fanatics.

IV

America Convalescent

The Big Red Scare was slowly—very slowly—dying.

What killed it?

The realization, for one thing, that there had never been any sufficient cause for such a panic as had convulsed the country. The localization of Communism in Europe, for another thing: when Germany and other European nations failed to be engulfed by the Bolshevist tide, the idea of its sweeping irresistibly across the Atlantic became a little less plausible. It was a fact, too, that radicalism was noticeably ebbing in the United States. The Fighting Quaker's inquisitorial methods, whatever one may think of them, had at least had the practical effect of scaring many Reds into a pale pinkness. By 1921 the A. F. of L. leaders were leaning over backward in their effort to appear as conservative as Judge Gary, college professors were canceling their subscriptions to liberal magazines on the ground that they could not afford to let such literature be seen on their tables, and the social reformers of a year or two before were tiring of what seemed a thankless and hopeless fight. There was also, perhaps, a perceptible loss of enthusiasm for governmental action against the Reds on the part of the growing company of the wets, who were acquiring a belated concern for personal liberty and a new distrust of federal snoopers. Yet there was another cause more important, perhaps, than any of these. The

temper of the aftermath of war was at last giving way to the
temper of peace. Like an overworked business man beginning
his vacation, the country had had to go through a period of
restlessness and irritability, but was finally learning how to
relax and amuse itself once more.

A sense of disillusionment remained; like the suddenly
liberated vacationist, the country felt that it ought to be enjoying itself more than it was, and that life was futile and nothing
mattered much. But in the meantime it might as well play—
follow the crowd, take up the new toys that were amusing the
crowd, go in for the new fads, savor the amusing scandals and
trivialities of life. By 1921 the new toys and fads and scandals
were forthcoming, and the country seized upon them fe-
verishly.

[2]

First of all was the radio, which was destined ultimately to
alter the daily habits of Americans as profoundly as anything
that the decade produced.

The first broadcasting station had been opened in East
Pittsburgh on November 2, 1920—a date which school children may some day have to learn—to carry the Harding-Cox
election returns. This was station KDKA, operated by the
Westinghouse Company. For a time, however, this new revolution in communication and public entertainment made slow
headway. Auditors were few. Amateur wireless operators
objected to the stream of music—mostly from phonograph
records—which issued from the Westinghouse station and
interfered with their important business. When a real orchestra
was substituted for the records, the resonance of the room in
which the players sat spoiled the effect. The orchestra was
placed out-of-doors, in a tent on the roof—and the tent blew
away. The tent was thereupon pitched in a big room indoors,
and not until then was it discovered that the cloth hangings
which subsequently became standard in broadcasting studios
would adequately muffle the sound.

Experiment proceeded, however; other radio stations were
opened, market reports were thrown on the air, Dr. Van Etten
of Pittsburgh permitted the services at Calvary Church to be
broadcasted, the University of Wisconsin gave radio concerts,
and politicians spouted into the strange instruments and won-

dered if anybody was really listening. Yet when Dempsey fought Carpentier in July, 1921, and three men at the ringside told the story of the slaughter into telephone transmitters to be relayed by air to eighty points throughout the country, their enterprise was reported in an obscure corner of the *New York Times* as an achievement in "wireless telephony"; and when the Unknown Soldier was buried at Arlington Cemetery the following November, crowds packed into Madison Square Garden in New York and the Auditorium in San Francisco to hear the speeches issue from huge amplifiers, and few in those crowds had any idea that soon they could hear all the orations they wanted without stirring from the easy-chair in the living-room. The great awakening had not yet come.

That winter, however—the winter of 1921-22—it came with a rush. Soon everybody was talking, not about wireless telephony, but about radio. A San Francisco paper described the discovery that millions were making: "There is radio music in the air, every night, everywhere. Anybody can hear it at home on a receiving set, which any boy can put up in an hour." In February President Harding had an outfit installed in his study, and the Dixmoor Golf Club announced that it would install a "telephone" to enable golfers to hear church services. In April, passengers on a Lackawanna train heard a radio concert, and Lieutenant Maynard broke all records for modernizing Christianity by broadcasting an Easter sermon from an airplane. Newspapers brought out radio sections and thousands of hitherto utterly unmechanical people puzzled over articles about regenerative circuits, sodion tubes, Grimes reflex circuits, crystal detectors, and neutrodynes. In the Ziegfeld "Follies of 1922" the popularity of "My Rambler Rose" was rivaled by that of a song about a man who hoped his love might hear him as she was "listening on the radio." And every other man you met on the street buttonholed you to tell you how he had sat up until two o'clock the night before, with earphones clamped to his head, and had actually *heard Havana!* How could one bother about the Red Menace if one was facing such momentous questions as how to construct a loop aërial?

In the *Readers' Guide to Periodical Literature* for the years 1919-21, in which were listed all the magazine articles appearing during those years, there were two columns of references to articles on Radicals and Radicalism and less than a quarter of a column of references to articles on Radio. In the *Readers'*

Guide for 1922-24, by contrast, the section on Radicals and Radicalism shrank to half a column and the section on Radio swelled to nineteen columns. In that change there is an index to something more than periodical literature.

[3]

Sport, too, had become an American obsession. When Jack Kearns persuaded Tex Rickard to bring together Dempsey and the worn-out but engaging Georges Carpentier at Boyle's Thirty Acres in Jersey City in 1921, the public responded as they had never before responded in the history of the country. Nearly seventy-five thousand people paid over a million and a half dollars—over three times as much as the Dempsey-Willard fight had brought in—to see the debonair Frenchman flattened in the fourth round, and the metropolitan papers, not content with a few columns in the sporting section, devoted page after page the next day to every conceivable detail of the fight. It was the first of the huge million-dollar bouts of the decade. Babe Ruth raised his home-run record to fifty-nine, and the 1921 World's Series broke records for gate receipts and attendance. Sport-hungry crowds who had never dreamed of taking a college-entrance examination swarmed to college football games, watched Captain Malcolm Aldrich of Yale and George Owen of Harvard, and devoured hundreds of columns of dopesters' gossip about Penn State and Pittsburgh and Iowa and the "praying Colonels" of Centre College. Racing had taken on a new lease of life with the unparalleled success of Man o' War in 1920. Tennis clubs were multiplying, and business men were discovering by the hundreds of thousands that a par-four hole was the best place to be in conference. There were food-fads, too, as well as sport-fads: such was the sudden and overwhelming craze for Eskimo Pie that in three months the price of cocoa beans on the New York market rose 50 per cent.

Another new American institution caught the public eye during the summer of 1921—the bathing beauty. In early July a Costume and Beauty Show was held at Washington's bathing beach on the Potomac, and the prize-winners were so little touched by the influence of Mack Sennett and his moving-picture bathers that they wore tunic bathing-suits, hats over their long curls, and long stockings—all but one, who daringly rolled her stockings below her knees. In early September Atlantic City held its first Beauty Pageant—a similar show, but with a difference. "For the time being, the censor ban on bare knees and skin-tight bathing suits was suspended," wrote an astonished reporter, "and thousands of spectators gasped as they applauded the girls." Miss Washington was declared the most beautiful girl of the cities of America, the one-piece suit became overnight the orthodox wear for bathing beauties (though taffetas and sateens remained good enough for genuine sea-going bathers for a season or two to come), promoters of seashore resorts began to plan new contests, and the rotogravure and tabloid editors faced a future bright with promise.

The tabloids, indeed, were booming—and not without effect. There was more than coincidence in the fact that as they rose, radicalism fell. They presented American life not as a political and economic struggle, but as a three-ring circus of sport, crime, and sex, and in varying degrees the other papers followed their lead under the pressure of competition. Workmen forgot to be class-conscious as they gloated over pictures of Miss Scranton on the Boardwalk and followed the Stillman case and the Arbuckle case and studied the racing dope about Morvich.

Readers with perceptibly higher brows, too, had their diversions from the affairs of the day. Though their heads still reeled from *The Education of Henry Adams,* they were wading manfully through paleontology as revealed in the *Outline of History* (and getting bogged, most of them, somewhere near the section on Genghis Khan). They were asking one another whether America was truly as ugly as Sinclair Lewis made it in *Main Street* and Tahiti truly as enchanting as Frederick O'Brien made it in *White Shadows of the South Seas*; they were learning about hot love in hot places from *The Sheik,* and lapping up Mrs. Asquith's gossip of the British ruling classes, and having a good old-fashioned cry over *If Winter Comes.*

Further diversions were on the way, too. If there had been any doubt, after the radio craze struck the country, that the American people were learning to enjoy such diversions with headlong unanimity, the events of 1922 and 1923 dispelled it. On the 16th of September, 1922, the murder of the decade took place: The Reverend Edward Wheeler Hall and Mrs. James Mills, the choir leader in his church, were found shot to death on an abandoned farm near New Brunswick, New

Jersey. The Hall-Mills case had all the elements needed to satisfy an exacting public taste for the sensational. It was better than the Elwell case of June, 1920. It was grisly, it was dramatic (the bodies being laid side by side as if to emphasize an unhallowed union), it involved wealth and respectability, it had just the right amount of sex interest—and in addition it took place close to the great metropolitan nerve-center of the American press. It was an illiterate American who did not shortly become acquainted with DeRussey's Lane, the crab-apple tree, the pig woman and her mule, the precise mental condition of Willie Stevens, and the gossip of the choir members.

[4]

By this time, too, a new game was beginning its conquest of the country. In the first year or two after the war, Joseph P. Babcock, Soochow representative of the Standard Oil Company, had become interested in the Chinese game of Mah Jong and had codified and simplified the rules for the use of Americans. Two brothers named White had introduced it to the English-speaking clubs of Shanghai, where it became popular. It was brought to the United States, and won such immediate favor that W. A. Hammond, a San Francisco lumber merchant, was encouraged to import sets on an ambitious scale. By September, 1922, he had already imported fifty thousand dollars' worth. A big campaign of advertising, with free lessons and exhibitions, pushed the game, and within the next year the Mah Jong craze had become so universal that Chinese makers of sets could no longer keep up with the demand and American manufacture was in full swing. By 1923, people who were beginning to take their radio sets for granted now simply left them turned on while they "broke the wall" and called "pung" or "chow" and wielded the Ming box and talked learnedly of bamboos, flowers, seasons, South Wind, and Red Dragon. The wealthy bought five-hundred-dollar sets; dozens of manufacturers leaped into the business; a Mah Jong League of America was formed; there was fierce debate as to what rules to play by, what system of scoring to use, and what constituted a "limit hand"; and the correct dinner party wound up with every one setting up ivory and bamboo tiles on green baize tables.

Even before Mah Jong reached its climax, however, Emil Coué had arrived in America, preceded by an efficient ballyhoo; in the early months of 1923 the little dried-up Frenchman from Nancy was suddenly the most-talked-of person in the country. Coué Institutes were established, and audiences who thronged to hear the master speak were hushed into awesome quiet as he repeated, himself, the formula which was already on everybody's lips: "Day by day in every way I am getting better and better." A few weeks later there was a new national thrill as the news of the finding of the tomb of King Tut-Ankh-Amen, cabled all the way from Egypt, overshadowed the news of the Radical trials and Ku-Klux Klan scandals, and dress manufacturers began to plan for a season of Egyptian styles. Finally, the country presently found still a new obsession—in the form of a song: a phrase picked up from an Italian fruit-vender and used some time before this as a "gag-line" by Tad Dorgan, the cartoonist, was worked into verse, put to music which drew liberally from the "Hallelujah Chorus" and "I Dreamt That I Dwelt in Marble Halls" and "Aunt Dinah's Quilting Party," was tried out in a Long Island roadhouse, and then was brought to New York, where it quickly superseded "Mr. Gallagher and Mr. Shean" in popular acclaim. Before long "Yes, We Have No Bananas" had penetrated to the remotest farmhouse in the remotest county.

Though the super-patriots still raged and federal agents still pursued the nimble Communists and an avowed Socialist was still regarded with as much enthusiasm as a leper, and the Ku-Klux Klan still grew, the Big Red Scare was dying. There were too many other things to think about.

Perhaps, though, there was still another reason for the passing of the Red Menace. Another Menace was endangering the land—and one which could not possibly be attributed to the machinations of Moscow. The younger generation was on the rampage, as we shall presently see.

[5]

Only one dispute, during the rest of the Post-war Decade, drew the old line of 1919 and 1920 between liberal and conservative throughout the nation.

At the height of the Big Red Scare—in April, 1920—there

had taken place at South Braintree, Massachusetts, a crime so unimportant that it was not even mentioned in the *New York Times* of the following day—or, for that matter, of the whole following year. It was the sort of crime which was taking place constantly all over the country. A paymaster and his guard, carrying two boxes containing the pay-roll of a shoe factory, were killed by two men with pistols, who thereupon leaped into an automobile which drew up at the curb, and drove away across the railroad tracks. Two weeks later a couple of Italian radicals were arrested as the murderers, and a year later—at about the time when the Washington bathing beauties were straightening their long stockings to be photographed and David Sarnoff was supervising the reporting of the Dempsey-Carpentier fight by "wireless telephone"—the Italians were tried before Judge Webster Thayer and a jury and found guilty. The trial attracted a little attention, but not much. A few months later, however, people from Maine to California began to ask what this Sacco-Vanzetti case was all about. For a very remarkable thing had happened.

Three men in a bleak Boston office—a Spanish carpenter, a Jewish youth from New York, and an Italian newspaper man —had been writing industriously about the two Italians to the radicals and the radical press of France and Italy and Spain and other countries in Europe and Central and South America. The result: A bomb exploded in Ambassador Herrick's house in Paris. Twenty people were killed by another bomb in a Paris Sacco-Vanzetti demonstration. Crowds menaced the American Embassy in Rome. There was an attempt to bomb the home of the Consul-General at Lisbon. There was a general strike and an attempt to boycott American goods at Montevideo. The case was discussed in the radical press of Algiers, Porto Rico, and Mexico. Under the circumstances it could not very well help becoming a *cause célèbre* in the United States.

But bombings and boycotts, though they attracted attention to the case, could never have aroused widespread public sympathy for Sacco and Vanzetti. What aroused it, as the case dragged on year after year and one appeal after another was denied, was the demeanor of the men themselves. Vanzetti in particular was clearly a remarkable man—an intellectual of noble character, a philosophical anarchist of a type which it seemed impossible to associate with a pay-roll murder. New evidence made the guilt of the men seem still more doubtful. When, in 1927—seven long years after the murder—Judge Thayer stubbornly denied the last appeal and pronounced the sentence of death, public opinion forced Governor Fuller of Massachusetts to review the case and consider pardoning Sacco and Vanzetti. The Governor named as an advisory committee to make a further study of the case, President Lowell of Harvard, President Stratton of the Massachusetts Institute of Technology, and Judge Robert Grant—all men respected by the community. A few weeks later the committee reported: they believed Sacco and Vanzetti to be guilty. There was no pardon. On the night of August 22, 1927, these two men who had gathered about their cause the hopes and fears of millions throughout the world were sent to the electric chair.

Whether they were actually guilty or not will probably never be definitely determined—though no one can read their speeches to the court and their letters without doubting if justice was done. The record of the case was of vast length and full of technicalities, it was discussed *ex-parte* by vehement propagandists on both sides, and the division of public opinion on the case was largely a division between those who thought radicals ought to be strung up on general principles and those who thought that the test of a country's civilization lay in the scrupulousness with which it protected the rights of minorities. The passions of the early days of the decade were revived as pickets marched before the Boston State House, calling on the Governor to release Sacco and Vanzetti, and the Boston police —whose strike not eight years before had put Calvin Coolidge in the White House which he now occupied—arrested the pickets and bore them off to the lock-up.

The bull market was now in full swing, the labor movement was enfeebled, prosperity had given radicalism what seemed to be its *coup de grâce*—but still the predicament of these two simple Italians had the power briefly to recall the days of Mitchell Palmer's Red raids and to arouse fears and hatreds long since quieted. People who had almost forgotten whether they were conservatives or liberals found themselves in bitter argument once more, and friendships were disrupted over the identification of Sacco's cap or the value of Captain Proctor's testimony about the fatal bullet. But only briefly. The headlines screamed that Sacco and Vanzetti had been executed, and men read them with a shiver, and wondered, perhaps, if this thing which had been done with such awful finality were the just deserts of crime or a hideous mistake—and glanced at another column to find where Lindbergh was flying today, and whipped open the paper to the financial page. . . . What was General Motors doing?

V

The Revolution in Manners and Morals

A first-class revolt against the accepted American order was certainly taking place during those early years of the Post-war Decade, but it was one with which Nikolai Lenin had nothing whatever to do. The shock troops of the rebellion were not alien agitators, but the sons and daughters of well-to-do American families, who knew little about Bolshevism and cared distinctly less, and their defiance was expressed not in obscure radical publications or in soap-box speeches, but right across the family breakfast table into the horrified ears of conservative fathers and mothers. Men and women were still shivering at the Red Menace when they awoke to the no less alarming Problem of the Younger Generation, and realized that if the Constitution were not in danger, the moral code of the country certainly was.

This code, as it currently concerned young people, might have been roughly summarized as follows: Women were the guardians of morality; they were made of finer stuff than men and were expected to act accordingly. Young girls must look forward in innocence (tempered perhaps with a modicum of physiological instruction) to a romantic love match which would lead them to the altar and to living-happily-ever-after; and until the "right man" came along they must allow no male to kiss them. It was expected that some men would succumb to the temptations of sex, but only with a special class of out-lawed women; girls of respectable families were supposed to have no such temptations. Boys and girls were permitted large freedom to work and play together, with decreasing and well-nigh nominal chaperonage, but only because the code worked so well on the whole that a sort of honor system was supplanting supervision by their elders; it was taken for granted that if they had been well brought up they would never take advantage of this freedom. And although the attitude toward smoking and drinking by girls differed widely in different strata of society and different parts of the country, majority opinion held that it was morally wrong for them to smoke and could hardly imagine them showing the effects of alcohol.

The war had not long been over when cries of alarm from parents, teachers, and moral preceptors began to rend the air. For the boys and girls just growing out of adolescence were making mincemeat of this code.

The dresses that the girls—and for that matter most of the older women—were wearing seemed alarming enough. In July, 1920, a fashion-writer reported in the *New York Times* that "the American woman . . . has lifted her skirts far beyond any modest limitation," which was another way of saying that the hem was now all of nine inches above the ground. It was freely predicted that skirts would come down again in the winter of 1920-21, but instead they climbed a few scandalous inches farther. The flappers wore thin dresses, short-sleeved and occasionally (in the evening) sleeveless; some of the wilder young things rolled their stockings below their knees, revealing to the shocked eyes of virtue a fleeting glance of shin-bones and knee-cap; and many of them were visibly using cosmetics. "The intoxication of rouge," earnestly explained Dorothy Speare in *Dancers in the Dark,* "is an insidious vintage known to more girls than mere man can ever believe." Useless for frantic parents to insist that no lady did such things; the answer was that the daughters of ladies were doing it, and even re-touching their masterpieces in public. Some of them, further-more, were abandoning their corsets. "The men won't dance with you if you wear a corset," they were quoted as saying.

The current mode in dancing created still more con-sternation. Not the romantic violin but the barbaric saxo-phone now dominated the orchestra, and to its passionate crooning and wailing the fox-trotters moved in what the editor of the Hobart College *Herald* disgustedly called a "syncopated embrace." No longer did even an inch of space separate them; they danced as if glued together, body to body, cheek to cheek. Cried the *Catholic Telegraph* of Cincinnati in righteous indignation, "The music is sensuous, the embracing of partners —the female only half dressed—is absolutely indecent; and the motions—they are such as may not be described, with any respect for propriety, in a family newspaper. Suffice it to say that there are certain houses appropriate for such dances; but those houses have been closed by law."

Supposedly "nice" girls were smoking cigarettes—openly and defiantly, if often rather awkwardly and self-consciously. They were drinking—somewhat less openly but often all too efficaciously. There were stories of daughters of the most exemplary parents getting drunk—"blotto," as their companions cheerfully put it—on the contents of the hip-flasks of the new prohibition régime, and going out joyriding with men at four in the morning. And worst of all, even at well-regulated dances they were said to retire where the eye of the most sharp-sighted chaperon could not follow, and in darkened rooms or in parked cars to engage in the unspeakable practice of petting and necking.

It was not until F. Scott Fitzgerald, who had hardly graduated from Princeton and ought to know what his generation was doing, brought out *This Side of Paradise* in April, 1920, that fathers and mothers realized fully what was afoot and how long it had been going on. Apparently the "petting party" had been current as early as 1916, and was now widely established as an indoor sport. "None of the Victorian mothers—and most of the mothers were Victorian—had any idea how casually their daughters were accustomed to be kissed," wrote Mr. Fitzgerald. ". . . Amory saw girls doing things that even in his memory would have been impossible: eating three-o'clock, after-dance suppers in impossible cafés, talking of every side of life with an air half of earnestness, half of mockery, yet with a furtive excitement that Amory considered stood for a real moral let-down. But he never realized how widespread it was until he saw the cities between New York and Chicago as one vast juvenile intrigue." The book caused a shudder to run down the national spine; did not Mr. Fitzgerald represent one of his well-nurtured heroines as brazenly confessing, "I've kissed dozens of men. I suppose I'll kiss dozens more"; and another heroine as saying to a young man (*to a young man!*), "Oh, just one person in fifty has any glimmer of what sex is. I'm hipped on Freud and all that, but it's rotten that every bit of real love in the world is ninety-nine per cent passion and one little *soupçon* of jealousy"?

It was incredible. It was abominable. What did it all mean? Was every decent standard being thrown over? Mothers read the scarlet words and wondered if they themselves "had any idea how often their daughters were accustomed to be kissed." . . . But no, this must be an exaggerated account of the misconduct of some especially depraved group. Nice girls couldn't behave like that and talk openly about passion. But in due course other books appeared to substantiate the findings of Mr. Fitzgerald: *Dancers in the Dark, The Plastic Age, Flaming Youth.* Magazine articles and newspapers reiterated the scandal. To be sure, there were plenty of communities where nice girls did not, in actual fact, "behave like that"; and even in the more sophisticated urban centers there were plenty of girls who did not. Nevertheless, there was enough fire beneath the smoke of these sensational revelations to make the Problem of the Younger Generation a topic of anxious discussion from coast to coast.

The forces of morality rallied to the attack. Dr. Francis E. Clark, the founder and president of the Christian Endeavor Society, declared that the modern "indecent dance" was "an offense against womanly purity, the very fountainhead of our family and civil life." The new style of dancing was denounced in religious journals as "impure, polluting, corrupting, debasing, destroying spirituality, increasing carnality," and the mothers and sisters and church members of the land were called upon to admonish and instruct and raise the spiritual tone of these dreadful young people. President Murphy of the University of Florida cried out with true Southern warmth, "The low-cut gowns, the rolled hose and short skirts are born of the Devil and his angels, and are carrying the present and future generations to chaos and destruction." A group of Episcopal church-women in New York, speaking with the authority of wealth and social position (for they included Mrs. J. Pierpont Morgan, Mrs. Borden Harriman, Mrs. Henry Phipps, Mrs. James Roosevelt, and Mrs. E. H. Harriman), proposed an organization to discourage fashions involving an "excess of nudity" and "improper ways of dancing." The Y.

W. C. A. conducted a national campaign against immodest dress among high-school girls, supplying newspapers with printed matter carrying headlines such as "Working Girls Responsive to Modesty Appeal" and "High Heels Losing Ground Even in France." In Philadelphia a Dress Reform Committee of prominent citizens sent a questionnaire to over a thousand clergymen to ask them what would be their idea of a proper dress, and although the gentlemen of the cloth showed a distressing variety of opinion, the committee proceeded to design a "moral gown" which was endorsed by ministers of fifteen denominations. The distinguishing characteristics of this moral gown were that it was very loose-fitting, that the sleeves reached just below the elbows, and that the hem came within seven and a half inches of the floor.

Not content with example and reproof, legislators in several states introduced bills to reform feminine dress once and for all. The *New York American* reported in 1921 that a bill was pending in Utah providing fine and imprisonment for those who wore on the streets "skirts higher than three inches above the ankle." A bill was laid before the Virginia legislature which would forbid any woman from wearing shirtwaists or evening gowns which displayed "more than three inches of her throat." In Ohio the proposed limit of decolletage was two inches; the bill introduced in the Ohio legislature aimed also to prevent the sale of any "garment which unduly displays or accentuates the lines of the female figure," and to prohibit any "female over fourteen years of age" from wearing "a skirt which does not reach to that part of the foot known as the instep."

Meanwhile innumerable families were torn with dissension over cigarettes and gin and all-night automobile rides. Fathers and mothers lay awake asking themselves whether their children were not utterly lost; sons and daughters evaded questions, lied miserably and unhappily, or flared up to reply rudely that at least they were not dirty-minded hypocrites, that they saw no harm in what they were doing and proposed to go right on doing it. From those liberal clergymen and teachers who prided themselves on keeping step with all that was new came a chorus of reassurance: these young people were at least franker and more honest than their elders had been; having experimented for themselves, would they not soon find out which standards were outworn and which represented the accumulated moral wisdom of the race? Hearing such hopeful words, many good people took heart again. Perhaps this flare-up of youthful passion was a flash in the pan, after all. Perhaps in another year or two the boys and girls would come to their senses and everything would be all right again.

They were wrong, however. For the revolt of the younger generation was only the beginning of a revolution in manners and morals that was already beginning to affect men and women of every age in every part of the country.

[2]

A number of forces were working together and interacting upon one another to make this revolution inevitable.

First of all was the state of mind brought about by the war and its conclusion. A whole generation had been infected by the eat-drink-and-be-merry-for-tomorrow-we-die spirit which accompanied the departure of the soldiers to the training camps and the fighting front. There had been an epidemic not only of abrupt war marriages, but of less conventional liaisons. In France, two million men had found themselves very close to filth and annihilation and very far from the American moral code and its defenders; prostitution had followed the flag and willing mademoiselles from Armentières had been plentiful; American girls sent over as nurses and war workers had come under the influence of continental manners and standards without being subject to the rigid protections thrown about their continental sisters of the respectable classes; and there had been a very widespread and very natural breakdown of traditional restraints and reticences and taboos. It was impossible for this generation to return unchanged when the ordeal was over. Some of them had acquired under the pressure of war-time conditions a new code which seemed to them quite defensible; millions of them had been provided with an emotional stimulant from which it was not easy to taper off. Their torn nerves craved the anodynes of speed, excitement, and passion. They found themselves expected to settle down into the humdrum routine of American life as if nothing had happened, to accept the moral dicta of elders who seemed to them still to be living in a Pollyanna land of rosy ideals which the war had killed for them. They couldn't do it, and they very disrespectfully said so.

"The older generation had certainly pretty well ruined this

world before passing it on to us," wrote one of them (John F. Carter in the *Atlantic Monthly*, September, 1920), expressing accurately the sentiments of innumerable contemporaries. "They give us this thing, knocked to pieces, leaky, red-hot, threatening to blow up; and then they are surprised that we don't accept it with the same attitude of pretty, decorous enthusiasm with which they received it, way back in the 'eighties."

The middle generation was not so immediately affected by the war neurosis. They had had time enough, before 1917, to build up habits of conformity not easily broken down. But they, too, as the let-down of 1919 followed the war, found themselves restless and discontented, in a mood to question everything that had once seemed to them true and worthy and of good report. They too had spent themselves and wanted a good time. They saw their juniors exploring the approaches to the forbidden land of sex, and presently they began to play with the idea of doing a little experimenting of their own. The same disillusion which had defeated Woodrow Wilson and had caused strikes and riots and the Big Red Scare furnished a culture in which the germs of the new freedom could grow and multiply.

The revolution was accelerated also by the growing independence of the American woman. She won the suffrage in 1920. She seemed, it is true, to be very little interested in it once she had it; she voted, but mostly as the unregenerate men about her did, despite the efforts of women's clubs and the League of Women Voters to awaken her to womanhood's civic opportunity; feminine candidates for office were few, and some of them—such as Governor Ma Ferguson of Texas—scarcely seemed to represent the starry-eyed spiritual influence which, it had been promised, would presently ennoble public life. Few of the younger women could rouse themselves to even a passing interest in politics: to them it was a sordid and futile business, without flavor and without hope. Nevertheless, the winning of the suffrage had its effect. It consolidated woman's position as man's equal.

Even more marked was the effect of woman's growing independence of the drudgeries of housekeeping. Smaller houses were being built, and they were easier to look after. Families were moving into apartments, and these made even less claim upon the housekeeper's time and energy. Women were learning how to make lighter work of the preparation of meals. Sales of canned foods were growing, the number of delicatessen stores had increased three times as fast as the population during the decade 1910-20, the output of bakeries increased by 60 per cent during the decade 1914-24. Much of what had once been housework was now either moving out of the home entirely or being simplified by machinery. The use of commercial laundries, for instance, increased by 57 per cent between 1914 and 1924. Electric washing-machines and electric irons were coming to the aid of those who still did their washing at home; the manager of the local electric power company at "Middletown," a typical small American city, estimated in 1924 that nearly 90 per cent of the homes in the city already had electric irons. The housewife was learning to telephone her shopping orders, to get her clothes ready-made and spare herself the rigors of dress-making, to buy a vacuum cleaner and emulate the lovely carefree girls in the magazine advertisements who banished dust with such delicate fingers. Women were slowly becoming emancipated from routine to "live their own lives."

And what were these "own lives" of theirs to be like? Well, for one thing, they could take jobs. Up to this time girls of the middle classes who had wanted to "do something" had been largely restricted to school-teaching, social-service work, nursing, stenography, and clerical work in business houses. But now they poured out of the schools and colleges into all manner of new occupations. They besieged the offices of publishers and advertisers; they went into tea-room management until there threatened to be more purveyors than consumers of chicken patties and cinnamon toast; they sold antiques, sold real estate, opened smart little shops, and finally invaded the department stores. In 1920 the department store was in the mind of the average college girl a rather bourgeois institution which employed "poor shop girls"; by the end of the decade college girls were standing in line for openings in the misses' sports-wear department and even selling behind the counter in the hope that some day fortune might smile upon them and make them buyers or stylists. Small-town girls who once would have been contented to stay in Sauk Center all their days were now borrowing from father to go to New York or Chicago to seek their fortunes—in Best's or Macy's or Marshall Field's.

Married women who were encumbered with children and could not seek jobs consoled themselves with the thought that home-making and child-rearing were really "professions," after all. No topic was so furiously discussed at luncheon tables from one end of the country to the other as the question whether the married woman should take a job, and whether the mother had a right to. And as for the unmarried woman, she no longer had to explain why she worked in a shop or an office; it was idleness, nowadays, that had to be defended.

With the job—or at least the sense that the job was a possibility—came a feeling of comparative economic independence. With the feeling of economic independence came a slackening of husbandly and parental authority. Maiden aunts and unmarried daughters were leaving the shelter of the family roof to install themselves in kitchenette apartments of their own. For city-dwellers the home was steadily becoming less of a shrine, more of a dormitory—a place of casual shelter where one stopped overnight on the way from the restaurant and the movie theater to the office. Yet even the job did not provide the American woman with that complete satisfaction which the management of a mechanized home no longer furnished. She still had energies and emotions to burn; she was ready for the revolution.

Like all revolutions, this one was stimulated by foreign propaganda. It came, however, not from Moscow, but from Vienna. Sigmund Freud had published his first book on psychoanalysis at the end of the nineteenth century, and he and Jung had lectured to American psychologists as early as 1909, but it was not until after the war that the Freudian gospel began to circulate to a marked extent among the American lay public. The one great intellectual force which had not suffered disrepute as a result of the war was science; the more-or-less educated public was now absorbing a quantity of popularized information about biology and anthropology which gave a general impression that men and women were merely animals of a rather intricate variety, and that moral codes had no universal validity and were often based on curious superstitions. A fertile ground was ready for the seeds of Freudianism, and presently one began to hear even from the lips of flappers that "science taught" new and disturbing things about sex. Sex, it appeared, was the central and pervasive force which

moved mankind. Almost every human motive was attributable
to it: if you were patriotic or liked the violin, you were in the
grip of sex—in a sublimated form. The first requirement of
mental health was to have an uninhibited sex life. If you would
be well and happy, you must obey your libido. Such was the
Freudian gospel as it imbedded itself in the American mind
after being filtered through the successive minds of interpreters
and popularizers and guileless readers and people who had
heard guileless readers talk about it. New words and phrases
began to be bandied about the cocktail-tray and the Mah Jong
table—inferiority complex, sadism, masochism, Œdipus complex. Intellectual ladies went to Europe to be analyzed; analysts
plied their new trade in American cities, conscientiously transferring the affections of their fair patients to themselves; and
clergymen who preached about the virtue of self-control were
reminded by outspoken critics that self-control was out-of-date
and really dangerous.

The principal remaining forces which accelerated the revolution in manners and morals were all 100 per cent American. They were prohibition, the automobile, the confession and
sex magazines, and the movies.

When the Eighteenth Amendment was ratified, prohibition
seemed, as we have already noted, to have an almost united
country behind it. Evasion of the law began immediately,
however, and strenuous and sincere opposition to it—especially in the large cities of the North and East—quickly gathered force. The results were the bootlegger, the speakeasy, and
a spirit of deliberate revolt which in many communities made
drinking "the thing to do." From these facts in turn flowed
further results: the increased popularity of distilled as against
fermented liquors, the use of the hip-flask, the cocktail party,
and the general transformation of drinking from a masculine
prerogative to one shared by both sexes together. The old-time
saloon had been overwhelmingly masculine; the speakeasy
usually catered to both men and women. As Elmer Davis put
it, "The old days when father spent his evenings at Cassidy's
bar with the rest of the boys are gone, and probably gone forever; Cassidy may still be in business at the old stand and
father may still go down there of evenings, but since prohibition mother goes down with him." Under the new régime not
only the drinks were mixed, but the company as well.

Meanwhile a new sort of freedom was being made possible by the enormous increase in the use of the automobile, and particularly of the closed car. (In 1919 hardly more than 10 per cent of the cars produced in the United States were closed; by 1924 the percentage had jumped to 43, by 1927 it had reached 82.8.) The automobile offered an almost universally available means of escaping temporarily from the supervision of parents and chaperons, or from the influence of neighborhood opinion. Boys and girls now thought nothing, as the Lynds pointed out in *Middletown,* of jumping into a car and driving off at a moment's notice—without asking anybody's permission—to a dance in another town twenty miles away, where they were strangers and enjoyed a freedom impossible among their neighbors. The closed car, moreover, was in effect a room protected from the weather which could be occupied at any time of the day or night and could be moved at will into a darkened byway or a country lane. The Lynds quoted the judge of the juvenile court in "Middletown" as declaring that the automobile had become a "house of prostitution on wheels," and cited the fact that of thirty girls brought before his court in a year on charges of sex crimes, for whom the place where the offense had occurred was recorded, nineteen were listed as having committed it in an automobile.

Finally, as the revolution began, its influence fertilized a bumper crop of sex magazines, confession magazines, and lurid motion pictures, and these in turn had their effect on a class of readers and movie-goers who had never heard and never would hear of Freud and the libido. The publishers of the sex adventure magazines, offering stories with such titles as "What I Told My Daughter the Night Before Her Marriage," "Indolent Kisses," and "Watch Your Step-Ins," learned to a nicety the gentle art of arousing the reader without arousing the censor. The publishers of the confession magazines, while always instructing their authors to provide a moral ending and to utter pious sentiments, concentrated on the description of what they euphemistically called "missteps." Most of their fiction was faked to order by hack writers who could write one day "The Confessions of a Chorus Girl" and the next day recount, again in the first person, the temptations which made it easy for the taxidriver to go wrong. Both classes of magazines became astonishingly numerous and successful. Bernarr Macfadden's *True-Story,* launched as late as 1919, had over

300,000 readers by 1923; 848,000 by 1924; over a million and a half by 1925; and almost two million by 1926—a record of rapid growth probably unparalleled in magazine publishing.

Crowding the news stands along with the sex and confession magazines were motion-picture magazines which depicted "seven movie kisses" with such captions as "Do you recognize your little friend, Mae Busch? She's had lots of kisses, but she never seems to grow *blasé*. At least you'll agree that she's giving a good imitation of a person enjoying this one." The movies themselves, drawing millions to their doors every day and every night, played incessantly upon the same lucrative theme. The producers of one picture advertised "brilliant men, beautiful jazz babies, champagne baths, midnight revels, petting parties in the purple dawn, all ending in one terrific smashing climax that makes you gasp"; the venders of another promised "neckers, petters, white kisses, red kisses, pleasure-mad daughters, sensation-craving mothers, . . . the truth—bold, naked, sensational." Seldom did the films offer as much as these advertisements promised, but there was enough in some of them to cause a sixteen-year-old girl (quoted by Alice Miller Mitchell) to testify, "Those pictures with hot love-making in them, they make girls and boys sitting together want to get up and walk out, go off somewhere, you know. Once I walked out with a boy before the picture was even over. We took a ride. But my friend, she all the time had to get up and go out with her boy friend."

A storm of criticism from church organizations led the motion-picture producers, early in the decade, to install Will H. Hays, President Harding's Postmaster-General, as their arbiter of morals and of taste, and Mr. Hays promised that all would be well. "This industry must have," said he before the Los Angeles Chamber of Commerce, "toward that sacred thing, the mind of a child, toward that clean virgin thing, that unmarked slate, the same responsibility, the same care about the impressions made upon it, that the best clergyman or the most inspired teacher of youth would have." The result of Mr. Hays's labors in behalf of the unmarked slate was to make the moral ending as obligatory as in the confession magazines, to smear over sexy pictures with pious platitudes, and to blacklist for motion-picture production many a fine novel and play which, because of its very honesty, might be construed as seriously or intelligently questioning the traditional sex ethics of the small town. Mr. Hays, being something of a genius, managed to keep the churchmen at bay. Whenever the threats of censorship began to become ominous he would promulgate a new series of moral commandments for the producers to follow. Yet of the practical effects of his supervision it is perhaps enough to say that the quotations given above all date from the period of his dictatorship. Giving lip-service to the old code, the movies diligently and with consummate vulgarity publicized the new.

Each of these diverse influences—the post-war disillusion, the new status of women, the Freudian gospel, the automobile, prohibition, the sex and confession magazines, and the movies —had its part in bringing about the revolution. Each of them, as an influence, was played upon by all the others; none of them could alone have changed to any great degree the folkways of America; together their force was irresistible.

[3]

The most conspicuous sign of what was taking place was the immense change in women's dress and appearance.

In Professor Paul H. Nystrom's *Economics of Fashion*, the trend of skirt-length during the Post-war Decade is ingeniously shown by the sort of graph with which business analysts delight to compute the ebb and flow of car-loadings or of stock averages. The basis of this graph is a series of measurements of fashion-plates in the *Delineator*; the statistician painstakingly measured the relation, from month to month, of the height of the skirt hem above the ground to the total height of the figure, and plotted his curve accordingly. This very unusual graph shows that in 1919 the average distance of the hem above the ground was about 10 per cent of the woman's height—or to put it in another way, about six or seven inches. In 1920 it curved upward from 10 to about 20 per cent. During the next three years it gradually dipped to 10 per cent again, reaching its low point in 1923. In 1924, however, it rose once more to between 15 and 20 per cent, in 1925 to more than 20 per cent; and the curve continued steadily upward until by 1927 it had passed the 25 per cent mark—in other words, until the skirt had reached the knee. There it remained until late in 1929.

This graph, as Professor Nystrom explains, does not accurately indicate what really happened, for it represents for any given year or month, not the average length of skirts actually worn, but the length of the skirt which the arbiters of fashion, not uninfluenced by the manufacturers of dress goods, expected and wanted women to wear. In actual fact, the dip between 1921 and 1924 was very slight. Paris dressmakers predicted the return of longer skirts, the American stylists and manufacturers followed their lead, the stores bought the longer skirts and tried to sell them, but women kept on buying the shortest skirts they could find. During the fall of 1923 and the spring of 1924, manufacturers were deluged with complaints from retailers that skirts would have to be shorter. Shorter they finally were, and still shorter. The knee-length dress proved to be exactly what women wanted. The unlucky manufacturers made valiant efforts to change the fashion. Despite all they could do, however, the knee-length skirt remained standard until the decade was approaching its end.

With the short skirt went an extraordinary change in the weight and material and amount of women's clothing. The boyishly slender figure became the aim of every woman's ambition, and the corset was so far abandoned that even in so short a period as the three years from 1924 to 1927 the combined sales of corsets and brassières in the department stores of the Cleveland Federal Reserve District fell off 11 per cent. Silk or rayon stockings and underwear supplanted cotton, to the distress of cotton manufacturers and the delight of rayon manufacturers; the production of rayon in American plants, which in 1920 had been only eight million pounds, had by 1925 reached fifty-three million pounds. The flesh-colored stocking became as standard as the short skirt. Petticoats almost vanished from the American scene; in fact, the tendency of women to drop off one layer of clothing after another became so pronounced that in 1928 the *Journal of Commerce* estimated that in 15 years the amount of material required for a woman's complete costume (exclusive of her stockings) had declined from 19¼ yards to 7 yards. All she could now be induced to wear, it seemed, was an overblouse (2 yards), a skirt (2¼ yards), vest or shirt (¾), knickers (2), and stockings—and all of them were made of silk or rayon! This latter statement, it is true, was a slight exaggeration; but a survey published in 1926 by the National Retail Dry Goods Association, on the basis of data from department stores all over the country, showed that only 33 per cent of the women's underwear sold was made of cotton, whereas 36 per cent was made of rayon, and 31 per cent of silk. No longer were silk stockings the mark of the rich; as the wife of a workingman with a total family income of $1,638 a year told the authors of *Middletown*, "No girl can wear cotton stockings to high school. Even in winter my children wear silk stockings with lisle or imitations underneath."

Not content with the freedom of short and skimpy clothes, women sought, too, the freedom of short hair. During the early years of the decade the bobbed head—which in 1918, as you may recall, had been regarded by the proprietor of the Palm Garden in New York as a sign of radicalism—became increasingly frequent among young girls, chiefly on the ground of convenience. In May, 1922, the *American Hairdresser* predicted that the bob, which persisted in being popular, "will probably last through the summer, anyway." It not only did this, it so increased in popularity that by 1924 the same journal was forced to feature bobbed styles and give its subscribers instructions in the new art, and was reporting the progress of a lively battle between the professional hairdressers and the barbers for the cream of this booming business. The ladies' hairdressers very naturally objected to women going to barbers' shops; the barbers, on the other hand, were trying to force legislation in various states which would forbid the "hairdressing profession" to cut hair unless they were licensed as barbers. Said the *Hairdresser*, putting the matter on the loftiest basis, "The effort to bring women to barber shops for haircutting is against the best interests of the public, the free and easy atmosphere often prevailing in barber shops being unsuitable to the high standard of American womanhood." But all that American womanhood appeared to insist upon was the best possible shingle. In the latter years of the decade bobbed hair became almost universal among girls in their twenties, very common among women in their thirties and forties, and by no means rare among women of sixty; and for a brief period the hair was not only bobbed, but in most cases cropped close to the head like a man's. Women universally adopted the small cloche hat which fitted tightly on the bobbed head, and the manufacturer of milliner's materials joined the hair-net

manufacturer, the hair-pin manufacturer, and the cotton goods
and woolen goods and corset manufacturers, among the ranks
of depressed industries.

For another industry, however, the decade brought new and
enormous profits. The manufacturers of cosmetics and the
proprietors of beauty shops had less than nothing to complain
of. The vogue of rouge and lipstick, which in 1920 had so
alarmed the parents of the younger generation, spread swiftly
to the remotest village. Women who in 1920 would have
thought the use of paint immoral were soon applying it reg-
ularly as a matter of course and making no effort to disguise
the fact; beauty shops had sprung up on every street to give
"facials," to apply pomade and astringents, to make war
against the wrinkles and sagging chins of age, to pluck and
trim and color the eyebrows, and otherwise to enhance and
restore the bloom of youth; and a strange new form of surgery,
"face-lifting," took its place among the applied sciences of the
day. Back in 1917, according to Frances Fisher Dubuc, only
two persons in the beauty culture business had paid an income
tax; by 1927 there were 18,000 firms and individuals in this
field listed as income-tax payers. The "beautician" had arrived.

As for the total amount of money spent by American
women on cosmetics and beauty culture by the end of the
decade, we may probably accept as conservative the prodigious
figure of three-quarters of a billion dollars set by Professor
Paul H. Nystrom in 1930; other estimates, indeed, ran as high
as two billion. Mrs. Christine Frederick tabulated in 1929
some other equally staggering figures: for every adult woman
in the country there were being sold annually over a pound of
face powder and no less than eight rouge compacts; there were
2,500 brands of perfume on the market and 1,500 face creams;
and if all the lipsticks sold in a year in the United States were
placed end to end, they would reach from New York to Reno
—which to some would seem an altogether logical destination.

Perhaps the readiest way of measuring the change in the
public attitude toward cosmetics is to compare the advertisements in a conservative periodical at the beginning of the
decade with those at its end. Although the June, 1919, issue of
the *Ladies' Home Journal* contained four advertisements which
listed rouge among other products, only one of them commented on its inclusion, and this referred to its rouge as one
that was "imperceptible if properly applied." In those days the

woman who used rouge—at least in the circles in which the *Journal* was read—wished to disguise the fact. (Advertisements of talc, in 1919, commonly displayed a mother leaning affectionately over a bouncing baby.) In the June, 1929, issue, exactly ten years later, the *Journal* permitted a lipstick to be advertised with the comment, "It's comforting to know that the alluring note of scarlet will stay with you for hours." (Incidentally, the examination of those two magazines offers another contrast: in 1919 the Listerine advertisement said simply, "The prompt application of Listerine may prevent a minor accident from becoming a major infection," whereas in 1929 it began a tragic rhapsody with the words, "Spring! for everyone but her . . .")

These changes in fashion—the short skirt, the boyish form, the straight, long-waisted dresses, the frank use of paint—were signs of a real change in the American feminine ideal (as well, perhaps, as in men's idea of what was the feminine ideal). Women were bent on freedom—freedom to work and to play without the trammels that had bound them heretofore to lives of comparative inactivity. But what they sought was not the the freedom from man and his desires which had put the suffragists of an earlier day into hard straw hats and mannish suits and low-heeled shoes. The woman of the nineteen-twenties wanted to be able to allure man even on the golf links and in the office; the little flapper who shingled her hair and wore a manageable little hat and put on knickerbockers for the weekends would not be parted from her silk stockings and her high-heeled shoes. Nor was the post-war feminine ideal one of fruitful maturity or ripened wisdom or practiced grace. On the contrary: the quest of slenderness, the flattening of the breasts, the vogue of short skirts (even when short skirts still suggested the appearance of a little girl), the juvenile effect of the long waist,—all were signs that, consciously or unconsciously, the women of this decade worshiped not merely youth, but unripened youth: they wanted to be—or thought men wanted them to be—men's casual and light-hearted companions; not broad-hipped mothers of the race, but irresponsible playmates. Youth was their pattern, but not youthful innocence: the adolescent whom they imitated was a hard-boiled adolescent, who thought not in terms of romantic love, but in terms of sex, and who made herself desirable not by that sly art which conceals art, but frankly and openly. In effect, the woman of the Post-war

Decade said to man, "You are tired and disillusioned, you do not want the cares of a family or the companionship of mature wisdom, you want exciting play, you want the thrills of sex without their fruition, and I will give them to you." And to herself she added, "But I will be free."

[4]

One indication of the revolution in manners which her headlong pursuit of freedom brought about was her rapid acceptance of the cigarette. Within a very few years millions of American women of all ages followed the lead of the flappers of 1920 and took up smoking. Custom still generally frowned upon their doing it on the street or in the office, and in the evangelical hinterlands the old taboo died hard; but in restaurants, at dinner parties and dances, in theater lobbies, and in a hundred other places they made the air blue. Here again the trend in advertising measured the trend in public opinion. At the beginning of the decade advertisers realized that it would have been suicidal to portray a woman smoking; within a few years, however, they ventured pictures of pretty girls imploring men to blow some of the smoke their way; and by the end of the decade billboards boldly displayed a smart-looking woman cigarette in hand, and in some of the magazines, despite floods of protests from rural readers, tobacco manufacturers were announcing that "now women may enjoy a companionable smoke with their husbands and brothers." In the ten years between 1918 and 1928 the total production of cigarettes in the United States *more than doubled*. Part of this increase was doubtless due to the death of the one-time masculine prejudice against the cigarette as unmanly, for it was accompanied by somewhat of a decrease in the production of cigars and smoking tobacco, as well as—mercifully—of chewing tobacco. Part of it was attributable to the fact that the convenience of the cigarette made the masculine smoker consume more tobacco than in the days when he preferred a cigar or a pipe. But the increase could never have been so large had it not been for the women who now strewed the dinner table with their ashes, snatched a puff between the acts, invaded the masculine sanctity of the club car, and forced department stores to place ornamental ash-trays between the chairs in their women's shoe departments. A formidable barrier between the sexes had broken down. The custom of separating them after formal dinners, for example, still lingered, but as an empty rite. Hosts who laid in a stock of cigars for their male guests often found them untouched; the men in the dining-room were smoking the very same brands of cigarettes that the ladies consumed in the living-room.

Of far greater social significance, however, was the fact that men and women were drinking together. Among well-to-do people the serving of cocktails before dinner became almost socially obligatory. Mixed parties swarmed up to the curtained grills of speakeasies and uttered the mystic password, and girls along with men stood at the speakeasy bar with one foot on the old brass rail. The late afternoon cocktail party became a new American institution. When dances were held in hotels, the curious and rather unsavory custom grew up of hiring hotel rooms where reliable drinks could be served in suitable privacy; guests of both sexes lounged on the beds and tossed off mixtures of high potency. As houses and apartments became smaller, the country club became the social center of the small city, the suburb, and the summer resort; and to its pretentious clubhouse, every Saturday night, drove men and women (after a round of cocktails at somebody's house) for the weekly dinner dance. Bottles of White Rock and of ginger ale decked the tables, out of capacious masculine hip pockets came flasks of gin (once the despised and rejected of bartenders, now the most popular of all liquors), and women who a few years before would have gasped at the thought that they would ever be "under the influence of alcohol" found themselves matching the men drink for drink and enjoying the uproarious release. The next day gossip would report that the reason Mrs. So-and-so disappeared from the party at eleven was because she had had too many cocktails and had been led to the dressing-room to be sick, or that somebody would have to meet the club's levy for breakage, or that Mrs. Such-and-such really oughtn't to drink so much because three cocktails made her throw bread about the table. A passing scandal would be created by a dance at which substantial married men amused themselves by tripping up waiters, or young people bent on petting parties drove right out on the golf-links and made wheel-tracks on the eighteenth green.

Such incidents were of course exceptional and in many communities they never occurred. It was altogether probable, though the professional wets denied it, that prohibition succeeded in reducing the total amount of drinking in the country as a whole and in reducing it decidedly among the workingmen of the industrial districts. The majority of experienced college administrators agreed—rather to the annoyance of some of their undergraduates—that there was less drinking among men students than there had been before prohibition and that drinking among girl students, at least while they were in residence, hardly offered a formidable problem. Yet the fact remained that among the prosperous classes which set the standards of national social behavior, alcohol flowed more freely than ever before and lubricated an unprecedented informality—to say the least—of manners.

It lubricated, too, a new outspokenness between men and women. Thanks to the spread of scientific skepticism and especially to Sigmund Freud, the dogmas of the conservative moralists were losing force and the dogma that salvation lay in facing the facts of sex was gaining. An upheaval in values was taking place. Modesty, reticence, and chivalry were going out of style; women no longer wanted to be "ladylike" or could appeal to their daughters to be "wholesome"; it was too widely suspected that the old-fashioned lady had been a sham and that the "wholesome" girl was merely inhibiting a nasty mind and would come to no good end. "Victorian" and "Puritan" were becoming terms of opprobrium: up-to-date people thought of Victorians as old ladies with bustles and inhibitions, and of Puritans as blue-nosed, ranting spoilsports. It was better to be modern,—everybody wanted to be modern,—and sophisticated, and smart, to smash the conventions and to be devastatingly frank. And with a cocktail glass in one's hand it was easy at least to be frank.

"Listen with a detached ear to a modern conversation," wrote Mary Agnes Hamilton in 1927, "and you will be struck, first, by the restriction of the vocabulary, and second, by the high proportion in that vocabulary of words such as, in the older jargon, 'no lady could use.' " With the taste for strong liquors went a taste for strong language. To one's lovely dinner partner, the inevitable antithesis for "grand" and "swell" had become "lousy." An unexpected "damn" or "hell" uttered on the New York stage was no longer a signal for the sudden sharp laughter of shocked surprise; such words were becoming the commonplace of everyday talk. The barroom anecdote of the decade before now went the rounds of aristocratic bridge tables. Every one wanted to be unshockable; it was delightful to be considered a little shocking; and so the competition in boldness of talk went on until for a time, as Mrs. Hamilton put it, a conversation in polite circles was like a room decorated entirely in scarlet—the result was over-emphasis, stridency, and eventual boredom.

Along with the new frankness in conversation went a new frankness in books and the theater. Consider, for example, the themes of a handful of the best plays produced in New York during the decade: *What Price Glory?*, which represented the amorous marines interlarding their talk with epithets new to the stage; *The Road to Rome*, the prime comic touch of which was the desire of a Roman matron to be despoiled by the Carthaginians; *Strange Interlude*, in which a wife who found there was insanity in her husband's family but wanted to give him a child decided to have the child by an attractive young doctor, instead of by her husband, and forthwith fell in love with the doctor; *Strictly Dishonorable*, in which a charming young girl walked blithely and open-eyed into an affair of a night with an opera-singer; and *The Captive*, which revealed to thousands of innocents the fact that the world contained such a phenomenon as homosexuality. None of these plays could have been tolerated even in New York before the Post-war Decade; all of them in the nineteen-twenties were not merely popular, but genuinely admired by intelligent audiences The effect of some of them upon these audiences is suggested by the story of the sedate old lady who, after two acts of *What Price Glory?*, reprimanded her grandson with a "God damn it, Johnny, sit down!"

The same thing was true of the novels of the decade; one after another, from *Jurgen* and *Dark Laughter* through the tales of Michael Arlen to *An American Tragedy* and *The Sun Also Rises* and *The Well of Loneliness* and *Point Counter Point*, they dealt with sex with an openness or a cynicism or an unmoral objectivity new to the English-speaking world. Bitterly the defenders of the Puritan code tried to stem the tide, but it was too strong for them. They banned *Jurgen*—and made a best seller of it and a public reputation for its author. They dragged Mary Ware Dennett into court for distributing a

pamphlet for children which explained some of the mysteries
of sex—only to have her upheld by a liberal judge and endorsed by intelligent public opinion. In Boston, where they
were backed by an alliance between stubborn Puritanism and
Roman Catholicism, they banned books wholesale, forbade
the stage presentation of *Strange Interlude*, and secured the
conviction of a bookseller for selling *Lady Chatterley's Lover*
—only to find that the intellectuals of the whole country were
laughing at them and that ultimately they were forced to allow
the publication of books which they would have moved to ban
ten years before. Despite all that they could do, the taste of the
country demanded a new sort of reading matter.

Early in the decade a distinguished essayist wrote an article
in which she contended that the physical processes of child-
birth were humiliating to many women. She showed it to the
editor of one of the best magazines, and he and she agreed that
it should not be printed: too many readers would be repelled
by the subject matter and horrified by the thesis. Only a few
years later, in 1927, the editor recalled this manuscript and
asked if he might see it again. He saw it—and wondered why it
had ever been disqualified. Already such frankness seemed
quite natural and permissible. The article was duly published,
and caused only the mildest of sensations.

If in 1918 the editors of a reputable magazine had accepted
a story in which one gangster said to another, "For Christ's
sake, Joe, give her the gas. Some lousy bastard has killed Eddie," they would have whipped out the blue pencil and changed
the passage to something like "For the love of Mike, Joe, give
her the gas. Some dirty skunk has killed Eddie." In 1929 that
sentence appeared in a story accepted by a magazine of the
most unblemished standing, and was printed without al-
teration. A few readers objected, but not many. Times had
changed. Even in the great popular periodicals with huge
circulations and a considerable following in the strongholds of
rural Methodism the change in standards was apparent. Said a
short-story writer in the late nineteen-twenties, "I used to write
for magazines like the *Saturday Evening Post* and the *Pictorial
Review* when I had a nice innocuous tale to tell and wanted the
money, and for magazines like *Harper's* and *Scribner's* when I
wanted to write something searching and honest. Now I find I
can sell the honest story to the big popular magazines too."

[5]

With the change in manners went an inevitable change in morals. Boys and girls were becoming sophisticated about sex at an earlier age; it was symptomatic that when the authors of *Middletown* asked 241 boys and 315 girls of high-school age to mark as true or false, according to their opinion, the extreme statement, "Nine out of every ten boys and girls of high-school age have petting parties," almost precisely half of them marked it as true. How much actual intercourse there was among such young people it is of course impossible to say; but the lurid stories told by Judge Lindsay—of girls who carried contraceptives in their vanity cases, and of "Caroline," who told the judge that fifty-eight girls of her acquaintance had had one or more sex experiences without a single pregnancy resulting—were matched by the gossip current in many a town. Whether prostitution increased or decreased during the decade is likewise uncertain; but certain it is that the prostitute was faced for the first time with an amateur competition of formidable proportions.

As for the amount of outright infidelity among married couples, one is again without reliable data, the private relations of men and women being happily beyond the reach of the statistician. The divorce rate, however, continued its steady increase; for every 100 marriages there were 8.8 divorces in 1910, 13.4 divorces in 1920, and 16.5 divorces in 1928—almost one divorce for every six marriages. There was a corresponding decline in the amount of disgrace accompanying divorce. In the urban communities men and women who had been divorced were now socially accepted without question; indeed, there was often about the divorced person just enough of an air of unconventionality, just enough of a touch of scarlet, to be considered rather dashing and desirable. Many young women probably felt as did the New York girl who said, toward the end of the decade, that she was thinking of marrying Henry, although she didn't care very much for him, because even if they didn't get along she could get a divorce and "it would be much more exciting to be a divorcée than to be an old maid."

The petting party, which in the first years of the decade had been limited to youngsters in their teens and twenties, soon made its appearance among older men and women: when the gin-flask was passed about the hotel bedroom during a dance, or the musicians stilled their saxophones during the Saturday-night party at the country club, men of affairs and women with half-grown children had their little taste of raw sex. One began to hear of young girls, intelligent and well born, who had spent week-ends with men before marriage and had told their prospective husbands everything and had been not merely forgiven, but told that there was nothing to forgive; a little "experience," these men felt, was all to the good for any girl. Millions of people were moving toward acceptance of what a *bon-vivant* of earlier days had said was his idea of the proper state of morality—"A single standard, and that a low one."

It would be easy, of course, to match every one of these cases with contrasting cases of men and women who still thought and behaved at the end of the decade exactly as the president of the Epworth League would have wished. Two women who conducted newspaper columns of advice in affairs of the heart testified that the sort of problem which was worrying young America, to judge from their bulging correspondence, was not whether to tell the boy friend about the illegitimate child, but whether it was proper to invite the boy friend up on the porch if he hadn't yet come across with an invitation to the movies, or whether the cake at a pie social should be cut with a knife. In the hinterlands there was still plenty of old-fashioned sentimental thinking about sex, of the sort which expressed itself in the slogan of a federated women's club: "Men are God's trees, women are His flowers." There were frantic efforts to stay the tide of moral change by law, the most picturesque of these efforts being the ordinance actually passed in Norphelt, Arkansas, in 1925, which contained the following provisions:

"Section 1. Hereafter it shall be unlawful for any man and woman, male or female, to be guilty of committing the act of sexual intercourse between themselves at any place within the corporate limits of said town.

"Section 3. Section One of this ordinance shall not apply to married persons as between themselves, and their husband and wife, unless of a grossly improper and lascivious nature."

Nevertheless, there was an unmistakable and rapid trend away from the old American code toward a philosophy of sex relations and of marriage wholly new to the country: toward a feeling that the virtues of chastity and fidelity had been rated too highly, that there was something to be said for what Mrs. Bertrand Russell defined as "the right, equally shared by men and women, to free participation in sex experience," that it was not necessary for girls to deny themselves this right before marriage or even for husbands and wives to do so after marriage. It was in acknowledgment of the spread of this feeling that Judge Lindsay proposed, in 1927, to establish "companionate marriage" on a legal basis. He wanted to legalize birth control (which, although still outlawed, was by this time generally practiced or believed in by married couples in all but the most ignorant classes) and to permit legal marriage to be terminated at any time in divorce by mutual consent, provided there were no children. His suggestion created great consternation and was widely and vigorously denounced; but the mere fact that it was seriously debated showed how the code of an earlier day had been shaken. The revolution in morals was in full swing.

[6]

A time of revolution, however, is an uneasy time to live in. It is easier to tear down a code than to put a new one in its place, and meanwhile there is bound to be more or less wear and tear and general unpleasantness. People who have been brought up to think that it is sinful for women to smoke or drink, and scandalous for sex to be discussed across the luncheon table, and unthinkable for a young girl to countenance strictly dishonorable attentions from a man, cannot all at once forget the admonitions of their childhood. It takes longer to hard-boil a man or a woman than an egg. Some of the apostles of the new freedom appeared to imagine that habits of thought could be changed overnight, and that if you only dragged the secrets of sex out into the daylight and let every one do just as he pleased at the moment, society would at once enter upon a state of barbaric innocence like that of the remotest South Sea Islanders. But it couldn't be done. When you drag the secrets of sex out into the daylight, the first thing that the sons and daughters of Mr. and Mrs. Grundy do is to fall all over themselves in the effort to have a good look, and for a time they can think of nothing else. If you let every one do just as he pleases, he is as likely as not to begin by making a nuisance of himself. He may even shortly discover that making a nuisance of himself is not, after all, the recipe for lasting happiness. So it happened when the old codes were broken down in the Post-war Decade.

One of the most striking results of the revolution was a widely pervasive obsession with sex. To listen to the conversation of some of the sons and daughters of Mr. and Mrs. Grundy was to be reminded of the girl whose father said that she would talk about anything; in fact, she hardly ever talked about anything else. The public attitude toward any number of problems of the day revealed this obsession: to give a single example, the fashionable argument against women's colleges at this period had nothing to do with the curriculum or with the intellectual future of the woman graduate, but pointed out that living with girls for four years was likely to distort a woman's sex life. The public taste in reading matter revealed it: to say nothing of the sex magazines and the tabloids and the acres of newspaper space devoted to juicy scandals like that of Daddy Browning and his Peaches, it was significant that almost every one of the novelists who were ranked most highly by the post-war intellectuals was at outs with the censors, and that the Pulitzer Prize juries had a hard time meeting the requirement that the prize-winning novel should "present the wholesome atmosphere of American life and the highest standard of American manners and manhood," and finally had to alter the terms of the award, substituting "whole" for "wholesome" and omitting reference to "highest standards." There were few distinguished novels being written which one could identify with a "wholesome atmosphere" without making what the Senate would call interpretive reservations. Readers who considered themselves "modern-minded" did not want them: they wanted the philosophical promiscuity of Aldous Huxley's men and women, the perfumed indiscretions of Michael Arlen's degenerates, Ernest Hemingway's unflinching account of the fleeting amours of the drunken Brett Ashley, Anita Loos's comedy of two kept women and their gentlemen friends, Radclyffe Hall's study of homosexuality. Young men and women who a few years before would have been championing radical economic or political doctrines were championing the new morality and talking about it everywhere and thinking of it incessantly. Sex was in the limelight, and the Grundy children could not turn their eyes away.

Another result of the revolution was that manners became not merely different, but—for a few years—unmannerly. It was no mere coincidence that during this decade hostesses—even at small parties—found that their guests couldn't be bothered to speak to them on arrival or departure; that "gate-crashing" at dances became an accepted practice; that thousands of men and women made a point of not getting to dinners within half an hour of the appointed time lest they seem insufficiently *blasé;* that house parties of flappers and their wide-trousered swains left burning cigarettes on the mahogany tables, scattered ashes light-heartedly on the rugs, took the porch cushions out in the boats and left them there to be rained on, without apology; or that men and women who had had—as the old phrase went—"advantages" and considered themselves highly civilized, absorbed a few cocktails and straightway turned a dinner party into a boisterous rout, forgetting that a general roughhouse was not precisely the sign of a return to the Greek idea of the good life. The old·bars were down, no new ones had been built, and meanwhile the pigs were in the pasture. Some day, perhaps, the ten years which followed the war may aptly be known as the Decade of Bad Manners.

Nor was it easy to throw overboard the moral code and substitute another without confusion and distress. It was one thing to proclaim that married couples should be free to find sex adventure wherever they pleased and that marriage was something independent of such casual sport; it was quite another thing for a man or woman in whom the ideal of romantic marriage had been ingrained since early childhood to tolerate infidelities when they actually took place. Judge Lindsay told the story of a woman who had made up her mind that her husband might love whom he pleased; she would be modern and think none the less of him for it. But whenever she laid eyes on her rival she was physically sick. Her mind, she discovered, was hard-boiled only on the surface. That woman had many a counterpart during the revolution in morals; behind the grim statistics of divorce there was many a case of husband and wife experimenting with the new freedom and suddenly finding that there was dynamite in it which wrecked that mutual confidence and esteem without which marriage—even for the sake of their children—could not be endured.

The new code had been born in disillusionment, and beneath all the bravado of its exponents and the talk about entering upon a new era the disillusionment persisted. If the decade was ill-mannered, it was also unhappy. With the old order of things had gone a set of values which had given richness and meaning to life, and substitute values were not easily found. If morality was dethroned, what was to take its place? Honor, said some of the prophets of the new day: "It doesn't matter much what you do so long as you're honest about it." A brave ideal—yet it did not wholly satisfy; it was too vague, too austere, too difficult to apply. If romantic love was dethroned, what was to take its place? Sex? But as Joseph Wood Krutch explained, "If love has come to be less often a sin, it has also come to be less often a supreme privilege." And as Walter Lippmann, in *A Preface to Morals*, added after quoting Mr. Krutch, "If you start with the belief that love is the pleasure of a moment, is it really surprising that it yields only a momentary pleasure?" The end of the pursuit of sex alone was emptiness and futility—the emptiness and futility to which Lady Brett Ashley and her friends in *The Sun Also Rises* were so tragically doomed.

There were not, to be sure, many Brett Ashleys in the United States during the Post-war Decade. Yet there were millions to whom in some degree came for a time the same disillusionment and with it the same unhappiness. They could not endure a life without values, and the only values they had been trained to understand were being undermined. Everything seemed meaningless and unimportant. Well, at least one could toss off a few drinks and get a kick out of physical passion and forget that the world was crumbling. . . . And so the saxophones wailed and the gin-flask went its rounds and the dancers made their treadmill circuit with half-closed eyes, and the outside world, so merciless and so insane, was shut away for a restless night. . . .

It takes time to build up a new code. Not until the decade was approaching its end did there appear signs that the revolutionists were once more learning to be at home in their world, to rid themselves of their obsession with sex, to adjust themselves emotionally to the change in conventions and standards, to live the freer and franker life of this new era gracefully, and to discover among the ruins of the old dispensation a new set of enduring satisfactions.

VI

Harding and the Scandals

Having been personal attorney for Warren G. Harding before
he was Senator from Ohio and while he was Senator, and thereafter until his death.

—And for Mrs. Harding for a period of several years, and before
her husband was elected President and after his death,

—And having been attorney for the Midland National Bank of
Washington Court House, O., and for my brother, M. S. Daugherty,

—And having been Attorney-General of the United States during
the time that President Harding served as President,

—And also for a time after President Harding's death under
President Coolidge,

—And with all of those named, as attorney, personal friend,
and Attorney-General, my relations were of the most confidential
character as well as professional,

—I refuse to testify and answer questions put to me, because:

The answer I might give or make and the testimony I might
give might tend to incriminate me.

> —*Harry M. Daugherty's written reply when called upon
> by Judge Thacher for information for the Federal
> Grand Jury in New York, March 31, 1926 (Punctuation
> revised.)*

On the morning of March 4, 1921—a brilliant morning
with a frosty air and a wind which whipped the flags of Wash-

ington—Woodrow Wilson, broken and bent and ill, limped from the White House door to a waiting automobile, rode down Pennsylvania Avenue to the Capitol with the stalwart President-elect at his side, and returned to the bitter seclusion of his private hôuse in S Street. Warren Gamaliel Harding was sworn in as President of the United States. The reign of normalcy had begun.

March 4, 1921: what do those cold figures mean to you? Let us turn back for a moment to that day and look about us.

The war had been over for more than two years, although, as the Treaty of Versailles had been thrown out by the Senate and Woodrow Wilson had refused to compromise with the gentlemen at the other end of the Avenue, a technical state of war still existed between Germany and the United States. Business, having boomed until the middle of 1920, was collapsing into the depths of depression and dragging down with it the price-level which had caused so much uproar about the High Cost of Living. The Big Red Scare was gradually ebbing, although the super-patriots still raged and Sacco and Vanzetti had not yet come to trial before Judge Thayer. The Ku-Klux Klan was acquiring its first few hundred thousand members. The Eighteenth Amendment was entering upon its second year, and rum-runners and bootleggers were beginning to acquire confidence. The sins of the flappers were disturbing the nation; it was at about this time that Philadelphia produced the "moral gown" and the *Literary Digest* featured a symposium entitled, "Is the Younger Generation in Peril?" The first radio broadcasting station in the country was hardly four months old and the radio craze was not yet. Skirts had climbed halfway to the knee and seemed likely to go down again, a crime commission had just been investigating Chicago's crime wave, Judge Landis had become the czar of baseball, Dempsey and Carpentier had signed to meet the following summer at Boyle's Thirty Acres, and *Main Street* and *The Outline of History* were becoming best sellers.

The nation was spiritually tired. Wearied by the excitements of the war and the nervous tension of the Big Red Scare, they hoped for quiet and healing. Sick of Wilson and his talk of America's duty to humanity, callous to political idealism, they hoped for a chance to pursue their private affairs without governmental interference and to forget about public affairs.

There might be no such word in the dictionary as normalcy, but normalcy was what they wanted.

Every new administration at Washington begins in an atmosphere of expectant good will, but in this case the airs which lapped the capital were particularly bland. The smile of the new President was as warming as a spring thaw after a winter of discontent. For four long years the gates of the White House had been locked and guarded with sentries. Harding's first official act was to throw them open, to permit a horde of sightseers to roam the grounds and flatten their noses against the executive window-panes and photograph one another under the great north portico; to permit flivvers and trucks to detour from Pennsylvania Avenue up the driveway and chortle right past the presidential front door. The act seemed to symbolize the return of the government to the people. Wilson had been denounced as an autocrat, had proudly kept his own counsel; Harding modestly said he would rely on the "best minds" to advise him, and took his oath of office upon the verse from Micah which asks, "What doth the Lord require of thee but to do justly, and to love mercy, and to walk humbly with thy God?" Wilson had seemed to be everlastingly prying into the affairs of business and had distrusted most business men; Harding meant to give them as free a hand as possible "to resume their normal onward way." And finally, whereas Wilson had been an austere academic theorist, Harding was "just folks"; he radiated an unaffected good nature, met reporters and White House visitors with a warm handclasp and a genial word, and touched the sentimental heart of America by establishing in the White House a dog named Laddie Boy. "The Washington atmosphere of today is like that of Old Home Week or a college class reunion," wrote Edward G. Lowry shortly after Harding took office. "The change is amazing. The populace is on a broad grin." An era of good will seemed to be beginning.

Warren Harding had two great assets, and these were already apparent. First, he looked as a President of the United States should. He was superbly handsome. His face and carriage had a Washingtonian nobility and dignity, his eyes were benign; he photographed well and the pictures of him in the rotogravure sections won him affection and respect. And he was the friendliest man who ever had entered the White House.

He seemed to like everybody, he wanted to do favors for everybody, he wanted to make everybody happy. His affability was not merely the forced affability of the cold-blooded politician; it was transparently and touchingly genuine. "Neighbor," he had said to Herbert Hoover at their first meeting, during the war, "I want to be helpful." He meant it; and now that he was President, he wanted to be helpful to neighbors from Marion and neighbors from campaign headquarters and to the whole neighborly American public.

His liabilities were not at first so apparent, yet they were disastrously real. Beyond the limited scope of his political experience he was "almost unbelievably ill-informed," as William Allen White put it. His mind was vague and fuzzy. Its quality was revealed in the clogged style of his public addresses, in his choice of turgid and maladroit language ("noninvolvement" in European affairs, "adhesion" to a treaty), and in his frequent attacks of suffix trouble ("normalcy" for normality, "betrothment" for betrothal). It was revealed even more clearly in his helplessness when confronted by questions of policy to which mere good nature could not find the answer. White tells of Harding's coming into the office of one of his secretaries after a day of listening to his advisers wrangling over a tax problem, and crying out: "John, I can't make a damn thing out of this tax problem. I listen to one side and they seem right, and then—God!—I talk to the other side and they seem just as right, and here I am where I started. I know somewhere there is a book that will give me the truth, but, hell, I couldn't read the book. I know somewhere there is an economist who knows the truth, but I don't know where to find him and haven't the sense to know him and trust him when I find him. God! what a job!" His inability to discover for himself the essential facts of a problem and to think it through made him utterly dependent upon subordinates and friends whose mental processes were sharper than his own.

If he had been discriminating in the choice of his friends and advisers, all might have been well. But discrimination had been left out of his equipment. He appointed Charles Evans Hughes and Herbert Hoover and Andrew Mellon to Cabinet positions out of a vague sense that they would provide his administration with the necessary amount of statesmanship, but he was as ready to follow the lead of Daugherty or Fall or Forbes. He had little notion of technical fitness for technical jobs. Offices were plums to him, and he handed them out like a benevolent Santa Claus—beginning with the boys from Marion. He made his brother-in-law Superintendent of Prisons; he not only kept the insignificant Doctor Sawyer, of Sawyer's Sanitarium at Marion, as his personal physician, but bestowed upon him what a White House announcement called a "brigadier-generalcy" (suffix trouble again) and deputed him to study the possible coordination of the health agencies of the government; and for Comptroller of the Currency he selected D. R. Crissinger, a Marion lawyer whose executive banking experience was limited to a few months as president of the National City Bank and Trust Company—of Marion.

Nor did Harding appear to be able to distinguish between honesty and rascality. He had been trained in the sordid school of practical Ohio politics. He had served for years as the majestic Doric false front behind which Ohio lobbyists and fixers and purchasers of privilege had discussed their "business propositions" and put over their "little deals"—and they, too, followed him to Washington, along with the boys from Marion. Some of them he put into positions of power, others he saw assuming positions of power; knowing them intimately, he must have known—if he was capable of a minute's clear and unprejudiced thought—how they would inevitably use those positions; but he was too fond of his old cronies, too anxious to have them share his good fortune, and too muddle-minded to face the issue until it was too late. He liked to slip away from the White House to the house in H Street where the Ohio gang and their intimates reveled and liquor flowed freely without undue regard for prohibition, and a man could take his pleasure at the poker table and forget the cares of state; and the easiest course to take was not to inquire too closely into what the boys were doing, to hope that if they were grafting a little on the side they'd be reasonable about it and not do anything to let old Warren down.

And why did he choose such company? The truth was that under his imposing exterior he was just a common small-town man, an "average sensual man," the sort of man who likes nothing better in the world than to be with the old bunch when they gather at Joe's place for an all-Saturday-night session, with waistcoats unbuttoned and cigars between their teeth and an ample supply of bottles and cracked ice at hand. His private life was one of cheap sex episodes; as one reads the confessions of his mistress, who claims that as President he was supporting an illegitimate baby born hardly a year before his election, one is struck by the shabbiness of the whole affair: the clandestine meetings in disreputable hotels, in the Senate Office Building (where Nan Britton believed their child to have been conceived), and even in a coat-closet in the executive offices of the White House itself. (Doubts have been cast upon the truth of the story told in *The President's Daughter*, but is it easy to imagine any one making up out of whole cloth a supposedly autobiographical story compounded of such ignoble adventures?) Even making due allowance for the refraction of Harding's personality through that of Nan Britton, one sees with deadly clarity the essential ordinariness of the man, the commonness of his "Gee, dearie" and "Say, you darling," his being swindled out of a hundred dollars by card sharpers on a train ride, his naïve assurance to Nan, when detectives broke in upon them in a Broadway hotel, that they could not be arrested because it was illegal to detain a Senator while "en route to Washington to serve the people." Warren Harding's ambitious wife had tailored and groomed him into outward respectability and made a man of substance of him; yet even now, after he had reached the White House, the rowdies of the Ohio gang were fundamentally his sort. He had risen above them, he could mingle urbanely with their superiors, but it was in the smoke-filled rooms of the house in H Street that he was really most at home.

Harding had no sooner arrived at the White House than a swarm of practical politicians of the McKinley-Foraker vintage reappeared in Washington. Blowsy gentlemen with cigars stuck in their cheeks and rolls of very useful hundred-dollar bills in their pockets began to infest the Washington hotels. The word ran about that you could do business with the government now—if you only fixed things up with the right man. The oil men licked their chops; had they not lobbied powerfully at the Chicago convention for the nomination of just such a man as Harding, who did not take this conservation nonsense too seriously, and would not Harding's Secretary of the Interior, Albert B. Fall, let them develop the national resources on friendly and not too stringent terms? The Ohio gang chuckled over the feast awaiting them: the chances for graft at Columbus had been a piker's chance compared with those which the mastery of the federal government would offer him. Warren Harding wanted to be helpful. Well, he would have a chance to be.

[2]

The public at large, however, knew little and cared less about what was happening behind the scenes. Their eyes—when they bothered to look at all—were upon the well-lighted stage where the Harding Administration was playing a drama of discreet and seemly statesmanship.

Peace with Germany, so long deferred, was made by a resolution signed by the President on July 2, 1921. The Government of the United States was put upon a unified budget basis for the first time in history by the passage of the Budget Act of 1921, and Charles G. Dawes, becoming Director of the Budget, entranced the newspaper-reading public with his picturesque language, his underslung pipe, and his broom-waving histrionics when he harangued the bureau chiefs on behalf of business efficiency. Immigration was restricted, being put upon a quota basis, to the satisfaction of labor and the relief of those who felt that the amount of melting being done in the melting-pot was disappointingly small. Congress raised the tariff, as all good Republican Congresses should. Secretary Mellon pleased the financial powers of the country by arguing for the lowering of the high surtaxes upon large incomes; and although an obstreperous Farm Bloc joined with the Democrats to keep the maximum surtax at 50 per cent, Wall Street at least felt that the Administration's heart was in the right place. Every foe of union labor was sure of this when Attorney-General Daugherty confronted the striking railway shopmen with an injunction worthy of Mitchell Palmer himself. In January, 1923, an agreement for the funding of the British war debt to the United States was made in Washington; it was shortly ratified by the Senate. The outstanding achievement of the Harding Administration, however, was undoubtedly the Washington Conference for the Limitation of Armaments—or, as the newspapers insisted upon calling it, the "Arms Parley."

Since the war the major powers of the world had begun once

more their race for supremacy in armament. England, the
United States, and Japan were all building ships for dear life.
The rivalry between them was rendered acute by the growing
tension in the Pacific. During the war Japan had seized her
golden opportunity for the expansion of her commercial empire: her rivals being very much occupied elsewhere, she had
begun to regard China as her special sphere of interest and to
treat it as a sort of protectorate where her commerce would
have prior rights to that of other nations. Her hand was
strengthened by an alliance with England. When Charles Evans
Hughes became Secretary of State and began to stand up for
American rights in the Orient, applying once more the traditional American policy of the Open Door, it was soon apparent
that the situation was ticklish. Japan wanted her own way; the
Americans opposed it; and there lay the Philippines, apparently right under Japan's thumb if trouble should break out!
All three powers, Britain, Japan, and the United States, would
be the gainers by an amicable agreement about the points
under dispute in the Pacific, by the substitution of a three-
cornered agreement for the Japanese-British alliance, and by
an arrangement for the limitation of fleets. Senator Borah
proposed an international conference. Harding and Hughes
took up his suggestion, the conference was called, and on
November 12, 1921—the day following the solemn burial of
America's Unknown Soldier at Arlington Cemetery—the delegates assembled in Washington.

President Harding opened the first session with a cordial if
profuse speech of welcome, and true to his policy of leaving
difficult problems to be solved by the "best minds," left Secretary Hughes and his associates to do the actual negotiating. In
this case his hands-off policy worked well. Hughes not only
had a brilliant mind, he had a definite program and a masterly
grasp of the complicated issues at stake. President Harding had
hardly walked out of Memorial Continental Hall when the
Secretary of State, installed as chairman of the conference,
began what seemed at first only the perfunctory address of
greeting—and then, to the amazement of the delegates assembled about the long conference tables, came out with a definite
and detailed program: a ten-year naval holiday, during which
no capital ships should be built; the abandonment of all capi-
tal-shipbuilding plans, either actual or projected; the scrapping,

by the three nations, of almost two million tons of ships built or building; and the limitation of replacement according to a 5-5-3 ratio: the American and British navies to be kept at parity and the Japanese at three-fifths of the size of each.

"With the acceptance of this plan," concluded Secretary Hughes amid a breathless silence, "the burden of meeting the demands of competition in naval armament will be lifted. Enormous sums will be released to aid the progress of civilization. At the same time the proper demands of national defense will be adequately met and the nations will have ample opportunity during the naval holiday of ten years to consider their future course. Preparation for offensive naval war will stop now."

The effect of this direct and specific proposal was prodigious. At the proposal of a naval holiday William Jennings Bryan, sitting among the newspaper men, expressed his enthusiasm with a yell of delight. At the conclusion of Hughes's speech the delegates broke into prolonged applause. It was echoed by the country and by the press of the world. People's imaginations were so stirred by the boldness and effectiveness of the Hughes plan that the success of the conference became almost inevitable.

After three months of negotiation the delegates of Japan, Great Britain, and the United States had agreed upon a treaty which followed the general lines of the Hughes program; had joined with the French in an agreement to respect one another's insular possessions in the Pacific, and to settle all disagreements by conciliatory negotiations; had prepared the way for the withdrawal of Japan from Shantung and Siberia; and had agreed to respect the principle of the open door in China. The treaties were duly ratified by the Senate. The immediate causes of friction in the Pacific were removed; and although cynics might point out that competition in cruisers and submarines was little abated and that battleships were almost obsolete anyhow, the Naval Treaty at least lessened the burden of competition, as Secretary Hughes had predicted, and in addition set a precedent of profound importance. The armaments which a nation built were now definitely recognized as being a matter of international concern, subject to international agreement.

Outwardly, then, things seemed to be going well for Warren

Harding. He was personally popular; his friendly attitude toward business satisfied the conservative temper of the country; his Secretary of the Treasury was being referred to, wherever two or three bankers or industrialists gathered together, as the "greatest since Alexander Hamilton"; his Secretary of Commerce, Herbert Hoover, was aiding trade as efficiently as he had aided the Belgians; and even discouraged idealists had to admit that the Washington Conference had been no mean achievement. Though there were rumors of graft and waste and mismanagement in some departments of the Government, and the director of the Veterans' Bureau had had to leave his office in disgrace, and there was noisy criticism in Congress of certain leases of oil lands to Messrs. Doheny and Sinclair, these things attracted only a mild public interest. When Harding left in the early summer of 1923 for a visit to Alaska, few people realized that anything was radically wrong with his administration. When, on his way home, he fell ill with what appeared to be ptomaine poisoning, and on his arrival at San Francisco his illness went into pneumonia, the country watched the daily headlines with affectionate concern. And when, just as the danger appeared to have been averted, he died suddenly—on August 2, 1923—of what his physicians took to be a stroke of apoplexy, the whole nation was plunged into deep and genuine grief.

The President's body was placed upon a special train, which proceeded across the country at the best possible speed to Washington. All along the route, thousands upon thousands of men, women, and children were gathered to see it slip by. Cowboys on the Western hills dismounted and stood uncovered as the train passed. In the cities the throngs of mourners were so dense that the engineer had to reduce his speed and the train fell hours behind schedule. "It is believed," wrote a reporter for the *New York Times*, "to be the most remarkable demonstration in American history of affection, respect, and reverence for the dead." When Warren Harding's body, after lying in state at Washington, was taken to Marion for burial, his successor proclaimed a day of public mourning, business houses were closed, memorial services were held from one end of the country to the other, flags hung at half mast, and buildings were draped in black.

The innumerable speeches made that day expressed no

merely perfunctory sentiments; everywhere people felt that a great-hearted man, bowed down with his labors in their behalf, had died a martyr to the service of his country. The dead President was called "a majestic figure who stood out like a rock of consistency"; it was said that "his vision was always on the spiritual"; and Bishop Manning of New York, speaking at a memorial service in the Cathedral of St. John the Divine, seemed to be giving the fallen hero no more than his due when he cried, "If I could write one sentence upon his monument it would be this, 'He taught us the power of brotherliness.' It is the greatest lesson that any man can teach us. It is the spirit of the Christian religion. In the spirit of brotherliness and kindness we can solve all the problems that confront us. . . . May God ever give to our country leaders as faithful, as wise, as noble in spirit, as the one whom we now mourn."

But as it happens, there are some problems—at least for a President of the United States—that the spirit of brotherliness and kindness will not alone solve. The problem, for example, of what to do when those to whom you have been all too brotherly have enmeshed your administration in graft, and you know that the scandal cannot long be concealed, and you feel your whole life-work toppling into disgrace. That was the problem which had killed Warren Harding.

A rumor that the President committed suicide by taking poison later gained wide currency through the publication of Samuel Hopkins Adams's *Revelry*, a novel largely based on the facts of the Harding Administration. Gaston B. Means, a Department of Justice detective and a member of the gang which revolved about Daugherty, implied only too clearly in *The Strange Death of President Harding* that the President was poisoned by his wife, with the connivance of Doctor Sawyer. The motive, according to Means, was a double one: Mrs. Harding had found out about Nan Britton and the illegitimate daughter and was consumed with a bitter and almost insane jealousy; and she had learned enough about the machinations of Harding's friends and the power that they had over him to feel that only death could save him from obloquy. Both the suicide theory and the Means story are very plausible. The ptomaine poisoning came, it was said, from eating crab meat on the presidential boat on the return from Alaska, but the list of supplies in the steward's pantry contained no crab meat and no one else in the presidential party was taken ill; furthermore, the fatal "stroke of apoplexy" occurred when the President was recovering from pneumonia, Mrs. Harding was apparently alone with him at the time, and the verdict of the physicians, not being based upon an autopsy, was hardly more than an expression of opinion. Yet it is not necessary to accept any such melodramatic version of the tragedy to acknowledge that Harding died a victim of the predicament in which he was caught. He knew too much of what had been going on in his administration to be able to face the future. On the Alaskan trip, he was clearly in a state of tragic fear; according to William Allen White, "he kept asking Secretary Hoover and the more trusted reporters who surrounded him what a President should do whose friends had betrayed him." Whatever killed him—poison or heart failure—did so the more easily because he had lost the will to live.

Of all this, of course, the country as a whole guessed nothing at the time. Their friend and President was dead, they mourned his death, and they applauded the plans of the Harding Memorial Association to raise a great monument in his honor. It was only afterward that the truth came out, piece by piece.

[3]

The martyred President had not been long in his grave when the peculiar circumstances under which the Naval Oil Reserves at Teapot Dome and Elk Hills had been leased began to be unearthed by the Senate Committee on Public Lands, and there was little by little disclosed what was perhaps the gravest and most far-reaching scandal of the Harding Administration. The facts of the case, as they were ultimately established, were, briefly, as follows:

Since 1909, three tracts of oil-bearing government land had been legally set aside for the future hypothetical needs of the United States navy—as a sort of insurance policy against a possible shortage of oil in time of emergency. They were Naval Reserve No. 1, at Elk Hills, California; No. 2, at Buena Vista, California; and No. 3, at Teapot Dome, Wyoming. As time went on, it became apparent that the oil under these lands might be in danger of being drawn off by neighboring wells, the flow of oil under the earth being such that if you dril: a well you are likely to bring up not only the oil from under your own land, but also that from under your neighbor's land. As to the extent of this danger to these particular properties there was wide disagreement; but when gushers were actually opened up right on the threshold of the Elk Hills Reserve, Congress took action. In 1920 it gave the Secretary of the Navy almost unlimited power to meet as he saw fit the problem of conserving the Reserves. Clearly there were at least two possible courses of action open to him. He might arrange to have offset wells drilled along the edge of the Reserves to neutralize the drainage, or he might lease the Reserves to private operators on condition that they store an equitable amount of the oil—or of fuel oil—for the future requirements of the national defense. Secretary Daniels preferred to have offset wells drilled.

But when Albert B. Fall became Secretary of the Interior under President Harding, he decided otherwise. During 1921 —on the eve of the Conference for the Limitation of Armaments—certain high officers in the navy were sufficiently nervous about possible trouble with Japan to declare that the navy must at once have fuel oil storage depots built and filled and ready for use at Pearl Harbor and other strategic points. This idea suited Mr. Fall perfectly. He had come into office as the ally of certain big oil interests, and being a politician without illusions, he saw a chance to do them a favor. He would lease the Reserves in their entirety to private operators, and meet the needs of the navy by using the royalty oil which these operators paid the Government for the purpose of buying fuel oil tanks and filling them with fuel oil. To be sure, the Secretary of the Navy alone had power to lease the Reserves, and Fall was not the Secretary of the Navy; but that was not an insuperable difficulty.

Less than three months after President Harding took office, he signed an Executive Order transferring the Reserves from the custody of the Secretary of the Navy to that of the Secretary of the Interior. On April 7, 1922, Fall secretly and without competitive bidding leased Reserve No. 3, the Teapot Dome Reserve, to Harry F. Sinclair's Mammoth Oil Company. On December 11, 1922, he secretly and without competitive bidding leased Reserve No. 1, the Elk Hills Reserve, to Edward F. Doheny's Pan-American Company. It has been argued that these leases were fair to the Government and that no undue profits would have accrued to the lessees if the contracts had been allowed to stand. It has been argued that the necessity for keeping secret what were thought of as military arrangements was sufficient excuse for the absence of competitive bidding and the complete absence of publicity. But it was later discovered that Fall had received from Sinclair some $260,000 in Liberty bonds, and that Fall had been "lent" by Doheny—without interest and without security—$100,000 in cash.

After a long series of Senate investigations, governmental lawsuits, and criminal trials which dragged out through the rest of the decade, the Doheny lease was voided by the Supreme Court as "illegal and fraudulent," the Sinclair lease was also voided, and Secretary Fall was found guilty of accepting a bribe from Doheny and sentenced to a year in prison. Secretary of the Navy Denby—who had amiably approved the transfer of the Reserves from his charge to that of Fall—was driven from office by public criticism. Paradoxically, both Doheny and Sinclair were acquitted. But Sinclair had to serve a double term in prison in 1929: first, for contempt of the Senate in refusing to answer questions put to him by the Committee on Public Lands, and second, for contempt of court in having the jury at his first trial shadowed by Burns detectives. (One of the jurors declared that a man had approached him with the suggestion that if he voted right he would have an automobile "as long as this block.")

Such are the bare facts of the oil lease transactions. But they are only a part of the story. For after the Senate Committee's first important disclosures, early in 1924, and President Coolidge's appointment of the useful Mr. Owen Roberts and the ornamental Ex-Senator Atlee Pomerene as a bi-partisan team of Government prosecutors to take whatever legal action might be called for on behalf of the Government, Messrs. Roberts and Pomerene discovered that certain bonds transferred by Sinclair to Fall had come from the exchequer of a hitherto unheard-of concern called the Continental Trading Company, Ltd., of Canada. And the history of the Continental Trading Company, Ltd., as it was gradually dragged to light, was not only highly sensational but highly illuminating as a case-study in current American business ethics. This is what had happened:

On the 17th of November, 1921—a few months before the Fall-Sinclair contract was made—a little group of men gathered in a room at the Hotel Vanderbilt in New York for a business session. They included Col. E. A. Humphreys, the owner of the rich Mexia oil field; Harry M. Blackmer of the Midwest Oil Company; James E. O'Neil of the Prairie Oil Company; Colonel Robert W. Stewart, chairman of the board of the Standard Oil Company of Indiana; and Harry F. Sinclair, head of the Sinclair Consolidated Oil Company. At that meeting Colonel Humphreys agreed to sell 33,333,333 barrels of oil from his oil field at $1.50 a barrel. But he discovered that he was not, as he had supposed, to sell this oil directly to the companies represented by the other men present. He was asked to sell it to a concern of which he had never heard, a concern which had only just been incorporated—the Continental Trading Company, Ltd. The contract of sale was guaranteed on behalf of the mysterious Continental Company by Sinclair and O'Neil. And the Continental straightway resold the oil to Sinclair's and O'Neil's companies, not at $1.50 a barrel, *but at $1.75 a barrel*—thereby diverting to the coffers of the Continental a nice profit of twenty-five cents a barrel which might otherwise have gone to the other companies whose executives were gathered together. A profit, it might be added, which in the course of time should amount to over eight million dollars.

As a matter of fact, it never amounted to as much as that. For after a year or more the Senate became unduly inquisitive and it was thought best to wind up the affairs of the Continental Trading Company, Ltd., and destroy its records. But before this was done, the profit of that little deal pulled off at the Hotel Vanderbilt had piled up to more than three millions.

With these millions, as they rolled in, President Osler, the distinguished Canadian attorney who headed the Continental, purchased Liberty bonds. And the bulk of these bonds (after taking out a 2-per-cent share for himself) he turned over, in packages, to four of the gentlemen who had sat in on the conference at the Vanderbilt, as follows:

To Harry M. Blackmer, approximately $763,000.

To James E. O'Neil, approximately $800,000.

To Colonel Robert W. Stewart, approximately $759,000.

To Harry F. Sinclair, approximately $757,000.

And did these gentlemen at once report to their directors

and stockholders the receipt of the bonds and put them into the corporate treasuries? They did not.

Blackmer, according to the subsequent (very subsequent) testimony of his counsel, put his share in a safety deposit box at the Equitable Trust Company in New York, where in 1928 it still remained.

O'Neil turned over his share to his company, but not until May, 1925.

Stewart handed his share to an employee of the Standard Oil Company of Indiana to be held in trust for the company in the vaults of the company, but never told any other associates of this except one member of the company's legal staff, and never disclosed to his directors what he had done until 1928, when he finally turned over the bonds to them. The trust agreement was written in pencil.

Sinclair, according to his own testimony, did not take the directors or officers of his company into his confidence until 1928, and kept his share of the bonds in a vault in his home. He did not keep all of them there very long, however, or the brave history of the Continental Trading Company, Ltd., might never have come to light. A goodly portion of them (as we have already seen) he turned over to Fall. Another goodly portion, amounting to $185,000, he "loaned" (in addition to an outright gift of $75,000), to the Republican National Committee, later getting back $100,000 of it. The "loan" was made to Will H. Hays, who had been chairman of the Republican National Committee during the Harding-Cox campaign of 1920, had later been appointed Postmaster-General by President Harding, and had finally resigned to become supervisor of morals for the motion-picture industry. Mr. Hays was czar of the movies by the time Sinclair handed him the bonds, but being a conscientious man, he was trying to get the 1920 Republican campaign debt paid off. To this end he attempted to use the Sinclair "loan" in a very interesting way. He and his lieutenants approached a number of wealthy men, potential donors to the cause, and told them that if they would contribute to meet the deficit they might have Sinclair bonds to the amount of their contributions. How long they might keep the bonds was not made clear—at least in Hays's testimony before the Senate Committee on Public Lands. This method of concealing an enormous Sinclair contribution was euphemistically called, by the moral supervisor of the movies, "using the bonds in efforts to raise money for the deficit."

[4]

So much for our little lesson in governmental practice and in the fiduciary duties of business executives in behalf of their stockholders. Now let us turn to the lighter side of the oil scandals. Lighter, that is, for those who were in no way implicated. There is a certain grim humor in the twistings and turnings of unwilling witnesses under the implacable cross-examination of Senator Walsh of Montana, without whose resourceful work the truth might never have been run to earth. Some of the scenes in the slowly-unfolding drama of the investigations, some of the sojourns of interested parties on foreign shores, some of the odd tricks of memory revealed, are not without an element of entertainment. Let us go back over the record of that long investigation and study a few of them, item by item.

Item One. Who Loaned Fall the Money?

In the autumn of 1923—not long after Harding's lamented death—Senator Walsh's committee learned of a recent sudden rise to affluence on the part of Secretary Fall. For some time previously Fall had been in financial straits; he had not even paid his local taxes for several years. But now all was changed. Mr. Fall had even purchased additional land near his New Mexican ranch, and in this purchase had used a considerable number of hundred-dollar bills. The Walsh committee at once became bloodhounds on the scent: hundred-dollar bills are as exciting to investigators as refusals to testify or refusals to waive immunity. From whom had Fall been receiving money? Fall wrote the committee a long letter, denying absolutely that he had ever received a dollar from Mr. Doheny or Mr. Sinclair, and in tones of outraged innocence explained that he had received a loan of $100,000 from Edward B. McLean of Washington, a millionaire newspaper-owner whose ample hospitality Harding and his associates had often enjoyed.

Mr. McLean was in Palm Beach and unable to come to

Washington to testify about this loan. The committee might perhaps have been expected to let the matter go at that. But they did not. Mr. McLean was wanted—and it began to appear that he was extremely unwilling to be examined. He and his friends engaged in a voluminous correspondence by coded telegrams with his aides in Washington, discussing the progress of affairs in messages such as

> *Haxpw sent over buy bonka and householder bonka sultry tkvouep prozoics sepic bepelt goal hocusing this pouted proponent*

Finally Senator Walsh all too obligingly journeyed to Palm Beach to take McLean's testimony there. Yes, McLean had made a loan to Fall. But he had made it in the form of three checks. Secretary Fall had shortly returned the checks; they had not even passed through the banks, and there was no record whatever of the transaction.

Clearly this brief and unusual financial transaction threw little light on the prosperity of the Ex-Secretary of the Interior or his use of cash in large denominations. Another explanation was necessary. Whereupon—on January 24, 1924—the lessee of Naval Reserve No. 1, Edward L. Doheny, took the stand. He, too, had loaned $100,000 to Fall. The money had been carried from New York to Washington in a satchel. But the loan had nothing to do with any lease of oil-bearing land. It was a bona fide loan made to accommodate an old friend. The elderly oil magnate drew a touching picture of his long years of comradeship with Fall. Was $100,000 a rather large sum to be loaned this way in cash? Why, no, it was "just a bagatelle" to him. It was not at all unusual for him "to make a remittance that way." Was there a note given for the loan? Yes; Doheny would search for it. Later he produced it—or rather, a fragment of it. The signature was missing. Fearing that he might die and that Fall might be unduly pressed for payment by cold-blooded executors, Doheny had torn the note in half and given the part with the signature to Mrs. Doheny—and she had mislaid it. The explanation was perfect—though some years later the Supreme Court seemed to regard it with skepticism.

Item Two. Six or Eight Cows

Just before the generous Doheny took the stand, the news-papers had been treated to a first-class front-page story. Archie Roosevelt, son of the great T. R. and brother of the lesser T. R. (who was Harding's Assistant Secretary of Navy), had come before the Walsh Committee as a volunteer witness. Archie Roosevelt was an officer in one of the Sinclair compa-nies, and he had something to get off his mind. His brother had urged him to tell all. He (Archie) had been told by one G. D. Wahlberg, confidential secretary to Sinclair, that Sinclair had paid $68,000 to the manager of Fall's ranch, a circumstance which, in view of the relentless way in which Senator Walsh was running down evidence, apparently had caused Wahlberg some uneasiness. Furthermore, Sinclair had sailed for Europe —not only had sailed, but had done so very quietly, without letting his name appear on the passenger list. The committee called Wahlberg. This gentleman was even more uneasy at the committee table than he had been in talking to Archie Roose-velt, but he had a charming explanation for what he was said to have said. Roosevelt must have misunderstood him. He had said nothing about $68,000. What he must have said was that Sinclair had sent "six or eight cows" to Fall's ranch. (Which was true, after a manner of speaking: Sinclair had indeed made a present of live stock to Fall; not precisely "six or eight cows," but a horse, six hogs, a bull, and six heifers.) You see how the misunderstanding arose? You see how much "sixty-eight thous" sounds like "six or eight cows"?

The Committee on Public Lands did not seem to see. They lifted a collective eyebrow. So a little later Wahlberg tried again. This time his explanation was even more delightful. He had been consulting his memory, and had decided that what he must actually have said when he sounded as if he were talking about $68,000 going to the manager of the Fall ranch, or the Fall farm, was that $68,000 was going to the manager of the "horse farm"—by which he had meant the trainer at Sinclair's celebrated Rancocas Stables. This $68,000 represented the salary of Hildreth, the trainer, together with his share of the winnings of Zev and other Sinclair horses.

"Horse farm"—there seemed to be something less than

idiomatic about the phrase. The collective eyebrow was not lowered.

Item Three. The Silences of Colonel Stewart—and Others

The Senate committee was hot on the trail—or rather on two trails. But then and thereafter the various gentlemen who could give it the greatest assistance in following these trails to the end revealed a strange reluctance to talk and a strange condition of memory when they did talk. Secretary Fall was declared by his physicians to be a "very sick man" who ought not to be pressed to testify. When he finally did testify, he refused to answer questions which might "tend to incriminate" him. Sinclair, as Archie Roosevelt had told the committee, had gone to Europe; after he returned, he too refused to answer questions; it was this refusal which led to his conviction for contempt. After his acquittal on the graver charge of conspiracy to defraud the government he at last spoke out; he admitted that he had turned over the bonds to Fall, but insisted that they were given in payment for a one-third interest in Fall's ranching and cattle business.

Blackmer had gone to Europe and could not be induced to return. O'Neil had gone to Europe and could not be induced to return. Osler of the Continental Trading Company was somewhere at the ends of the earth. And as for Colonel Stewart, only the insistence of John D. Rockefeller, Jr., induced him to come from Cuba to face the committee. When he did face it, early in 1928, he testified as follows: "I did not personally receive any of these bonds. I did not make one dollar out of the transaction." Less than two months later, after Sinclair's acquittal had somewhat reduced the tension, he admitted that over three-quarters of a million dollars' worth of these bonds had been delivered to him, and that he had not told the directors of his company about them for several years.

Item Four. The Testimony of Mr. Hays

In 1924 Will H. Hays, preceptor of motion-picture morality, was called before the Senate committee. He was asked how much money Sinclair had contributed to the Republican Party. Seventy-five thousand dollars, he said.

In 1928, after the history of the Continental bonds had become somewhat clearer, Mr. Hays was asked to face the committee again. He told them the full story of Sinclair's "loan" of $185,000 in addition to his gift. Why had he not told this before? He had not been "asked about any bonds."

Item Five. The Reticence of Mr. Mellon

A few days after Mr. Hays gave his second and improved version of the Sinclair contributions, the cashier of Charles Pratt & Company was called before the committee to testify about $50,000 worth of Sinclair-Continental Liberty bonds which had been left by Hays with the late John T. Pratt, to be held against a contribution of the same amount—after the ingenious Hays plan—by Mr. Pratt to the Republican Committee. The cashier produced a card on which Mr. Pratt had noted the disposal of the bonds and the payment of his contribution. And in the corner of this card was a minute notation in pencil, as follows:

> *$50,000*
> *Andy*   *Weeks*
> *DuPont*
> *Butler*

Senator Walsh examined the card.

Senator Walsh: I can make out "Weeks," and I can make out "DuPont," and I can make out "Butler," but what is this other name? It looks like Andy.

The Cashier (*using a magnifying glass*): It's Weeks, Du-Pont, Butler, and the other name must be Candy. . . . Yes, it might be Andy.

Senator Nye: And who is Andy?

The Cashier: I have no idea who Andy can be. I can think of no one known as Andy.

There was a roar from the crowd in the room. Everybody knew who Andy must be. Senator Walsh dispatched a note to Andrew W. Mellon, Secretary of the Treasury, to ask him if he could explain the notation. This Mr. Mellon obligingly did without delay.

Late in 1923, Mr. Mellon explained—at just about the time when the Teapot Dome investigation was getting under way— Hays had sent him some bonds. "When Mr. Hays called shortly thereafter, he told me that he had received the bonds from Mr. Sinclair and suggested that I hold the bonds and contribute an equal amount to the fund. This I declined to do."

The Secretary had acted with strict integrity. He had sent the bonds back, and instead of following Hays's suggestion he had made an outright contribution of $50,000. He added that he had "had no knowledge of what has developed since, that is, of the Teapot Dome lease matter."

It is perhaps worth noting, however, that this testimony was given in 1928. For more than three years not only the Senate committee, but Messrs. Roberts and Pomerene, the public attorneys appointed by President Coolidge to prosecute the government suits, had been trying to discover just what had become of the Continental bonds, and during all that time the Secretary of the Treasury was aware that in 1923 he had been offered Liberty bonds which came from Sinclair. He said nothing until that little card turned up with Andy (or possibly Candy) penciled on it. A small matter, perhaps; but surely it revealed the Secretary as a paragon of reticence when his testimony might cast discredit on the money-raising methods of his party.

Thus comes to an end—as of this writing, at least—the remarkable story of Teapot Dome and Elk Hills and the Continental Trading Company, Ltd. The Executive Order transferring the leases, which may be said to have begun it all, was promulgated in June, 1921, when Harding was new in office, and the Stillman divorce trial was impending, and Dempsey was preparing to meet Carpentier, and young Charles Lindbergh had not yet taken his first ride in an airplane. By the time Sinclair and Stewart had told their stories and Hays had revised himself and Secretary Mellon had overcome his reticence, Lindbergh had flown to Europe and Herbert Hoover was corralling delegates for the Republican nomination; by the time Harry Sinclair emerged from his unwelcome term of service as apothecary in the Washington jail, the bull market had come down in ruin and the Post-war Decade was dying. Secretary Fall's term as guardian of the national resources for the Harding Administration had been brief, but the aftermath had been as long and harrowing as it was instructive.

Oh yes—there is one more thing to add. The oil: what became of the oil that started it all, the oil that the patriots of the Navy Department had been so anxious to have immediately available in case of trouble in the Pacific? There had been a good deal of excitement about bonds and hundred-thousand-dollar loans, but everybody seemed to have forgotten about that oil. Production in the properties leased to Sinclair and Doheny was stopped; but you may recall that the danger of drainage into neighboring wells had been much discussed in 1921. The neighboring wells went right on producing, and it is said that part of the oil from them—including, in all probability, some drawn from within the Reserves—was sold to the Japanese Government!

[5]

The oil cases were the aristocrats among the scandals of the Harding Administration, but there were other scandals juicier and more reeking. Let us hold our noses for a moment and examine a few of them briefly.

There was, for example, the almost incredible extravagance and corruption of the Veterans' Bureau under Charles R. Forbes, a buccaneer of fortune (and one-time deserter from the army) whom Harding had fallen in with on a visit to Hawaii. Harding was so taken with Forbes that in 1921 he put him in charge of the Government's work for those disabled war heroes in whose behalf every public man considered it his duty to shed an appreciative tear. Forbes held office for less than two years, and during that time it was estimated that over two hundred million dollars went astray in graft and flagrant waste on the part of his Bureau. Forbes went on a notorious junket through the country, supposedly selecting hospital sites which in reality had already been chosen. His Bureau let contracts for veterans' hospitals almost without regard for price; for instance, a contract for a hospital at Northampton was let to a firm which asked some thirty thousand dollars more than the lowest bidder. It was charged that Forbes had an arrangement with the builders of some hospitals whereby he was to pocket a third of the profits. Preposterous purchases of hospital supplies were made: the Veterans' Bureau bought $70,000 worth of floor wax and floor cleaner, for instance—enough, it was said, to last a hundred years—and for the cleaner it paid 98 cents a gallon, although expert testimony later brought out the fact that it was worth less than 4 cents a gallon exclusive of the water which it contained. Quantities of surplus goods were sold with the same easy disregard for price: 84,000 brand-new sheets which had cost $1.37 each were sold at 26 or 27 cents apiece, although at that very moment the Bureau was purchasing 25,000 new ones at $1.03 apiece. "At one time," reported Bruce Bliven, "sheets just bought were actually going in at one end of the warehouse [at Perryville, Maryland] as the ones just sold were going out the other, and some of them by mistake went straight in and out again." More than 75,000 towels which had cost 19 cents each were sold for 3⅜ cents each. These few facts are enough to show with what generous abandon Forbes spent the money appropriated to care for the defenders of the Republic. Forbes went to Leavenworth in 1926 for fraud.

There was rampant graft in the office of the Alien Property Custodian as well. Gaston B. Means has charged that attorneys who came to Washington to file claims for the return of properties taken over from Germans during the war were advised to consult a Boston lawyer named Thurston, that Thurston would charge them a big fee for his services, the claim would be allowed, and the fee would be split with those in authority. Be that as it may, the evidence brought out in the American Metal Company case was sufficient to indicate the sort of transaction which was permitted to take place.

The American Metal Company was an internationally-owned concern 49 per cent of whose stock had been taken over by the Alien Property Custodian during the war on the ground that it belonged to Germans. This stock had been sold for $6,-000,000. In 1921 a certain Richard Merton appeared at the Custodian's office with the claim that this 49 per cent had not been German, but Swiss, and that the Swiss owners, whom he represented, should be reimbursed. The claim was allowed after Merton had paid $441,000 in Liberty bonds to John T. King, Republican National Committeeman from Connecticut, for "services" which consisted of introducing him to Colonel T. W. Miller, the Custodian, and to Jess Smith, Attorney-General Daugherty's man Friday. It was brought out at Miller's trial that at least $200,000 of this $441,000 was paid over to Jess Smith "for expediting the claim through his acquaintance in Washington"; that Mal S. Daugherty, brother of the

Attorney-General, sold at least $40,000 worth of Merton Liberty bonds and shortly thereafter deposited $49,165 to his brother's account; and that Colonel Miller also got a share of the money. Miller was convicted in 1927 of conspiracy to defraud the Government of his unbiased services and was sentenced to eighteen months in prison. Daugherty was also brought to trail, but got off. After two juries had been unable to agree as to his guilt or innocence, the indictment against him was dismissed—but not before it had been brought out that in 1925 this former chief legal officer of the Government had gone to his brother's bank at Washington Court House, Ohio, and had taken out and burned the ledger sheets covering his own account there, and his brother's account, and another account known as "Jesse Smith Extra."

It was during the grand jury investigation which preceded the American Metal Company case that Harding's Attorney-General wrote the remarkable statement which appears at the head of this chapter. During his trial Daugherty failed to take the stand in his own defense, and his attorney, Max Steuer, later explained this failure in another equally remarkable statement:

"It was not anything connected with this case which impelled him to refrain from so doing. . . . He feared . . . that Mr. Buckner would cross-examine him about matters political that would not involve Mr. Daugherty, concerning which he knew and as to which he would never make disclosure. . . . If the jury knew the real reason for destroying the ledger sheets they would commend rather than condemn Mr. Daugherty, but he insisted on silence."

Could there be more deliberate implication that Harding's Attorney-General could not tell the truth for fear of blackening the reputation of his dead chief? Call Daugherty's silence, if you wish, the silence of loyalty, or call those statements an effort to hide behind the dead President; in either case the Harding Administration appears in a strange light.

Charges still more damaging were boldly made by Gaston B. Means in 1930. He stated that as a henchman of the Ohio gang he used to engage two adjoining rooms at a New York hotel for the collection of prohibition graft from bootleggers who were willing to pay for federal protection; that he would place a big goldfish-bowl in one of the rooms, on a table which he could see by peeping through the door from the next room; that each bootlegger would come at his appointed hour and minute and leave in the bowl huge amounts of cash in thousand-dollar or five-hundred-dollar bills; that as soon as the bootlegger left, Means would enter, count the money, and check off the contribution; and that in this way he collected a total of fully seven million dollars which he turned over to Jess Smith, the collector-in-chief for the Ohio Gang, who shared an apartment in Washington with Attorney-General Daugherty.

Means further asserted that the swag from this and other forms of graft was kept hidden—many thousand dollars at a time—in a metal box buried in the back yard of the house which he occupied at 903 Sixteenth Street in Washington; he described this house and yard as being protected with a high wire fence and fitted out with a code signal system and other secret devices such as would delight a gang of small boys playing pirate.

Jess Smith committed suicide—at least that was the official verdict—in 1923 in the apartment which he shared with Harry Daugherty. Means claimed that just before this tragedy took place, the gang had discovered that Smith—like the careful shopkeeper he had been before he was brought to Washington by Daugherty to occupy a desk in the Department of Justice—had kept a record of all the cash which had passed through his hands, and that Smith, terrified at the thought of his guilt and his secret knowledge, had been playing with the idea of turning state's witness against the gang. According to Means, the gang thereupon decided that Smith must be disposed of. Although Smith was afraid of firearms, he was persuaded to purchase a revolver on one of his trips to Ohio. And the "suicide" which followed—so Means plainly indicated, as many others had already suspected—was no suicide at all.

Finally, Means drew attention to the astonishing mortality among those who had been in on the secrets of the gang. Not only had Smith dropped out of the picture, but also John T. King (who had received the Merton bonds), C. F. Hately (a Department of Justice agent), C. F. Cramer (attorney for the Veterans' Bureau), Thurston (the Boston lawyer who represented many clients before the Alien Property Custodian), T. B. Felder (attorney for the Harding group), President Harding, Mrs. Harding, and General Sawyer. They had all died—most of them suddenly—within a few years of the end of the Harding Administration.

No matter how much or how little credence one may give to these latter charges and their implications, the proved evidence is enough to warrant the statement that the Harding Administration was responsible in its short two years and five months for more concentrated robbery and rascality than any other in the whole history of the Federal Government.

[6]

And how did the American people take these disclosures? Did they rise in wrath to punish the offenders?

When the oil scandals were first spread across the front pages of the newspapers, early in 1924, there was a wave of excitement sufficient to force the resignation of Denby and Daugherty and to bring about the appointment by the new President, Calvin Coolidge, of special Government counsel to deal with the oil cases. But the harshest condemnation on the part of the press and the public was reserved, not for those who had defrauded the government, but for those who insisted on bringing the facts to light. Senator Walsh, who led the investigation of the oil scandals, and Senator Wheeler, who investigated the Department of Justice, were called by the *New York Tribune* "the Montana scandal-mongers." The *New York Evening Post* called them "mud-gunners." The *New York Times,* despite its Democratic leanings, called them "assassins of character." In these and other newspapers throughout the country one read of the "Democratic lynching-bee" and "poison-tongued partisanship, pure malice, and twittering hysteria," and the inquiries were called "in plain words, contemptible and disgusting."

Newspaper-readers echoed these amiable sentiments. Substantial business men solemnly informed one another that mistakes might have been made but that it was unpatriotic to condemn them and thus to "cast discredit on the Government," and that those who insisted on probing them to the bottom were "nothing better than Bolsheviki." One of the leading super-patriots of the land, Fred R. Marvin of the Key Men of America, said the whole oil scandal was the result of "a gigantic international conspiracy . . . of the internationalists, or shall we call them socialists and communists?" A commuter riding daily to New York from his suburb at this period observed that on the seven-o'clock train there was some indignation at the scandals, but that on the eight-o'clock train there was only indignation at their exposure and that on the nine-o'clock train they were not even mentioned. When, a few months later, John W. Davis, campaigning for the Presidency on the Democratic ticket, made political capital of the Harding scandals, the opinion of the majority seemed to be that what he said was in bad taste, and Davis was snowed under at the polls. The fact was that any relentless investigation of the scandals threatened to disturb, if only slightly, the *status quo,* and disturbance of the *status quo* was the last thing that the dominant business class or the country at large wanted.

They had voted for normalcy and they still believed in it. The most that they required of the United States Government was that it should keep its hands off business (except to give it a lift now and then through the imposition of favorable tariffs and otherwise) and be otherwise unobtrusive. They did not look for bold and far-seeing statesmanship at Washington; their idea of statesmanship on the part of the President was that he should let things alone, give industry and trade a chance to garner fat profits, and not "rock the boat." They realized that their selection of Harding had been something of a false start toward the realization of this modest ideal. Harding had been a little too hail-fellow-well-met, and his amiability had led him into associations which brought about unfortunate publicity, and unfortunate publicity had a tendency to rock the boat. But the basic principle remained sound: all the country needed now was a President who combined with unobtrusiveness and friendliness toward business an unimpeachable integrity and an indisposition to have his leg pulled; and this sort of President they now had. The inscrutable workings of Providence had placed in the office left vacant by Harding the precise embodiment of this revised presidential ideal. Calvin Coolidge was unobtrusive to the last degree; he would never try to steer the ship of state into unknown waters; and at the same time he was sufficiently honest and circumspect to prevent any unseemly revelry from taking place on the decks. Everything was, therefore, as it should be. Why weaken public confidence in Harding's party, and thus in Harding's successor, by going into the unfortunate episodes of the past? The best thing to do was to let bygones be bygones.

As the years went by and the scandals which came to light grew in number and in scope, it began to appear that the "mistakes" of 1921-23 had been larger than the friends of normalcy had supposed when they vented their spleen upon Senator Walsh. But the testimony, coming out intermittently as it did, was confusing and hard to piece together; plain citizens could not keep clear in their minds such complicated facts as those relating to the Continental bonds or the Daugherty bank-accounts; and the steady passage of time made the later investigations seem like a washing of very ancient dirty linen. Business was good, the Coolidge variety of normalcy was working to the satisfaction of the country, Coolidge was honest; why dwell unnecessarily on the past? Resentment at the scandals and resentment at the scandal-mongers both gave way to a profound and untroubled apathy. When the full story of the Continental Trading Company deal became known, John D. Rockefeller, Jr., as a large stockholder in the Standard Oil of Indiana, waged war against Colonel Stewart and managed to put him out of the chairmanship of the company; but the business world as a whole seemed to find nothing wrong in Colonel Stewart's performance. The voice of John the Baptist was a voice crying in the wilderness.

Yet the reputation of the martyred President sank slowly and quietly lower. For years the great tomb at Marion, Ohio, that noble monument to which a sorrowing nation had so freely subscribed, remained undedicated. Clearly a monument to a President of the United States could hardly be dedicated by anybody but a President of the United States; Harding's successors, however, seemed to find it inconvenient to come to Marion for the ceremony. Late in 1930, over seven years after Harding's death, the Harding Memorial Association met to consider what should be done in this embarrassing situation. That dauntless friend of the late President, Harry M. Daugherty, who had once refrained from testifying because he knew things "as to which he would never make disclosure," made a florid speech in which he declared that the American people had never been swayed "by the lip of libel or the tongue of falsehood." He proposed that the dedication be indefinitely postponed. The resolution was duly passed. Later, however, it was decided by those in high position that the matter could not very well be left in this unsatisfactory position, and that good Republicans had better swallow their medicine and be done with it. President Hoover and ex-President Coolidge accepted invitations to take part in the dedication of the tomb in June, 1931, and the dedication accordingly took place at last. But a certain restraint was manifest in the proceedings. It was not so easy in 1931 as it had been in 1923 to compose panegyrics upon the public virtues of that good-natured man who had "taught us the power of brotherliness."

VII

Coolidge Prosperity

Business was booming when Warren Harding died, and in a primitive Vermont farmhouse, by the light of an old-fashioned kerosene lamp, Colonel John Coolidge administered to his son Calvin the oath of office as President of the United States. The hopeless depression of 1921 had given way to the hopeful improvement of 1922 and the rushing revival of 1923.

The prices of common stocks, to be sure, suggested no unreasonable optimism. On August 2, 1923, the day of Harding's death, United States Steel (paying a five-dollar dividend) stood at 87, Atchison (paying six dollars) at 95, New York Central (paying seven) at 97, and American Telephone and Telegraph (paying nine) at 122; and the total turnover for the day on the New York Stock Exchange amounted to only a little over 600,000 shares. The Big Bull Market was still far in the future. Nevertheless the tide of prosperity was in full flood.

Pick up one of those graphs with which statisticians measure the economic ups and downs of the Post-war Decade. You will find that the line of business activity rises to a jagged peak in 1920, drops precipitously into a deep valley in late 1920 and 1921, climbs uncertainly upward through 1922 to another peak at the middle of 1923, dips somewhat in 1924 (but not nearly so far as in 1921), rises again in 1925 and 1926, dips momentarily but slightly toward the end of 1927, and then zigzags up to a perfect Everest of prosperity in 1929—only to plunge down at last into the bottomless abyss of 1930 and 1931.

Hold the graph at arm's-length and glance at it again, and you will see that the clefts of 1924 and 1927 are mere indentations in a lofty and irregular plateau which reaches from early 1923 to late 1929. That plateau represents nearly seven years of unparalleled plenty; nearly seven years during which men and women might be disillusioned about politics and religion and love, but believed that at the end of the rainbow there was at least a pot of negotiable legal tender consisting of the profits of American industry and American salesmanship; nearly seven years during which the business man was, as Stuart Chase put it, "the dictator of our destinies," ousting "the statesman, the priest, the philosopher, as the creator of standards of ethics and behavior" and becoming "the final authority on the conduct of American society." For nearly seven years the prosperity band-wagon rolled down Main Street.

Not everyone could manage to climb aboard this wagon. Mighty few farmers could get so much as a fingerhold upon it. Some dairymen clung there, to be sure, and fruit-growers and truck-gardeners. For prodigious changes were taking place in the national diet as the result of the public's discovery of the useful vitamin, the propaganda for a more varied menu, and the invention of better methods of shipping perishable foods. Between 1919 and 1926 the national production of milk and milk products increased by one-third and that of ice-cream alone took a 45-per-cent jump. Between 1919 and 1928, as families learned that there were vitamins in celery, spinach, and carrots, and became accustomed to serving fresh vegetables the year round (along with fresh fruits), the acreage of nineteen commercial truck vegetable crops nearly doubled. But the growers of staple crops such as wheat and corn and cotton were in a bad way. Their foreign markets had dwindled under competition from other countries. Women were wearing less and less cotton. Few agricultural raw materials were used in the new economy of automobiles and radios and electricity. And the more efficient the poor farmer became, the more machines he bought to increase his output and thus keep the wolf from the door, the more surely he and his fellows were faced by the specter of overproduction. The index number of all farm prices, which had coasted from 205 in 1920 to 116 in

1921—"perhaps the most terrible toboggan slide in all American agricultural history," to quote Stuart Chase again—regained only a fraction of the ground it had lost: in 1927 it stood at 131. Loudly the poor farmers complained, desperately they and their Norrises and Brookharts and Shipsteads and La Follettes campaigned for federal aid, and by the hundreds of thousands they left the farm for the cities.

There were other industries unrepresented in the triumphal march of progress. Coal-mining suffered, and textile-manufacturing, and shipbuilding, and shoe and leather manufacturing. Whole regions of the country felt the effects of depression in one or more of these industries. The South was held back by cotton, the agricultural Northwest by the dismal condition of the wheat growers, New England by the paralysis of the textile and shoe industries. Nevertheless, the prosperity band-wagon did not lack for occupants, and their good fortune outweighed and outshouted the ill fortune of those who lamented by the roadside.

[2]

In a position of honor rode the automobile manufacturer. His hour of destiny had struck. By this time paved roads and repair shops and filling stations had become so plentiful that the motorist might sally forth for the day without fear of being stuck in a mudhole or stranded without benefit of gasoline or crippled by a dead spark plug. Automobiles were now made with such precision, for that matter, that the motorist need hardly know a spark plug by sight; thousands of automobile owners had never even lifted the hood to see what the engine looked like. Now that closed cars were in quantity production, furthermore, the motorist had no need of Spartan blood, even in January. And the stylish new models were a delight to the eye. At the beginning of the decade most cars had been somber in color, but with the invention of pyroxylin finishes they broke out (in 1925 and 1926) into a whole rainbow of colors, from Florentine cream to Versailles violet. Bodies were swung lower, expert designers sought new harmonies of line, balloon tires came in, and at last even Henry Ford capitulated to style and beauty.

If any sign had been needed of the central place which the automobile had come to occupy in the mind and heart of the average American, it was furnished when the Model A Ford was brought out in December, 1927. Since the previous spring, when Henry Ford had shut down his gigantic plant, scrapped his Model T and the thousands of machines which brought it into being, and announced that he was going to put a new car on the market, the country had been in a state of suspense. Obviously he would have to make drastic changes. Model T had been losing to Chevrolet its leadership in the enormous low-priced-car market, for the time had come when people were no longer content with ugliness and a maximum speed of forty or forty-five miles an hour; no longer content, either, to roar slowly uphill with a weary left foot jammed against the low-speed pedal while robin's-egg blue Chevrolets swept past in second. Yet equally obviously Henry Ford was the mechanical genius of the age. What miracle would he accomplish?

Rumor after rumor broke into the front pages of the newspapers. So intense was the interest that even the fact that an automobile dealer in Brooklyn had "learned something of the new car through a telegram from his brother Henry" was headline stuff. When the editor of the Brighton, Michigan, *Weekly Argus* actually snapped a photograph of a new Ford out for a trial spin, newspaper-readers pounced on the picture and avidly discussed its every line. The great day arrived when this newest product of the inventive genius of the age was to be shown to the public. The Ford Motor Company was running in 2,000 daily newspapers a five-day series of full-page advertisements at a total cost of $1,300,000; and everyone who could read was reading them. On December 2, 1927, when Model A was unveiled, one million people—so the *Herald-Tribune* figured—tried to get into the Ford headquarters in New York to catch a glimpse of it; as Charles Merz later reported in his life of Ford, "one hundred thousand people flocked into the showrooms of the Ford Company in Detroit; mounted police were called out to patrol the crowds in Cleveland; in Kansas City so great a mob stormed Convention Hall that platforms had to be built to lift the new car high enough for everyone to see it." So it went from one end of the United States to the other. Thousands of orders piled up on the Ford books for Niagara Blue roadsters and Arabian Sand phaetons. For weeks and months, every new Ford that appeared on the streets drew a crowd. To the motor-minded American people the first showing of a new kind of automobile was no matter of merely cas-

ual or commercial interest. It was one of the great events of
the year 1927; not so thrilling as Lindbergh's flight, but rival-
ing the execution of Sacco and Vanzetti, the Hall-Mills murder trial, the Mississippi flood, and the Dempsey-Tunney fight
at Chicago in its capacity to arouse public excitement.

In 1919 there had been 6,771,000 passenger cars in service
in the United States; by 1929 there were no less than 23,121,-
000. There you have possibly the most potent statistic of Coolidge Prosperity. As a footnote to it I suggest the following.
Even as early as the end of 1923 there were two cars for every
three families in "Middletown," a typical American city. The
Lynds and their investigators interviewed 123 working-class
families of "Middletown" and found that 60 of them had cars.
Of these 60, 26 lived in such shabby-looking houses that the
investigators thought to ask whether they had bathtubs, and
discovered that as many as 21 of the 26 had none. The automobile came even before the tub!

And as it came, it changed the face of America. Villages
which had once prospered because they were "on the railroad"
languished with economic anæmia; villages on Route 6!
bloomed with garages, filling stations, hot-dog stands, chicken-
dinner restaurants, tearooms, tourists' rests, camping sites, and
affluence. The interurban trolley perished, or survived only as
a pathetic anachronism. Railroad after railroad gave up its
branch lines, or saw its revenues slowly dwindling under the
competition of mammoth interurban busses and trucks snort-
ing along six-lane concrete highways. The whole country was
covered with a network of passenger bus-lines. In thousands of
towns, at the beginning of the decade a single traffic officer at
the junction of Main Street and Central Street had been
sufficient for the control of traffic. By the end of the decade,
what a difference!—red and green lights, blinkers, one-way
streets, boulevard stops, stringent and yet more stringent park-
ing ordinances—and still a shining flow of traffic that backed
up for blocks along Main Street every Saturday and Sunday
afternoon. Slowly but surely the age of steam was yielding to
the gasoline age.

[3]

The radio manufacturer occupied a less important seat than
the automobile manufacturer on the prosperity bandwagon,

but he had the distinction of being the youngest rider. You will remember that there was no such thing as radio broadcasting to the public until the autumn of 1920, but that by the spring of 1922 radio had become a craze—as much talked about as Mah Jong was to be the following year or cross-word puzzles the year after. In 1922 the sales of radio sets, parts, and accessories amounted to $60,000,000. People wondered what would happen when the edge wore off the novelty of hearing a jazz orchestra in Schenectady or in Davenport, Iowa, play "Mr. Gallagher and Mr. Shean." What actually did happen is suggested by the cold figures of total annual radio sales for the next few years:

1922—$ 60,000,000	(as we have just seen)
1923—$136,000,000	
1924—$358,000,000	
1925—$430,000,000	
1926—$506,000,000	
1927—$425,600,000	
1928—$650,550,000	
1929—$842,548,000	(an increase over the 1922 figures of 1,400 per cent!)

Don't hurry past those figures. Study them a moment, remembering that whenever there is a dip in the curve of national prosperity there is likely to be a dip in the sales of almost every popular commodity. There was a dip in national prosperity in 1927, for instance; do you see what it did to radio sales? But there was also a dip in 1924, a worse one in fact. Yet radio sales made in that year the largest proportional increase in the whole period. Why? Well, for one thing, that was the year in which the embattled Democrats met at Madison Square Garden in New York to pick a standard-bearer, and the deadlock between the hosts of McAdoo and the hosts of Al Smith lasted day after day after day, and millions of Americans heard through loud-speakers the lusty cry of, "Alabama, twenty-four votes for Underwoo—ood!" and discovered that a political convention could be a grand show to listen to and that a seat by the radio was as good as a ticket to the Garden. Better, in fact; for at any moment you could turn a knob and get "Barney Google" or "It Ain't Gonna Rain No More" by way of respite. At the age of three and a half years, radio broadcasting had attained its majority.

Behind those figures of radio sales lies a whole chapter of the life of the Post-war Decade: radio penetrating every third home in the country; giant broadcasting stations with nation-wide hook-ups; tenement-house roofs covered with forests of antennæ; Roxy and his Gang, the Happiness Boys, the A & P Gypsies, and Rudy Vallee crooning from antique Florentine cabinet sets; Graham McNamee's voice, which had become more familiar to the American public than that of any other citizen of the land, shouting across your living room and mine: "*And* he did it! Yes, sir, he did it! It's a touchdown! Boy, I want to tell you this is one of the finest games . . ."; the Government belatedly asserting itself in 1927 to allocate wave-lengths among competing radio stations; advertisers paying huge sums for the privilege of introducing Beethoven with a few well-chosen words about yeast or toothpaste; and Michael Meehan personally conducting the common stock of the Radio Corporation of America from a 1928 low of 85¼ to a 1929 high of 549.

There were other riders on the prosperity band-wagon. Rayon, cigarettes, refrigerators, telephones, chemical prep-arations (especially cosmetics), and electrical devices of various sorts all were in growing demand. While the inde-pendent storekeeper struggled to hold his own, the amount of retail business done in chain stores and department stores jumped by leaps and bounds. For every $100 worth of business done in 1919, by 1927 the five-and-ten-cent chains were doing $260 worth, the cigar chains $153 worth, the drug chains $224 worth, and the grocery chains $387 worth. Mrs. Smith no longer patronized her "naborhood" store; she climbed into her two-thousand-dollar car to drive to the red-fronted chain grocery and save twenty-seven cents on her daily purchases. The movies prospered, sending their celluloid reels all over the world and making Charlie Chaplin, Douglas Fairbanks, Gloria Swanson, Rudolph Valentino, and Clara Bow familiar figures to the Eskimo, the Malay, and the heathen Chinee; while at home the attendance at the motion-picture houses of "Middletown" during a single month (December, 1923) amounted to four and a half times the entire population of the city. Men, women, and children, rich and poor, the Middle-towners went to the movies at an average rate of better than once a week!

Was this Coolidge Prosperity real? The farmers did not

think so. Perhaps the textile manufacturers did not think so. But the figures of corporation profits and wages and incomes left little room for doubt. Consider, for example, two significant facts at opposite ends of the scale of wealth. Between 1922 and 1927, the purchasing power of American wages increased at the rate of more than two per cent annually. And during the three years between 1924 and 1927 alone there was a leap from 75 to 283 in the number of Americans who paid taxes on incomes of more than a million dollars a year.

[4]

Why did it happen? What made the United States so prosperous?

Some of the reasons were obvious enough. The war had impoverished Europe and hardly damaged the United States at all; when peace came the Americans found themselves the economic masters of the world. Their young country, with enormous resources in materials and in human energy and with a wide domestic market, was ready to take advantage of this situation. It had developed mass production to a new point of mechanical and managerial efficiency. The Ford gospel of high wages, low prices, and standardized manufacture on a basis of the most minute division of machine-tending labor was working smoothly not only at Highland Park, but in thousands of other factories. Executives, remembering with a shudder the piled-up inventories of 1921, had learned the lesson of cautious hand-to-mouth buying; and they were surrounded with more expert technical consultants, research men, personnel managers, statisticians, and business forecasters than had ever before invaded that cave of the winds, the conference room. Their confidence was strengthened by their almost superstitious belief that the Republican Administration was their invincible ally. And they were all of them aided by the boom in the automobile industry. The phenomenal activity of this one part of the body economic—which was responsible, directly or indirectly, for the employment of nearly four million men—pumped new life into all the rest.

Prosperity was assisted, too, by two new stimulants to purchasing, each of which mortgaged the future but kept the factories roaring while it was being injected. The first was the increase in installment buying. People were getting to consider it old-fashioned to limit their purchases to the amount of their cash balance; the thing to do was to "exercise their credit." By the latter part of the decade, economists figured that 15 per cent of all retail sales were on an installment basis, and that there were some six billions of "easy payment" paper outstanding. The other stimulant was stock-market speculation. When stocks were skyrocketing in 1928 and 1929 it is probable that hundreds of thousands of people were buying goods with money which represented, essentially, a gamble on the business profits of the nineteen-thirties. It was fun while it lasted.

If these were the principal causes of Coolidge Prosperity, the salesman and the advertising man were at least its agents and evangels. Business had learned as never before the immense importance to it of the ultimate consumer. Unless he could be persuaded to buy and buy lavishly, the whole stream of six-cylinder cars, super-heterodynes, cigarettes, rouge compacts, and electric ice-boxes would be dammed at its outlet. The salesman and the advertising man held the key to this outlet. As competition increased their methods became more strenuous. No longer was it considered enough to recommend one's goods in modest and explicit terms and to place them on the counter in the hope that the ultimate consumer would make up his mind to purchase. The advertiser must plan elaborate national campaigns, consult with psychologists, and employ all the eloquence of poets to cajole, exhort, or intimidate the consumer into buying,—to "break down consumer resistance." Not only was each individual concern struggling to get a larger share of the business in its own field, but whole industries shouted against one another in the public's ear. The embattled candy manufacturers took full-page space in the newspapers to reply to the American Tobacco Company's slogan of "Reach for a Lucky instead of a sweet." Trade journals were quoted by the *Reader's Digest* as reporting the efforts of the furniture manufacturers to make the people "furniture conscious" and of the clothing manufacturers to make them "tuxedo conscious." The salesman must have the ardor of a zealot, must force his way into people's houses by hook or by crook, must let nothing stand between him and the consummation of his sale. As executives put it, "You can't be an order-taker any longer—you've got to be a *salesman*." The public, generally speaking, could be relied upon to regard with complacence the most flagrant assaults upon its credulity by the advertiser and the most outrageous invasions of its privacy by the salesman; for the public was in a mood to forgive every sin committed in the holy name of business.

Never before had such pressure been exerted upon salesmen to get results. Many concerns took up the quota system, setting as the objective for each sales representative a figure 20 or 25 per cent beyond that of the previous year, and putting it up to him to reach this figure or lose his employer's favor and perhaps his job. All sorts of sales contests and other ingenious devices were used to stimulate the force. Among the schemes suggested by the Dartnell Company of Chicago, which had more than ten thousand American business organizations subscribing to its service, was that of buying various novelties and sending them to the salesman at weekly intervals: one week a miniature feather duster with a tag urging him to "dust his territory," another week an imitation cannon cracker with the injunction to "make a big noise," and so on. The American Slicing Machine Company offered a turkey at Christmas to every one of its salesmen who beat his quota for the year. "We asked each man," explained the sales manager afterward, "to appoint a child in his family as a mascot, realizing that every one of them would work his head off to make some youngster happy at Christmas. The way these youngsters took hold of the plan was amusing, and at times the intensity of their interest was almost pathetic." The sales manager of another concern reported cheerfully that "one of his stunts" was "to twit one man at the good work of another until he is almost sore enough to be ready to fight." And according to Jesse Rainsford Sprague, still another company invented—and boasted of—a method of goading its salesmen which for sheer inhumanity probably set a record for the whole era of Coolidge Prosperity. It gave a banquet at which the man with the best score was served with oysters, roast turkey, and a most elaborate ice; the man with the second best score had the same dinner but without the oysters; and so on down to the man with the worst score, before whom was laid a small plate of boiled beans and a couple of crackers.

If the salesman was sometimes under pressure such as this, it is not surprising that the consumer felt the pressure, too. Let two extreme instances (both cited by Jesse Rainsford Sprague) suffice to suggest the trend in business methods. A wholesale drug concern offered to the trade a small table with a railing

round its top for the display of "specials"; it was to be set up
directly in the path of customers, "whose attention," according
to *Printer's Ink*, "will be attracted to the articles when they fall
over it, bump into it, kick their shins upon it, or otherwise
come in contact with it." And *Selling News* awarded one of its
cash prizes for "sales ideas" to a vender of electric cleaners
who told the following story of commercial prowess. One day
he looked up from the street and saw a lady shaking a rug out
of a second-story window. "The door leading to her upstairs
rooms was open. I went right in and up those stairs without
knocking, greeting the lady with the remark: 'Well, I am here
right on time. What room do you wish me to start in?' She was
very much surprised, assuring me that I had the wrong number. But during my very courteous apologies I had managed to
get my cleaner connected and in action. The result was that I
walked out minus the cleaner, plus her contract and check for
a substantial down payment." The readers of *Selling News*
were apparently not expected to be less than enthusiastic at the
prospect of a man invading a woman's apartment and setting
up a cleaner in it without permission and under false pre-
tenses. For if you could get away with such exploits, it helped
business, and good business helped prosperity, and prosperity
was good for the country.

[5]

The advertisers met the competition of the new era with
better design, persuasively realistic photographs, and sheer
volume: the amount of advertising done in 1927, according to
Francis H. Sisson, came to over a billion and a half dollars.
They met it with a new frankness, introducing to staid magazine readers the advantages of Odo-ro-no and Kotex. And they
met it, furthermore, with a subtle change in technic. The copy-
writer was learning to pay less attention to the special qualities
and advantages of his product, and more to the study of what
the mass of unregenerate mankind wanted—to be young and
desirable, to be rich, to keep up with the Joneses, to be envied.
The winning method was to associate his product with one or
more of these ends, logically or illogically, truthfully or
cynically; to draw a lesson from the dramatic case of some
imaginary man or woman whose fate was altered by the use of
X's soap, to show that in the most fashionable circles people

were choosing the right cigarette in blindfold tests, or to suggest by means of glowing testimonials—often bought and paid for—that the advertised product was used by women of fashion, movie stars, and non-stop flyers. One queen of the films was said to have journeyed from California all the way to New York to spend a single exhausting day being photographed for testimonial purposes in dozens of costumes and using dozens of commercial articles, many of which she had presumably never laid eyes on before—and all because the appearance of these testimonials would help advertise her newest picture. Of what value were sober facts from the laboratory: did not a tooth-powder manufacturer try to meet the hokum of emotional toothpaste advertising by citing medical authorities, and was not his counter-campaign as a breath in a gale? At the beginning of the decade advertising had been considered a business; in the early days of Coolidge Prosperity its fulsome prophets were calling it a profession; but by the end of the decade many of its practitioners, observing the overwhelming victory of methods taken over from tabloid journalism, were beginning to refer to it—among themselves—as a racket.

A wise man of the nineteen-twenties might have said that he cared not who made the laws of the country if he only might write its national advertising. For here were the sagas of the age, romances and tragedies depicting characters who became more familiar to the populace than those in any novel. The man who distinctly remembered Mr. Addison Sims of Seattle. . . . The four out of five who, failing to use Forhan's, succumbed to pyorrhea, each of them with a white mask mercifully concealing his unhappy mouth. . . . The pathetic figure of the man, once a golf champion, "now only a wistful onlooker" creeping about after the star players, his shattered health due to tooth neglect. . . . The poor fellow sunk in the corner of a taxicab, whose wife upbraided him with not having said a word all evening (when he might so easily have shone with the aid of the *Elbert Hubbard Scrap Book*). . . . The man whose conversation so dazzled the company that the envious dinner-coated bystanders could only breathe in amazement, "I think he's quoting from Shelley." . . . The woman who would undoubtedly do something about B. O. if people only said to her what they really thought. . . . The man whose friends laughed when the waiter spoke to him in French. . . . The girl who thought filet mignon was a kind of fish. . . . The poor couple who faced one another in humiliation after their guests were gone, the wife still holding the door knob and struggling against her tears, the husband biting his nails with shame (When Your Guests Are Gone— Are You Sorry You Ever Invited Them? . . . Be Free From All Embarrassment! Let the Famous *Book of Etiquette* Tell You Exactly What to Do, Say, Write, or Wear on Every Occasion). . . . The girl who merely carried the daisy chain, yet she had athlete's foot. . . . These men and women of the advertising pages, suffering or triumphant, became a part of the folklore of the day.

Sometimes their feats were astonishing. Consider, for example, the man who had purchased Nelson Doubleday's *Pocket University,* and found himself, one evening, in a group in which some one mentioned Ali Baba:

"Ali Baba? I sat forward in my chair. I could tell them all about this romantic, picturesque figure of fiction.

"I don't know how it happened, but they gathered all around me. And I told them of golden ships that sailed the seven seas, of a famous man and his donkey who wandered unknown ways, of the brute-man from whom we are all descended. I told them things they never knew of Cleopatra, of the eccentric Diogenes, of Romulus and the founding of Rome. I told them of the unfortunate death of Sir Raleigh (*sic*), of the tragic end of poor Anne Boleyn. . . .

" 'You must have traveled all over the world to know so many marvelous things.' "

Skeptics might smile, thanking themselves that they were not of the company on that interminable evening; but the advertisement stuck in their minds. And to others, less sophisticated, it doubtless opened shining vistas of delight. They, too, could hold the dinner party spellbound if only they filled out the coupon. . . .

By far the most famous of these dramatic advertisements of the Post-war Decade was the long series in which the awful results of halitosis were set forth through the depiction of a gallery of unfortunates whose closest friends would not tell them. "Often a bridesmaid but never a bride. . . . Edna's case was really a pathetic one." . . . "Why did she leave him that way?" . . . "*That's* why you're a failure," . . . and then that devilishly ingenious display which capitalized on the fears aroused by earlier tragedies in the series: the picture of a girl looking at a Listerine advertisement and saying to herself, "This *can't* apply to me!" Useless for the American Medical Association to insist that Listerine was "not a true deodorant," that it simply covered one smell with another. Just as useless as for the Life Extension Institute to find "one out of twenty with pyorrhea, rather than Mr. Forhan's famous four-out-of-five" (to quote Stuart Chase once more). Halitosis had the power of dramatic advertising behind it, and Listerine swept to greater and greater profits on a tide of public trepidation.

[6]

As year followed year of prosperity, the new diffusion of wealth brought marked results. There had been a great boom in higher education immediately after the war, and the boom continued, although at a somewhat slackened pace, until college trustees were beside themselves wondering how to find room for the swarming applicants. There was an epidemic of outlines of knowledge and books of etiquette for those who had got rich quick and wanted to get cultured quick and become socially at ease. Wells's *Outline of History*, the best-selling non-fiction book of 1921 and 1922, was followed by Van Loon's *Story of Mankind*, J. Arthur Thomson's *Outline of Science* (both of them best sellers in 1922), the Doubleday mail-order *Book of Etiquette* and Emily Post's *Book of Etiquette* (which led the non-fiction list in 1923), *Why We Behave Like Human Beings* (a big success of 1926), and *The Story of Philosophy*, which ran away from all other books in the non-fiction list of 1927.

There was a rush of innocents abroad. According to the figures of the Department of Commerce, over 437,000 people left the United States by ship for foreign parts in the year 1928 alone, to say nothing of 14,000 odd who entered Canada and Mexico by rail, and over three million cars which crossed into Canada for a day or more. The innocents spent freely: the money that they left abroad, in fact (amounting in 1928 to some $650,000,000), solved for a time a difficult problem in international finance: how the United States could continue to receive interest on her foreign debts and foreign investments without permitting foreign goods to pass the high tariff barrier in large quantities.

The United States became the banker and financial arbitrator for the world. When the financial relations between Germany and the Allies needed to be straightened out, it was General Charles G. Dawes and Owen D. Young who headed the necessary international commissions—not only because their judgment was considered wise, and impartial as between the countries of Europe, but because the United States was in a position to call the tune. Americans were called in to reorganize the finances of one country after another. American investments abroad increased by leaps and bounds. The squat limestone building at the corner of Broad and Wall Streets, still wearing the scars of the shrapnel which had struck it during the 1920 explosion, had become the undisputed financial center of the world. Only occasionally did the United States have to intervene by force of arms in other countries. The Marines ruled Haiti and restored order in Nicaragua; but in general the country extended its empire not by military conquest or political dictation, but by financial penetration.

At home, one of the most conspicuous results of prosperity was the conquest of the whole country by urban tastes and urban dress and the urban way of living. The rube disappeared. Girls in the villages of New Hampshire and Wyoming wore the same brief skirts and used the same lipsticks as their sisters in New York. The proletariat—or what the radicals of the Big Red Scare days had called the proletariat—gradually lost its class consciousness; the American Federation of Labor dwindled in membership and influence; the time had come when workingmen owned second-hand Buicks and applauded Jimmy Walker, not objecting in the least, it seemed, to his exquisite clothes, his valet, and his frequent visits to the millionaire-haunted sands of Palm Beach. It was no accident that men like Mellon and Hoover and Morrow found their wealth an asset rather than a liability in public office, or that there was a widespread popular movement to make Henry Ford President in 1924. The possession of millions was a sign of success, and success was worshiped the country over.

[7]

Business itself was regarded with a new veneration. Once it had been considered less dignified and distinguished than the learned professions, but now people thought they praised a clergyman highly when they called him a good business man. College alumni, gathered at their annual banquets, fervently applauded the banker trustees who spoke of education as one of the greatest American industries and compared the president and the dean to business executives. The colleges themselves organized business courses and cheerfully granted credit to candidates for degrees in the arts and sciences for their work in advertising copy-writing, marketing methods, elementary stenography, and drug-store practice. Even Columbia University drew men and women into its home-study courses by a system of follow-up letters worthy of a manufacturer of refrigerators, and sent out salesmen to ring the door bells of those who expressed a flicker of interest; even the great University of Chicago made use of what André Siegfried has called "the mysticism of success" by heading an advertisement of its correspondence courses with the admonition to "DEVELOP POWER AT HOME, to investigate, persevere, achieve." . . . The Harvard Business School established annual advertising awards, conferring academic *éclat* upon well-phrased sales arguments for commercial products. It was not easy for the churches to resist the tide of business enthusiasm. The Swedish Immanuel Congregational Church in New York, according to an item in the *American Mercury*, recognized the superiority of the business to the spiritual appeal by offering to all who contributed one hundred dollars to its building fund "an engraved certificate of investment in preferred capital stock in the Kingdom of God." And a church billboard in uptown New York struck the same persuasive note: "Come to Church. Christian Worship Increases Your Efficiency. Christian F. Reisner, Pastor."

In every American city and town, service clubs gathered the flower of the middle-class citizenry together for weekly luncheons noisy with good fellowship. They were growing fast, these service clubs. Rotary, the most famous of them, had been founded in 1905; by 1930 it had 150,000 members and boasted—as a sign of its international influence—as many as 3,000 clubs in 44 countries. The number of Kiwanis Clubs rose from 205 in 1920 to 1,800 in 1929; the Lions Clubs, of which the first was not formed until 1917, multiplied until at the end of the decade there were 1,200 of them. Nor did these clubs content themselves with singing songs and conducting social-

service campaigns; they expressed the national faith in what
one of their founders called "the redemptive and regenerative
influence of business." The speakers before them pictured the
business man as a builder, a doer of great things, yes, and a
dreamer whose imagination was ever seeking out new ways of
serving humanity. It was a popular note, for in hundreds of
directors' rooms, around hundreds of conference tables, the
American business men of the era of Coolidge Prosperity were
seeing themselves as men of vision with eyes steadfastly fixed
on the long future. At the end of the decade, a cartoon in the
New Yorker represented an executive as saying to his heavy-
jowled colleagues at one of these meetings: "We have ideas.
Possibly we tilt at windmills—just seven Don Juans tilting at
windmills." It was a perfect bit of satire on business sentimentality. The service club specialized in this sort of mysticism:
was not a speaker before the Rotarians of Waterloo, Iowa,
quoted by the *American Mercury* as declaring that "Rotary is
a manifestation of the divine"?

Indeed, the association of business with religion was one of
the most significant phenomena of the day. When the National
Association of Credit Men held their annual convention at
New York, there were provided for the three thousand delegates a special devotional service at the Cathedral of St. John
the Divine and five sessions of prayer conducted by Protestant
clergymen, a Roman Catholic priest, and a Jewish rabbi; and
the credit men were uplifted by a sermon by Dr. S. Parkes
Cadman on "Religion in Business." Likewise the Associated
Advertising Clubs, meeting in Philadelphia, listened to a keynote address by Doctor Cadman on "Imagination and Advertising," and at the meeting of the Church Advertising Department the subjects discussed included "Spiritual Principles
in Advertising" and "Advertising the Kingdom through Press-
Radio Service." The fact that each night of the session a cab-
aret entertainment was furnished to the earnest delegates from
11.30 to 2 and that part of the Atlantic City Beauty Pageant
was presented was merely a sign that even men of high faith
must have their fun.

So frequent was the use of the Bible to point the lessons of
business and of business to point the lessons of the Bible that it
was sometimes difficult to determine which was supposed to
gain the most from the association. Fred F. French, a New

York builder and real-estate man, told his salesmen, "There is no such thing as a reason why not," and continued: "One evidence of the soundness of this theory may be found in the command laid down in Matthew vii:7 by the Greatest Human-nature Expert that ever lived, 'Knock and it shall be opened unto you.'" He continued by quoting "the greatest command of them all—'Love Thy Neighbor as Thyself'"—and then stated that by following such high principles the Fred F. French salesmen had "immeasurably strengthened their own characters and power, so that during this year they will serve our stockholders at a lower commission rate, and yet each one earn more money for himself than in nineteen hundred twenty-five." In this case Scripture was apparently taken as setting a standard for business to meet—to its own pecuniary profit. Yet in other cases it was not so certain that business was not the standard, and Scripture complimented by being lifted to the business level.

Witness, for example, the pamphlet on *Moses, Persuader of Men* issued by the Metropolitan Casualty Insurance Company (with an introduction by the indefatigable Doctor Cadman), which declared that "Moses was one of the greatest salesmen and real-estate promoters that ever lived," that he was a "Dominant, Fearless, and Successful Personality in one of the most magnificent selling campaigns that history ever placed upon its pages." And witness, finally, the extraordinary message preached by Bruce Barton in *The Man Nobody Knows*, which so touched the American heart that for two successive years—1925 and 1926—it was the best-selling non-fiction book in the United States. Barton sold Christianity to the public by showing its resemblance to business. Jesus, this book taught, was not only "the most popular dinner guest in Jerusalem" and "an outdoor man," but a great executive. "He picked up twelve men from the bottom ranks of business and forged them into an organization that conquered the world. . . . Nowhere is there such a startling example of executive success as the way in which that organization was brought together." His parables were "the most powerful advertisements of all time. . . . He would be a national advertiser today." In fact, Jesus was "the founder of modern business." Why, you ask? Because he was the author of the ideal of service.

The Gospel According to Bruce Barton met a popular demand. Under the beneficent influence of Coolidge Prosperity, business had become almost the national religion of America. Millions of people wanted to be reassured that this religion was altogether right and proper, and that in the rules for making big money lay all the law and the prophets.

Was it strange that during the very years when the Barton Gospel was circulating most vigorously, selling and advertising campaigns were becoming more cynical and the American business world was refusing to exercise itself over the Teapot Dome disclosures and the sordid history of the Continental Trading Company? Perhaps; but it must be remembered that in all religions there is likely to be a gap between faith and works. The business man's halo did not always fit, but he wore it proudly.

[8]

So the prosperity band-wagon rolled along with throttle wide open and siren blaring. But what of the man on the driver's seat, the man whose name this era bore?

He did not have a jutting chin, a Powerful Personality, or an irresistible flow of selling talk. If you had come from Timbuctoo and found him among a crowd of Chamber of Commerce boosters, he would have been the last man you would have picked as their patron saint. He had never been in business. His canonization by the hosts of quantity production and high-pressure salesmanship was a sublime paradox—and yet it was largely justified. Almost the most remarkable thing about Coolidge Prosperity was Calvin Coolidge.

He was a meager-looking man, a Vermonter with a hatchet face, sandy hair, tight lips, and the expression, as William Allen White remarked, of one "looking down his nose to locate that evil smell which seemed forever to affront him." He was pale and diffident. In private he could be garrulous, but in public he was as silent as a cake of ice. When his firmness in the Boston police strike captured the attention of the country and brought him to Washington as Vice-President, not even the affable warmth of the Harding Administration could thaw him. The Vice-President has to go to many a formal dinner; Coolidge went—and said nothing. The hostesses of Washington were dismayed and puzzled. "Over the Alps lay Italy, they thought, but none of them had won the summit and so they couldn't be sure that the view was worth the climb," wrote Edward G. Lowry. Coolidge became President, and still the frost continued.

Nor did this silence cloak a wide-ranging mind. Coolidge knew his American history, but neither he nor his intellect had ever ventured far abroad. Go through his addresses and his smug *Autobiography*, and the most original thing you will find in them is his uncompromising unoriginality. Calvin Coolidge still believed in the old American copy-book maxims when almost everybody else had half forgotten them or was beginning to doubt them. "The success which is made in any walk of life is measured almost exactly by the amount of hard work that is put into it. . . . There is only one form of political strategy in which I have any confidence, and that is to try to do the right thing and sometimes be able to succeed. . . . If society lacks learning and virtue it will perish. . . . The nation with the greatest moral power will win. . . ." This philosophy of hard work and frugal living and piety crowned with success might have been brought down from some Vermont attic where *McGuffy's Reader* gathered dust. But it was so old that it looked new; it was so exactly what uncounted Americans had been taught at their mother's knee that it touched what remained of the pioneer spirit in their hearts; and Coolidge set it forth with refreshing brevity. So completely did it win over the country that if the President had declared that a straight line is the shortest distance between two points, one wonders if editorial pages would not have paid tribute to his concise wisdom.

He was not a bold leader, nor did he care to be. He followed no gleam, stormed no redoubt. Considering the fact that he was in the White House for five years and seven months, his presidential record was surprisingly negative. But it was just the sort of record that he preferred.

In its foreign policy, his Administration made little effort to persuade the American people that they were not happily isolated from the outside world. Bankers might engage in determining the amount of German reparations, unofficial observers might sit in on European negotiations, but the Government, remembering the decline and fall of Woodrow Wilson, shrewdly maintained an air of magnificent unconcern.

Coolidge proposed, as had Harding before him, that the United States should join the World Court, but so gently that when the Senate eventually ratified the proposal with reservations which the other member nations were unable to accept, and the President went out of office without having achieved his end, nobody felt that his prestige suffered much thereby. A second naval conference was held at Geneva in 1927, but ended in failure. A Nicaraguan revolution was settled—after considerable turmoil and humiliation—with the aid of the Marines and of Henry L. Stimson's plan for a new election under American supervision. An even more bitter dispute with Mexico over the legal status of oil lands owned by American interests was finally moderated through the wisdom and tact of Coolidge's Amherst classmate and ambassador, Dwight W. Morrow. But the most conspicuous achievement of the Coolidge Administration in foreign affairs was the leading part it took in securing the Kellogg-Briand Treaty renouncing war as an instrument of national policy—a fine gesture which every nation was delighted to make but which had very little noticeable influence on the actualities of international relations. Aside from the belated solution of the Nicaraguan and Mexican difficulties and the championship of this somewhat innocuous treaty, the policy of the Coolidge Administration was to collect the money due it (even at the expense of considerable ill-feeling), to keep a watchful eye on the expansion of the American financial empire, and otherwise to let well enough alone.

Coolidge's record in domestic affairs was even less exciting. He was nothing if not cautious. When the Harding scandals came to light, he did what was necessary to set in motion an official prosecution, he adroitly jockeyed the notorious Daugherty out of the Cabinet, and from that moment on he exhibited an unruffled and altogether convincing calm. When there was a strike in the anthracite coal mines he did not leap into the breach; he let Governor Gifford Pinchot of Pennsylvania do it. On the one burning political issue of the day, that of prohibition, he managed to express no opinion except that the laws should be enforced. There was dynamite in prohibition; Calvin Coolidge remained at a safe distance and looked the other way.

He maintained the *status quo* for the benefit of business. Twice he vetoed farm relief legislation—to the immense satisfaction of the industrial and banking community which constituted his strongest support—on the ground that the McNary-Haugen bills were economically unsound. He vetoed the soldier bonus, too, on the ground of its expense, though in this case his veto was overruled. His proudest boast was that he cut down the cost of running the Government by systematic cheeseparing, reduced the public debt, and brought about four reductions in federal taxes, aiding not only those with small incomes but even more conspicuously those with large. Meanwhile his Secretary of Commerce, Herbert Hoover, ingeniously helped business to help itself; on the various governmental commissions, critics of contemporary commercial practices were replaced, as far as possible, by those who would look upon business with a lenient eye; and the serene quiet which lay about the White House was broken only by occasional flattering pronouncements upon business and assurances that prosperity was securely founded.

An uninspired and unheroic policy, you suggest? But it was sincere: Calvin Coolidge honestly believed that by asserting himself as little as possible and by lifting the tax burdens of the rich he was benefiting the whole country—as perhaps he was. And it was perfectly in keeping with the uninspired and unheroic political temper of the times. For the lusty business men who in these fat years had become the arbiters of national opinion did not envisage the Government as an agency for making over the country into something a little nearer to their hearts' desire, as a champion of human rights or a redresser of wrongs. The prosperity band-wagon was bringing them rapidly toward their hearts' desire, and politics might block the traffic. They did not want a man of action in the Presidency; they wanted as little government as possible, at as low cost as possible, and this dour New Englander who drove the prosperity band-wagon with so slack a rein embodied their idea of supreme statesmanship.

Statesmanship of a sort Calvin Coolidge certainly represented. Prosperity has its undeniable advantages, and a President who is astute enough to know how to encourage it without getting himself into hot water may possibly be forgiven such complacency as appears in his *Autobiography*. There is perhaps a cool word to be said, too, for the prudence which deliberately accepts the inevitable, which does not even try to be bolder or more magnanimous than circumstances will safely permit. The great god business was supreme in the land, and Calvin Coolidge was fortunate enough to become almost a demi-god by doing discreet obeisance before the altar.

VIII

The Ballyhoo Years

All nations, in all eras of history, are swept from time to time by waves of contagious excitement over fads or fashions or dramatic public issues. But the size and frequency of these waves is highly variable, as is the nature of the events which set them in motion. One of the striking characteristics of the era of Coolidge Prosperity was the unparalleled rapidity and unanimity with which millions of men and women turned their attention, their talk, and their emotional interest upon a series of tremendous trifles—a heavyweight boxing-match, a murder trial, a new automobile model, a transatlantic flight.

Most of the *causes célèbres* which thus stirred the country from end to end were quite unimportant from the traditional point of view of the historian. The future destinies of few people were affected in the slightest by the testimony of the "pig woman" at the Hall-Mills trial or the attempt to rescue Floyd Collins from his Kentucky cave. Yet the fact that such things could engage the hopes and fears of unprecedented numbers of people was anything but unimportant. No account of the Coolidge years would be adequate which did not review that strange procession of events which a nation tired of "important issues" swarmed to watch, or which did not take account of that remarkable chain of circumstances which produced as the hero of the age, not a great public servant, not a

155

reformer, not a warrior, but a stunt flyer who crossed the ocean to win a money prize.

By the time Calvin Coolidge reached the White House, the tension of the earlier years of the Post-war Decade had been largely relaxed. Though Woodrow Wilson still clung feebly to life in the sunny house in S Street, the League issue was dead and only handfuls of irreconcilable idealists imagined it to have a chance of resuscitation. The radicals were discouraged, the labor movement had lost energy and prestige since the days of the Big Red Scare, and under the beneficent influence of easy riches—or at least of easy Fords and Chevrolets—individualistic capitalism had settled itself securely in the saddle. The Ku-Klux Klan numbered its millions, yet already it was beginning to lose that naïve ardor which had lighted its fires on a thousand hilltops; it was becoming less of a crusade and more of a political racket. Genuine public issues, about which the masses of the population could be induced to feel intensely, were few and far between. There was prohibition, to be sure; anybody could get excited about prohibition; but because the division of opinion on liquor cut across party lines, every national politician, almost without exception, did his best to thrust this issue into the background. In the agricultural Northwest and Middle West there was a violent outcry for farm relief, but it could command only a scattered and half-hearted interest throughout the rest of a nation which was becoming progressively urbanized. Public spirit was at low ebb; over the World Court, the oil scandals, the Nicaraguan situation, the American people as a whole refused to bother themselves. They gave their energies to triumphant business, and for the rest they were in holiday mood. "Happy," they might have said, "is the nation which has no history—and a lot of good shows to watch." They were ready for any good show that came along.

It was now possible in the United States for more people to enjoy the same good show at the same time than in any other land on earth or at any previous time in history. Mass production was not confined to automobiles; there was mass production in news and ideas as well. For the system of easy nation-wide communication which had long since made the literate and prosperous American people a nation of faddists was rapidly becoming more widely extended, more centralized, and more effective than ever before.

To begin with, there were fewer newspapers, with larger circulations, and they were standardized to an unprecedented degree by the increasing use of press-association material and syndicated features. Between 1914 and 1926, as Silas Bent has pointed out, the number of daily papers in the country dropped from 2,580 to 2,001, the number of Sunday papers dropped from 571 to 541, and the aggregate circulation per issue rose from somewhat over 28,000,000 to 36,000,000. The city of Cleveland, which a quarter of a century before had had three morning papers, now had but one; Detroit, Minneapolis, and St. Louis had lost all but one apiece; Chicago during a period in which it had doubled in population, had seen the number of its morning dailies drop from seven to two. Newspapers all over the country were being gathered into chains under more or less centralized direction: by 1927 the success of the Hearst and Scripps-Howard systems and the hope of cutting down overhead costs had led to the formation of no less than 55 chains controlling 230 daily papers with a combined circulation of over 13,000,000.

No longer did the local editor rely as before upon local writers and cartoonists to fill out his pages and give them a local flavor; the central office of the chain, or newspaper syndicates in New York, could provide him with editorials, health talks, comic strips, sob-sister columns, household hints, sports gossip, and Sunday features prepared for a national audience and guaranteed to tickle the mass mind. Andy Gump and Dorothy Dix had their millions of admirers from Maine to Oregon, and the words hammered out by a reporter at Jack Dempsey's training-camp were devoured with one accord by real-estate men in Florida and riveters in Seattle.

Meanwhile, the number of national magazines with huge circulations had increased, the volume of national advertising had increased, a horde of publicity agents had learned the knack of associating their cause or product with whatever happened to be in the public mind at the moment, and finally there was the new and vastly important phenomenon of radio broadcasting, which on occasion could link together a multitude of firesides to hear the story of a World's Series game or a Lindbergh welcome. The national mind had become as never before an instrument upon which a few men could play. And these men were learning, as Mr. Bent has also shown, to play upon it in a new way—to concentrate upon *one tune at a time*.

Not that they put their heads together and deliberately decided to do this. Circumstances and self-interest made it the almost inevitable thing for them to do. They discovered—the successful tabloids were daily teaching them—that the public tended to become excited about one thing at a time. Newspaper owners and editors found that whenever a Dayton trial or a *Vestris* disaster took place, they sold more papers if they gave it all they had—their star reporters, their front-page display, and the bulk of their space. They took full advantage of this discovery: according to Mr. Bent's compilations, the insignificant Gray-Snyder murder trial got a bigger "play" in the press than the sinking of the *Titanic*; Lindbergh's flight, than the Armistice and the overthrow of the German Empire. Syndicate managers and writers, advertisers, press agents, radio broadcasters, all were aware that mention of the leading event of the day, whatever it might be, was the key to public interest. The result was that when something happened which promised to appeal to the popular mind, one had it hurled at one in huge headlines, waded through page after page of syndicated discussion of it, heard about it on the radio, was reminded of it again and again in the outpourings of publicity-seeking orators and preachers, saw pictures of it in the Sunday papers and in the movies, and (unless one was a perverse individualist) enjoyed the sensation of vibrating to the same chord which thrilled a vast populace.

The country had bread, but it wanted circuses—and now it could go to them a hundred million strong.

[2]

Mah Jong was still popular during the winter of 1923-24—the winter when Calvin Coolidge was becoming accustomed to the White House, and the Bok Peace Prize was awarded, and the oil scandals broke, and Woodrow Wilson died, and General Dawes went overseas to preside over the reparations conference, and *So Big* outsold all other novels, and people were tiring of "Yes, We Have No Bananas," and to the delight of every rotogravure editor the lid of the stone sarcophagus of King Tutankhamen's tomb was raised at Luxor. Mah Jong was popular, but it had lost its novelty.

It was during that winter—on January 2, 1924, to be pre-

cise—that a young man in New York called on his aunt. The
aunt had a relative who was addicted to the cross-word puzzles
which appeared every Sunday in the magazine supplement of
the *New York World*, and asked the young man whether there
was by any chance a book of these puzzles; it might make a
nice present for her relative. The young man, on due inquiry,
found that there was no such thing as a book of them, although
cross-word puzzles dated back at least to 1913 and had been
published in the *World* for years. But as it happened, he himself (his name was Richard Simon) was at that very moment
launching a book-publishing business with his friend Schuster
—and with one girl as their entire staff. Simon had a bright
idea, which he communicated to Schuster the next day: *they*
would bring out a cross-word-puzzle book. The two young
men asked Prosper Buranelli, F. Gregory Hartswick, and
Margaret Petherbridge, the puzzle editors of the *World*, to
prepare it; and despite a certain coolness on the part of the
book-sellers, who told them that the public "wasn't interested
in puzzle books," they brought it out in mid-April.

Their promotion campaign was ingenious and proved to be
prophetic, for from the very beginning they advertised their
book by drawing the following parallel:

     1921—Coué
     1922—Mah Jong
     1923—Bananas
     1924—THE CROSS-WORD-PUZZLE BOOK

Within a month this odd-looking volume with a pencil
attached to it had become a best seller. By the following winter
its sales had mounted into the hundreds of thousands, other
publishers were falling over themselves to get out books which
would reap an advantage from the craze, it was a dull newspaper which did not have its daily puzzle, sales of dictionaries
were bounding, there was a new demand for that ancient and
honorable handmaid of the professional writer, Roget's *The-
saurus*, a man had been sent to jail in New York for refusing to
leave a restaurant after four hours of trying to solve a puzzle,
and Mrs. Mary Zaba of Chicago was reported to be a "cross-
word widow," her husband apparently being so busy with
puzzles that he had no time to support her. The newspapers
carried the news that a Pittsburgh pastor had put the text of his

sermon into a puzzle. The Baltimore and Ohio Railroad placed dictionaries in all the trains on its main line. A traveler between New York and Boston reported that 60 per cent of the passengers were trying to fill up the squares in their puzzles, and that in the dining-car five waiters were trying to think of a five-letter word which meant "serving to inspire fear." Anybody you met on the street could tell you the name of the Egyptian sun-god or provide you with the two-letter word which meant a printer's measure.

The cross-word puzzle craze gradually died down in 1925. It was followed by a minor epidemic of question-and-answer books; there was a time when ladies and gentlemen with vague memories faced frequent humiliation after dinner because they were unable to identify John Huss or tell what an ohm was. Not until after contract bridge was introduced in the United States in 1926 did they breathe easily. Despite the decline of the cross-word puzzle, however, it remained throughout the rest of the decade a daily feature in most newspapers; and Simon and Schuster, bringing out their sixteenth series in 1930, figured their total sales since early 1924 at nearly three-quarters of a million copies, and the grand total, including British and Canadian sales, at over two millions.

[3]

This craze, like the Mah Jong craze which preceded it, was a fresh indication of the susceptibility of the American people to fads, but it was not in any real sense a creature of the new ballyhoo newspaper technic. The newspapers did not pick it up until it was well on its way. The greatest demonstrations of the power of the press to excite the millions over trifles were yet to come.

There was, of course, plenty to interest the casual newspaper reader in 1924 and early 1925, when everybody was doing puzzles. There was the presidential campaign, though this proved somewhat of an anti-climax after the sizzling Democratic Convention at Madison Square Garden, that long-drawn-out battle between the forces of William G. McAdoo and Al Smith which ended in a half-hearted stampede to John W. Davis; so much emotional energy had been expended by the Westerners in hating the Tammany Catholic and by the

Tammanyites in singing "The Sidewalks of New York," that the Democratic party never really collected itself, and the unimpassioned Calvin, with his quiet insistence upon economy and tax reduction and his knack for making himself appear the personal embodiment of prosperity, was carried into office by a vast majority. There was also the trial of Leopold and Loeb for the murder of Bobby Franks in Chicago. There was the visit of the Prince of Wales to Long Island, during which he danced much, played polo, went motor-boating, and was detected in the act of reading *The Life and Letters of Walter Hines Page*. (It was in 1924, by the way, that those other importations from Britain, the voluminous gray flannel trousers known as Oxford bags, first hung about the heels of the up-and-coming young male.) There was a noteworthy alliance between a representative of the nobility of France and a representative of the nobility of Hollywood: Gloria Swanson married the Marquis de la Falaise de la Coudray. There was a superb eclipse of the sun, providentially arranged for the delectation of the Eastern seaboard cities. There was Paavo Nurmi: watch in hand, his heels thudding on the board track, Nurmi outran the chesty taxi-driver, Joie Ray, and later performed the incredible feat of covering two miles in less than nine minutes. There was the hullabaloo over bringing the serum to Nome to end a diphtheria epidemic, which for a few days made national heroes of Leonard Seppalla, Gunnar Kasson, and the dog Balto. And there was Floyd Collins imprisoned in his cave.

It was the tragedy of Floyd Collins, perhaps, which gave the clearest indication up to that time of the unanimity with which the American people could become excited over a quite unimportant event if only it were dramatic enough.

Floyd Collins was an obscure young Kentuckian who had been exploring an underground passage five miles from Mammoth Cave, with no more heroic purpose than that of finding something which might attract lucrative tourists. Some 125 feet from daylight he was caught by a cave-in which pinned his foot under a huge rock. So narrow and steep was the passage that those who tried to dig him out had to hitch along on their stomachs in cold slime and water and pass back from hand to hand the earth and rocks that they pried loose with hammers and blow-torches. Only a few people might have heard of Collins's predicament if W. B. Miller of the *Louisville Courier-*

Journal had not been slight of stature, daring, and an able reporter. Miller wormed his way down the slippery, tortuous passageway to interview Collins, became engrossed in the efforts to rescue the man, described them in vivid dispatches— and to his amazement found that the entire country was turning to watch the struggle. Collins's plight contained those elements of dramatic suspense and individual conflict with fate which make a great news story, and every city editor, day after day, planted it on page one. When Miller arrived at Sand Cave he had found only three men at the entrance, warming themselves at a fire and wondering, without excitement, how soon their friend would extricate himself. A fortnight later there was a city of a hundred or more tents there and the milling crowds had to be restrained by barbed-wire barriers and state troops with drawn bayonets; and on February 17, 1925, even the *New York Times* gave a three-column page-one headline to the news of the dénouement:

> FIND FLOYD COLLINS DEAD IN CAVE TRAP ON
> 18TH DAY; LIFELESS AT LEAST 24 HOURS; FOOT
> MUST BE AMPUTATED TO GET BODY OUT

Within a month, as Charles Merz later reminded the readers of the *New Republic*, there was a cave-in in a North Carolina mine in which 71 men were caught and 53 actually lost. It attracted no great notice. It was "just a mine disaster." Yet for more than two weeks the plight of a single commonplace prospector for tourists riveted the attention of the nation on Sand Cave, Kentucky. It was an exciting show to watch, and the dispensers of news were learning to turn their spotlights on one show at a time.

Even the Collins thriller, however, was as nothing beside the spectacle which was offered a few months later when John Thomas Scopes was tried at Dayton, Tennessee, for teaching the doctrine of evolution in the Central High School.

The Scopes case had genuine significance. It dramatized one of the most momentous struggles of the age—the conflict between religion and science. Yet even this trial, so diligently and noisily was it ballyhooed, took on some of the aspects of a circus.

[4]

If religion lost ground during the Post-war Decade, the best available church statistics gave no sign of the fact. They showed, to be sure, a very slow growth in the number of churches in use; but this was explained partly by the tendency toward consolidation of existing churches and partly by the trend of population toward the cities—a trend which drew the church-going public into fewer churches with larger congregations. The number of church *members,* on the other hand, grew just about as fast as the population, and church wealth and expenditures grew more rapidly still. On actual attendance at services there were no reliable figures, although it was widely believed that an increasing proportion of the nominally faithful were finding other things to do on Sunday morning. Statistically, the churches apparently just about maintained their position in American life.

Yet it is difficult to escape the conclusion that they maintained it chiefly by the force of momentum—and to some extent, perhaps, by diligent attention to the things which are Cæsar's: by adopting, here and there, the acceptable gospel according to Bruce Barton; by strenuous membership and money-raising campaigns (such as Bishop Manning's high-pressure drive in New York for a "house of prayer for all people," which proved to be a house of prayer under strictly Episcopal auspices); and by the somewhat secular lure of church theatricals, open forums, basket-ball and swimming pools, and muscular good fellowship for the young. Something spiritual had gone out of the churches—a sense of certainty that theirs was the way to salvation. Religion was furiously discussed; there had never been so many books on religious topics in circulation, and the leading divines wrote constantly for the popular magazines; yet all this discussion was itself a sign that for millions of people religion had become a debatable subject instead of being accepted without question among the traditions of the community.

If church attendance declined, it was perhaps because, as Walter Lippmann put it, people were not so certain that they were going to meet God when they went to church. If the minister's prestige declined, it was in many cases because he had lost his one-time conviction that he had a definite and authoritative mission. The Reverend Charles Stelzle, a shrewd observer of religious conditions, spoke bluntly in an article in the *World's Work*: the church, he said, was declining largely because "those who are identified with it do not actually believe in it." Mr. Stelzle told of asking groups of Protestant ministers what there was in their church programs which would prompt them, if they were outsiders, to say, "That is great; that is worth lining up for," and of receiving in no case an immediate answer which satisfied even the answerer himself. In the congregations, and especially among the younger men and women, there was an undeniable weakening of loyalty to the church and an undeniable vagueness as to what it had to offer them—witness, for example, the tone of the discussions which accompanied the abandonment of compulsory chapel in a number of colleges.

This loss of spiritual dynamic was variously ascribed to the general let-down in moral energy which followed the strain of the war; to prosperity, which encouraged the comfortable belief that it profited a man very considerably if he gained a Cadillac car and a laudatory article in the *American Magazine;* to the growing popularity of Sunday golf and automobiling; and to disapproval in some quarters of the political lobbying of church organizations, and disgust at the connivance of many ministers in the bigotry of the Klan. More important than any of these causes, however, was the effect upon the churches of scientific doctrines and scientific methods of thought.

The prestige of science was colossal. The man in the street and the woman in the kitchen, confronted on every hand with new machines and devices which they owed to the laboratory, were ready to believe that science could accomplish almost anything; and they were being deluged with scientific information and theory. The newspapers were giving columns of space to inform (or misinform) them of the latest discoveries: a new dictum from Albert Einstein was now front-page stuff even though practically nobody could understand it. Outlines of knowledge poured from the presses to tell people about the planetesimal hypothesis and the constitution of the atom, to describe for them in unwarranted detail the daily life of the cave-man, and to acquaint them with electrons, endocrines, hormones, vitamins, reflexes, and psychoses. On the lower intellectual levels, millions of people were discovering for the first time that there was such a thing as the venerable theory of evolution. Those who had assimilated this doctrine without disaster at an early age were absorbing from Wells, Thomson, East, Wiggam, Dorsey, and innumerable other popularizers and interpreters of science a collection of ideas newer and more disquieting: that we are residents of an insignificant satellite of a very average star obscurely placed in one of who-knows-how-many galaxies scattered through space; that our behavior depends largely upon chromosomes and ductless glands; that the Hottentot obeys impulses similar to those which activate the pastor of the First Baptist Church, and is probably already better adapted to his Hottentot environment than he would be if he followed the Baptist code; that sex is the most important thing in life, that inhibitions are not to be tolerated, that sin is an out-of-date term, that most untoward behavior is the result of complexes acquired at an early age, and that men and women are mere bundles of behavior-patterns, anyhow. If some of the scientific and pseudo-scientific principles which lodged themselves in the popular mind contradicted one another, that did not seem to matter: the popular mind appeared equally ready to believe with East and Wiggam in the power of heredity and with Watson in the power of environment.

Of all the sciences it was the youngest and least scientific which most captivated the general public and had the most disintegrating effect upon religious faith. Psychology was king. Freud, Adler, Jung, and Watson had their tens of thousands of votaries; intelligence-testers invaded the schools in quest of I. Q.s; psychiatrists were installed in business houses to hire and fire employees and determine advertising policies; and one had only to read the newspapers to be told with complete assurance that psychology held the key to the problems of waywardness, divorce, and crime.

The word science had become a shibboleth. To preface a statement with "Science teaches us" was enough to silence argument. If a sales manager wanted to put over a promotion scheme or a clergyman to recommend a charity, they both hastened to say that it was scientific.

The effect of the prestige of science upon churchmen was well summed up by Dr. Harry Emerson Fosdick at the end of the decade:

"The men of faith might claim for their positions ancient

tradition, practical usefulness, and spiritual desirability, but one query could prick all such bubbles: Is it scientific? That question has searched religion for contraband goods, stripped it of old superstitions, forced it to change its categories of thought and methods of work, and in general has so cowed and scared religion that many modern-minded believers . . . instinctively throw up their hands at the mere whisper of it. . . . When a prominent scientist comes out strongly for religion, all the churches thank Heaven and take courage as though it were the highest possible compliment to God to have Eddington believe in Him. Science has become the arbiter of this generation's thought, until to call even a prophet and a seer scientific is to cap the climax of praise."

So powerful was the invasion of scientific ideas and of the scientific habit of reliance upon proved acts that the Protestant churches—which numbered in their membership five out of every eight adult church members in the United States— were broken into two warring camps. Those who believed in the letter of the Bible and refused to accept any teaching, even of science, which seemed to conflict with it, began in 1921 to call themselves Fundamentalists. The Modernists (or Liberals), on the other hand, tried to reconcile their beliefs with scientific thought; to throw overboard what was out of date, to retain what was essential and intellectually respectable, and generally to mediate between Christianity and the skeptical spirit of the age.

The position of the Fundamentalists seemed almost hopeless. The tide of all rational thought in a rational age seemed to be running against them. But they were numerous, and at least there was no doubt about where they stood. Particularly in the South they controlled the big Protestant denominations. And they fought strenuously. They forced the liberal Doctor Fosdick out of the pulpit of a Presbyterian church and back into his own Baptist fold, and even caused him to be tried for heresy (though there was no churchman in America more influential than he). They introduced into the legislatures of nearly half the states of the Union bills designed to forbid the teaching of the doctrine of evolution; in Texas, Louisiana, Arkansas, and South Carolina they pushed such bills through one house of the legislature only to fail in the other; and in Tennessee, Oklahoma, and Mississippi they actually succeeded in writing their anachronistic wishes into law.

The Modernists had the *Zeitgeist* on their side, but they were not united. Their interpretations of God—as the first cause, as absolute energy, as idealized reality, as a righteous will working in creation, as the ideal and goal toward which all that is highest and best is moving—were confusingly various and ambiguous. Some of these interpretations offered little to satisfy the worshiper: one New England clergyman said that when he thought of God he thought of "a sort of oblong blur." And the Modernists threw overboard so many doctrines in which the bulk of American Protestants had grown up believing (such as the Virgin birth, the resurrection of the body, and the Atonement) that they seemed to many to have no religious cargo left except a nebulous faith, a general benevolence, and a disposition to assure everyone that he was really just as religious as they. Gone for them, as Walter Lippmann said, was "that deep, compulsive, organic faith in an external fact which is the essence of religion for all but that very small minority who can live within themselves in mystical communion or by the power of their understanding." The Modernists, furthermore, had not only Fundamentalism to battle with, but another adversary, the skeptic nourished on outlines of science; and the sermons of more than one Modernist leader gave the impression that Modernism, trying to meet the skeptic's arguments without resorting to the argument from authority, was being forced against its will to whittle down its creed to almost nothing at all.

All through the decade the three-sided conflict reverberated. It reached its climax in the Scopes case in the summer of 1925.

The Tennessee legislature, dominated by Fundamentalists, passed a bill providing that "it shall be unlawful for any teacher in any of the universities, normals and all other public schools of the State, which are supported in whole or in part by the public school funds of the State, to teach any theory that denies the story of the Divine creation of man as taught in the Bible, and to teach instead that man has descended from a lower order of animals."

This law had no sooner been placed upon the books than a little group of men in the sleepy town of Dayton, Tennessee, decided to put it to the test. George Rappelyea, a mining engineer, was drinking lemon phosphates in Robinson's drug store with John Thomas Scopes, a likeable young man of twenty-four who taught biology at the Central High School, and two or three others. Rappelyea proposed that Scopes should allow himself to be caught red-handed in the act of teaching the theory of evolution to an innocent child, and Scopes—half serious, half in joke—agreed. Their motives were apparently mixed; it was characteristic of the times that (according to so friendly a narrator of the incident as Arthur Garfield Hays) Rappelyea declared that their action would put Dayton on the map. At all events, the illegal deed was shortly perpetrated and Scopes was arrested. William Jennings Bryan forthwith volunteered his services to the prosecution; Rappelyea wired the Civil Liberties Union in New York and secured for Scopes the legal assistance of Clarence Darrow, Dudley Field Malone, and Arthur Garfield Hays; the trial was set for July, 1925, and Dayton suddenly discovered that it was to be put on the map with a vengeance.

There was something to be said for the right of the people to decide what should be taught in their tax-supported schools, even if what they decided upon was ridiculous. But the issue of the Scopes case, as the great mass of newspaper readers saw it, was nothing so abstruse as the rights of taxpayers versus academic freedom. In the eyes of the public, the trial was a battle between Fundamentalism on the one hand and twentieth-century skepticism (assisted by Modernism) on the other. The champions of both causes were headliners. Bryan had been three times a candidate for the Presidency, had been Secretary of State, and was a famous orator; he was the perfect embodiment of old-fashioned American idealism—friendly, naïve, provincial. Darrow, a radical, a friend of the underdog, an agnostic, had recently jumped into the limelight of publicity through his defense of Leopold and Loeb. Even Tex Rickard could hardly have staged a more promising contest than a battle between these two men over such an emotional issue.

It was a strange trial. Into the quiet town of Dayton flocked gaunt Tennessee farmers and their families in mule-drawn wagons and ramshackle Fords; quiet, godly people in overalls and gingham and black, ready to defend their faith against the "foreigners," yet curious to know what this new-fangled evolutionary theory might be. Revivalists of every sort flocked there, too, held their meetings on the outskirts of the town under the light of flares, and tacked up signs on the trees about the courthouse—"Read Your Bible Daily for One Week," and "Be Sure Your Sins Will Find You Out," and at the very courthouse gate:

THE KINGDOM OF GOD

The sweetheart love of Jesus Christ and Paradise Street is at hand. Do you want to be a sweet angel? Forty days of prayer. Itemize your sins and iniquities for eternal life. If you come clean, God will talk back to you in voice.

Yet the atmosphere of Dayton was not simply that of rural piety. Hot-dog venders and lemonade venders set up their stalls along the streets as if it were circus day. Booksellers hawked volumes on biology. Over a hundred newspaper men poured into the town. The Western Union installed twenty-two telegraph operators in a room off a grocery store. In the courtroom itself, as the trial impended, reporters and camera men crowded alongside grim-faced Tennessee countrymen; there was a buzz of talk, a shuffle of feet, a ticking of telegraph instruments, an air of suspense like that of a first-night performance at the theater. Judge, defendant, and counsel were stripped to their shirt sleeves—Bryan in a pongee shirt turned in at the neck, Darrow with lavender suspenders, Judge Raulston with galluses of a more sober judicial hue—yet fashion was not wholly absent: the news was flashed over the wires to the whole country that the judge's daughters, as they entered the courtroom with him, wore rolled stockings like any metropolitan flapper's. Court was opened with a pious prayer—and motion-picture operators climbed upon tables and chairs to photograph the leading participants in the trial from every possible angle. The evidence ranged all the way from the admission of fourteen-year-old Howard Morgan that Scopes had told him about evolution and that it hadn't hurt him any, to the estimate of a zoölogist that life had begun something like six hundred million years ago (an assertion which caused gasps and titters of disbelief from the rustics in the audience). And meanwhile two million words were being telegraphed out of Dayton, the trial was being broadcast by the *Chicago Tribune*'s station WGN, the Dreamland Circus at Coney Island offered "Zip" to the Scopes defense as a "missing link," cable companies were reporting enormous increases in transatlantic cable tolls, and news agencies in London were being besieged with requests for more copy from Switzerland, Italy, Germany, Russia, China, and Japan. Ballyhoo had come to Dayton.

It was a bitter trial. Attorney-General Stewart of Tennessee cried out against the insidious doctrine which was "undermining the faith of Tennessee's children and robbing them of their chance of eternal life." Bryan charged Darrow with having only one purpose, "to slur at the Bible." Darrow spoke of Bryan's "fool religion." Yet again and again the scene verged on farce. The climax—both of bitterness and of farce—came on the afternoon of July 20th, when on the spur of the moment Hays asked that the defense be permitted to put Bryan on the stand as an expert on the Bible, and Bryan consented.

So great was the crowd that afternoon that the judge had decided to move the court outdoors, to a platform built against the courthouse under the maple trees. Benches were set out before it. The reporters sat on the benches, on the ground, anywhere, and scribbled their stories. On the outskirts of the seated crowd a throng stood in the hot sunlight which streamed down through the trees. And on the platform sat the shirt-sleeved Clarence Darrow, a Bible on his knee, and put the Fundamentalist champion through one of the strangest examinations which ever took place in a court of law.

He asked Bryan about Jonah and the whale, Joshua and the the sun, where Cain got his wife, the date of the Flood, the significance of the Tower of Babel. Bryan affirmed his belief that the world was created in 4004 B.C. and the Flood occurred in or about 2348 B.C.; that Eve was literally made out of Adam's rib; that the Tower of Babel was responsible for the diversity of languages in the world; and that a "big fish" had swallowed Jonah. When Darrow asked him if he had ever discovered where Cain got his wife, Bryan answered: "No, sir; I leave the agnostics to hunt for her." When Darrow inquired, "Do you say you do not believe that there were any civilizations on this earth that reach back beyond five thousand years?" Bryan stoutly replied, "I am not satisfied by any evidence I have seen." Tempers were getting frazzled by the strain and the heat; once Darrow declared that his purpose in examining Bryan was "to show up Fundamentalism . . . to prevent bigots and ignoramuses from controlling the educational system of the United States," and Bryan jumped up, his face purple, and shook his fist at Darrow, crying, "To protect the word of God against the greatest atheist and agnostic in the United States!"

It was a savage encounter, and a tragic one for the ex-Secretary of State. He was defending what he held most dear. He was making—though he did not know it—his last appearance before the great American public which had once done him honor (he died scarcely a week later). And he was being covered with humiliation. The sort of religious faith which he represented could not take the witness stand and face reason as a prosecutor.

On the morning of July 21st Judge Raulston mercifully refused to let the ordeal of Bryan continue and expunged the testimony of the previous afternoon. Scopes's lawyers had been unable to get any of their scientific evidence before the jury, and now they saw that their only chance of making the sort of defense they had planned for lay in giving up the case and bringing it before the Tennessee Supreme Court on appeal. Scopes was promptly found guilty and fined one hundred dollars. The State Supreme Court later upheld the anti-evolution law but freed Scopes on a technicality, thus preventing further appeal.

Theoretically, Fundamentalism had won, for the law stood. Yet really Fundamentalism had lost. Legislators might go on passing anti-evolution laws, and in the hinterlands the pious might still keep their religion locked in a science-proof compartment of their minds; but civilized opinion everywhere had regarded the Dayton trial with amazement and amusement, and the slow drift away from Fundamentalist certainty continued.

The reporters, the movie men, the syndicate writers, the telegraph operators shook the dust of Dayton from their feet. This monkey trial had been a good show for the front pages, but maybe it was a little too highbrow in its implications. What next? . . . How about a good clean fight without any biology in it?

[5]

The year 1925 drew slowly toward its close. The *Shenandoah*—a great navy dirigible—was wrecked, and for a few days the country supped on horror. The Florida real-estate boom reached its dizziest height And then the football season revealed what the ballyhoo technic could do for a football star. Nobody needed a course in biology to appreciate Red Grange.

The Post-war Decade was a great sporting era. More men were playing golf than ever before—playing it in baggy plus-fours, with tassels at the knee and checked stockings. There were five thousand golf-courses in the United States, there were said to be two million players, and it was estimated that half a billion dollars was spent annually on the game. The ability to play it had become a part of the almost essential equipment of the aspiring business executive. The country club had become the focus of social life in hundreds of communities. But it was an even greater era for watching sports than for taking part in them. Promoters, chambers of commerce, newspaper-owners, sports writers, press agents, radio broadcasters, all found profit in exploiting the public's mania for sporting shows and its willingness to be persuaded that the great athletes of the day were supermen. Never before had such a blinding light of publicity been turned upon the gridiron, the diamond, and the prize ring.

Men who had never learned until the nineteen-twenties the difference between a brassie and a niblick grabbed their five-star editions to read about Bobby Jones's exploits with his redoubtable putter, Calamity Jane. There was big money in being a successful golf professional: Walter Hagen's income for several years ranged between forty and eighty thousand dollars, and for a time he received thirty thousand a year and a house for lending the prestige of his presence and his name to a Florida real-estate development. World's Series baseball crowds broke all records. So intense was the excitement over football that stadia seating fifty and sixty and seventy thousand people were filled to the last seat when the big teams met, while scores of thousands more sat in warm living-rooms to hear the play-by-play story over the radio and to be told by Graham McNamee that it certainly was cold on the upper rim of the amphitheater. The Yale Athletic Association was said to have taken in over a million dollars in ticket money in a single season. Teams which represented supposed institutions of learning went barnstorming for weeks at a time, imbibing what academic instruction they might on the sleeping-car between the Yankee Stadium and Chicago or between Texas and the

Tournament of Roses at Pasadena. More Americans could identify Knute Rockne as the Notre Dame coach than could tell who was the presiding officer of the United States Senate. The fame of star football players, to be sure, was ephemeral compared with that of Jones in golf, or of Ruth in baseball, or of Tilden in tennis. Aldrich, Owen, Bo McMillin, Ernie Nevers, Grange, the Four Horsemen, Benny Friedman, Caldwell, Cagle, and Albie Booth all reigned briefly. But the case of Red Grange may illustrate to what heights a hero of the stadium could rise in the consulship of Calvin Coolidge, when pockets were full and the art of ballyhoo was young and vigorous.

"Harold E. Grange—the middle name is Edward—was born in Forksville, Sullivan County, Pennsylvania, on June 13, 1903," announced a publicity item sent out to the press to put the University of Illinois on the map by glorifying its greatest product. "His father, Lyle N. Grange, in his youth had been the king of lumberjacks in the Pennsylvania mountains, being renowned for his strength, skill, and daring. His mother, a sweet and lovely girl, died when 'Red' was five years old, and it was this which determined his father to move from Pennsylvania to Wheaton, Illinois. . . . The father, who never married again, is deputy sheriff at Wheaton."

But the publicity item (which continues in this rhapsodic tone for many a paragraph) is perhaps too leisurely. Suffice it to say that Red Grange—the "Wheaton iceman," as they called him—played football exceedingly well for the University of Illinois, so well that at the end of the season of 1925 (his senior year) he decided not to bother any further with education at the moment, but to reap the harvest of his fame. Let a series of items summarizing the telegraphic press dispatches tell the story:

Nov. 2–Grange is carried two miles by students.

Nov. 3–His football jersey will be framed at Illinois.

Nov. 11–Admirers circulate petition nominating him for Congress despite his being under age. Is silent on $40,000 offer from New York Giants for three games.

Nov. 17–Is offered $120,000 a year by real-estate firm.

Nov. 21–Plays last game with Illinois, turns professional.

Nov. 22–Signs with Chicago Bears.

Nov. 26–Plays first professional game with Bears and collects $12,000.

Dec.   6–Collects $30,000 in first New York game.
Dec.   7–Signs $300,000 movie contract with Arrow Picture Corporation; may earn $100,000 by June.
Dec.   8–Is presented to President Coolidge.

The public is fickle, however. Within a few months Gertrude Ederle and the first mother to swim the English Channel were being welcomed in New York with thunderous applause. Dempsey and Tunney were preparing for their Philadelphia fight, and the spotlight had left Red Grange. Five years later he was reported to be working in a night club in Hollywood, while that other hero of the backfield, Caldwell of Yale, was running a lunchroom in New Haven. *Sic transit*.

The public mania for vicarious participation in sport reached its climax in the two Dempsey-Tunney fights, the first at Philadelphia in September, 1926, the second at Chicago a year later. Prize-fighting, once outlawed, had become so respectable in American eyes that gentlefolk crowded into the ringside seats and a clergyman on Long Island had to postpone a meeting of his vestrymen so that they might listen in on one of the big bouts. The newspapers covered acres of paper for weeks beforehand with gossip and prognostications from the training-camps; public interest was whipped up by such devices as signed articles—widely syndicated—in which the contestants berated each other (both sets of articles, in one case, being written by the same "ghost"), and even a paper so traditionally conservative in its treatment of sports as the *New York Times* announced the result of a major bout with three streamer headlines running all the way across its front page. One hundred and thirty thousand people watched Tunney outbox a weary Dempsey at Philadelphia and paid nearly two million dollars for the privilege; one hundred and forty-five thousand people watched the return match at Chicago and the receipts reached the incredible sum of $2,600,000. Compare that sum with the trifling $452,000 taken in when Dempsey gained his title from Willard in 1919 and you have a measure of what had happened in a few years. So enormous was the amphitheater at Chicago that two-thirds of the people in the outermost seats did not know who had won when the fight was over. Nor was the audience limited to the throng in Chicago, for millions more—forty millions, the radio people claimed—heard the breathless story of it, blow by blow, over the radio.

During the seventh round—when Tunney fell and the referee, by delaying the beginning of his count until Dempsey had reached his corner, gave Tunney some thirteen seconds to recover—five Americans dropped dead of heart failure at their radios. Five other deaths were attributed to the excitement of hearing the radio story of the fight.

Equally remarkable was the aftermath of these two mighty contests. Dempsey had been a mauler at the beginning of the decade; he was an ex-mauler at its end. Not so Tunney. From the pinnacle of his fame he stepped neatly off on to those upper levels of literary and fashionable society in which heavyweight champions, haloed by publicity, were newly welcome. Having received $1,742,282 in three years for his prowess in the ring, Tunney lectured on Shakespeare before Professor Phelps's class at Yale, went for a walking trip in Europe with Thornton Wilder (author of the best-selling novel of the year, *The Bridge of San Luis Rey*), married a young gentlewoman of Greenwich, Connecticut, and after an extensive stay abroad returned to the United States with his bride, giving out on his arrival a prepared statement which, if not quite Shakespearian or Wilderesque in its style, at least gave evidence of effort:

It is hard to realize as our ship passes through the Narrows that fifteen months have elapsed since the *Mauretania* was carrying me in the other direction. During those fifteen months Mrs. Tunney and I have visited many countries and have met some very interesting people. We thoroughly enjoyed our travels, but find the greatest joy of all in again being home with our people and friends.

The echo of a rumor at home that I am contemplating returning to the boxing game to defend the heavyweight championship reached me in Italy. This is in no sense true, for I have permanently ended my public career. My great work now is to live quietly and simply, for this manner of living brings me most happiness.

The sports writers were decidedly cool toward Tunney's post-boxing career. But he was simply exercising the ancient democratic prerogative of rising higher than his source. Ballyhoo had exalted him to the skies, and he took advantage of it to leave the dubious atmosphere of the pugilistic world and seek more salubrious airs.

[6]

As 1925 gave way to 1926, the searchlight of public attention had shifted from Red Grange to the marriage of Irving Berlin and Ellin Mackay, showing that the curiosity of millions is no respecter of personal privacy; to the gallant rescue of the men of the steamship *Antinoë* in mid-ocean by Captain Fried of the *President Roosevelt*; to the exclusion from the United States of Vera, Countess Cathcart, on the uncomplimentary ground of moral turpitude; to Byrd's daring flight over the North Pole; and, as the summer of 1926 arrived, to the disappearance from a bathing beach of Aimee Semple McPherson, evangelist of a Four-Square Gospel made in California—a disappearance that was to prove the first of a series of opera-bouffe episodes which for years attracted wide-eyed tourists in droves to Mrs. McPherson's Angelus Temple.

The summer passed—the summer when the English Channel was full of swimmers, and the brown jacket of *The Private Life of Helen of Troy* ornamented thousands of cottage tables, girls in knee-length skirts and horizontally striped sweaters were learning to dance the Charleston, and the Philadelphia Sesquicentennial was sinking deeper and deeper into the red despite the aid of the Dempsey-Tunney fight. Toward the season's end there was a striking demonstration of what astute press-agentry could do to make a national sensation. A young man named Rudolph Alfonzo Raffaele Pierre Filibert Guglielmi di Valentina d'Antonguolla died in New York at the age of thirty-one. The love-making of Rudolph Valentino (as he had understandably preferred to call himself) had quickened the pulses of innumerable motion-picture addicts; with his sideburns and his passionate air, "the sheik" had set the standard for masculine sex appeal. But his lying in state in an undertaker's establishment on Broadway would hardly have attracted a crowd which stretched through eleven blocks if his manager had not arranged the scenes of grief with uncanny skill, and if Harry C. Klemfuss, the undertaker's press agent, had not provided the newspapers with everything they could desire—such as photographs, distributed in advance, of the chamber where the actor's body would lie, and posed photographs of the funeral cortège. (One of these latter pictures, ac-

cording to Silas Bent, was on the streets in one newspaper
before the funeral procession started.) With such practical
assistance, the press gave itself to the affair so whole-heartedly
that mobs rioted about the undertaker's and scores of people
were injured. Sweet are the uses of publicity: Valentino had
been heavily in debt when he died, but his posthumous films,
according to his manager's subsequent testimony, turned the
debt into a $600,000 balance to the credit of his estate. High-
minded citizens regretted that the death of Charles William
Eliot, which occurred at about the same time, occasioned no
such spectacular lamentations. But the president emeritus of
Harvard had had no professional talent to put over his funeral
in a big way.

Tunney beat Dempsey, a hurricane contributed the *coup-de-
grâce* to the Florida boom, Queen Marie of Rumania sniffed
the profits of ballyhoo from afar and made a royal visit to the
United States; and then for months on end in the winter of
1926-27 the American people waded deep in scandal and
crime.

It was four long years since the Reverend Edward W. Hall
and Mrs. Eleanor R. Mills had been found murdered near the
crab-apple tree by DeRussey's Lane outside New Brunswick,
New Jersey. In 1922 the grand jury had found no indictment.
But in 1926 a tabloid newspaper in search of more circulation
dug up what purported to be important new evidence and got
the case reopened. Mrs. Hall was arrested—at such an unholy
hour of the night that the reporters and photographers of this
tabloid got a scoop—and she and her two brothers, Henry and
Willie Stevens, were brought to trial, thus providing thrills for
the readers not only of the tabloid in question, but of every
other newspaper in the United States.

The most sensational scene in this most sensational trial of
the decade took place when Jane Gibson, the "pig woman,"
who was supposed to be dying, was brought from her hospital
to the courtroom on a stretcher and placed on a bed facing the
jury. Mrs. Gibson told a weird story. She had been pestered by
corn-robbers, it seemed, and on the night of the murder, hearing the rattle of a wagon that she thought might contain the
robbers, she saddled Jenny, her mule, and followed the wagon
down DeRussey's Lane, "peeking and peeking and peeking."
She saw a car in the Lane, with two people in it whom she

identified as Mrs. Hall and Willie Stevens. She tethered Jenny
to a cedar tree, heard the sound of a quarrel and a voice saying, "Explain these letters"; she saw Henry and Willie Stevens
in the gleam of a flashlight, she heard shots, and then she fled
in terror all the way home—only to find that she had left a
moccasin behind. Despite her fear, she went all the way back
to get that moccasin, and heard what she thought was the
screeching of an owl, but found it was a woman crying—"a big
white-haired woman doing something with her hand, crying
something." She said this woman was Mrs. Hall. All this testimony the "pig woman" gave from her bed in a wailing voice,
while trained nurses stood beside her and took her pulse; then,
crying out to the defendants, "I have told the truth! So help me
God! And you know I've told the truth!" she was borne from
the room.

The testimony of the "pig woman" did not gain in force
from what was brought out about her previous checkered
career; it would have made even less impression upon the jury
had they known that their "dying witness," whose appearance
in the courtroom had been so ingeniously staged, was destined
to live four years more. Mrs. Hall and her brothers came
magnificently through their ordeal, slow-witted Willie Stevens
in particular delighting millions of murder-trial fans by the
way in which he stoutly resisted the efforts of Senator Simpson
to bullyrag him into confusion. The new evidence dug up by
the tabloid—consisting chiefly of a calling-card which was
supposed to have Willie Stevens's fingerprint on it—did not
impress the jury.

But though the prosecution's case thus collapsed, the reputation of the Stevens family had been butchered to make a
Roman holiday of the first magnitude for newspaper readers.
Five million words were written and sent from Somerville,
New Jersey, during the first eleven days of the trial. Twice as
many newspaper men were there as at Dayton. The reporters
included Mary Roberts Rinehart, the novelist, Billy Sunday,
the revivalist, and James Mills, the husband of the murdered
choir-singer; and the man who had claimed the mantle of
Bryan as the leader of Fundamentalism, the Reverend John
Roach Straton, wrote a daily editorial moralizing about the
case. Over wires jacked into the largest telegraph switchboard
in the world traveled the tidings of lust and crime to every

corner of the United States, and the public lapped them up and cried for more.

So insistently did they cry that when, a few short months later, an art editor named Albert Snyder was killed with a sash-weight by his wife and her lover, a corset salesman named Judd Gray, once more the forces of ballyhoo got into action. In this case there was no mystery, nor was the victim highly placed; the only excuses for putting the Snyder-Gray trial on the front page were that it involved a sex triangle and that the Snyders were ordinary people living in an ordinary New York suburb—the sort of people with whom the ordinary reader could easily identify himself. Yet so great was the demand for vicarious horrors that once more the great Western Union switchboard was brought into action, an even more imposing galaxy of special writers interpreted the sordid drama (including David Wark Griffith, Peggy Joyce, and Will Durant, as well as Mrs. Rinehart, Billy Sunday, and Doctor Straton), and once more the American people tasted blood.

In the interval between the Hall-Mills case and the Snyder-Gray case, they had had a chance to roll an even riper scandal on their tongues. Frances Heenan Browning, known to the multitude as "Peaches," brought suit for separation from Edward W. Browning, a New York real-estate man who had a penchant for giving to very young girls the delights of a Cinderella. Supposedly sober and reputable newspapers recited the unedifying details of "Daddy" Browning's adventures; and when the *New York Graphic,* a tabloid, printed a "composograph" of Browning in pajamas shouting "Woof! Woof! Don't be a goof!" to his half-clad wife because—according to the caption—she "refused to parade nude," even the *Daily News,* which in the past had shown no distaste for scandal, expressed its fear that if such things went on the public would be "drenched in obscenity."

A great many people felt as the *Daily News* did, and regarded with dismay the depths to which the public taste seemed to have fallen. Surely a change must come, they thought. This carnival of commercialized degradation could not continue.

The change came—suddenly.

[7]

The owner of the Brevoort and Lafayette Hotels in New York, Raymond Orteig, had offered—way back in 1919—a prize of $25,000 for the first non-stop flight between New York and Paris. Only a few days after the conclusion of the Snyder-Gray trial, three planes were waiting for favorable weather conditions to hop off from Roosevelt Field, just outside New York, in quest of this prize: the *Columbia*, which was to be piloted by Clarence Chamberlin and Lloyd Bertaud; the *America*, with Lieutenant-Commander Byrd of North Pole fame in command; and the *Spirit of St. Louis*, which had abruptly arrived from the Pacific coast with a lone young man named Charles A. Lindbergh at the controls. There was no telling which of the three planes would get off first, but clearly the public favorite was the young man from the West. He was modest, he seemed to know his business, there was something particularly daring about his idea of making the perilous journey alone, and he was as attractive-looking a youngster as ever had faced a camera man. The reporters—to his annoyance—called him "Lucky Lindy" and the "Flying Fool." The spotlight of publicity was upon him. Not yet, however, was he a god.

On the evening of May 19, 1927, Lindbergh decided that although it was drizzling on Long Island, the weather reports gave a chance of fair skies for his trip and he had better get ready. He spent the small hours of the next morning in sleepless preparations, went to Curtiss Field, received further weather news, had his plane trundled to Roosevelt Field and fueled, and a little before eight o'clock—on the morning of May 20th—climbed in and took off for Paris.

Then something very like a miracle took place.

No sooner had the word been flashed along the wires that Lindbergh had started than the whole population of the country became united in the exaltation of a common emotion. Young and old, rich and poor, farmer and stockbroker, Fundamentalist and skeptic, highbrow and lowbrow, all with one accord fastened their hopes upon the young man in the *Spirit of St. Louis*. To give a single instance of the intensity of their mood: at the Yankee Stadium in New York, where the Maloney-Sharkey fight was held on the evening of the 20th, forty thousand hard-boiled boxing fans rose as one man and stood with bared heads in impressive silence when the announcer asked them to pray for Lindbergh. The next day came the successive reports of Lindbergh's success—he had reached the Irish coast, he was crossing over England, he was over the Channel, he had landed at Le Bourget to be enthusiastically mobbed by a vast crowd of Frenchmen—and the American people went almost mad with joy and relief. And when the reports of Lindbergh's first few days in Paris showed that he was behaving with charming modesty and courtesy, millions of his countrymen took him to their hearts as they had taken no other human being in living memory.

Every record for mass excitement and mass enthusiasm in the age of ballyhoo was smashed during the next few weeks. Nothing seemed to matter, either to the newspapers or to the people who read them, but Lindbergh and his story. On the day the flight was completed the *Washington Star* sold 16,000 extra copies, the *St. Louis Post-Dispatch* 40,000, the *New York Evening World* 114,000. The huge headlines which described Lindbergh's triumphal progress from day to day in newspapers from Maine to Oregon showed how thorough was public agreement with the somewhat extravagant dictum of the *Evening World* that Lindbergh had performed "the greatest feat of a solitary man in the records of the human race." Upon his return to the United States, a single Sunday issue of a single paper contained one hundred columns of text and pictures devoted to him. Nobody appeared to question the fitness of President Coolidge's action in sending a cruiser of the United States navy to bring this young private citizen and his plane back from France. He was greeted in Washington at a vast open-air gathering at which the President made—according to Charles Merz—"the longest and most impressive address since his annual message to Congress." The Western Union having provided form messages for telegrams of congratulations to Lindbergh on his arrival, 55,000 of them were sent to him— and were loaded on a truck and trundled after him in the parade through Washington. One telegram, from Minneapolis, was signed with 17,500 names and made up a scroll 520 feet long, under which ten messenger boys staggered. After the public welcome in New York, the Street Cleaning Department

gathered up 1,800 tons of paper which had been torn up and
thrown out of windows of office buildings to make a snow-
storm of greeting—1,800 tons as against a mere 155 tons
swept up after the premature Armistice celebration of November 7, 1918!

Lindbergh was commissioned Colonel, and received the
Distinguished Flying Cross, the Congressional Medal of
Honor, and so many foreign decorations and honorary
memberships that to repeat the list would be a weary task. He
was offered two and a half million dollars for a tour of the
world by air, and $700,000 to appear in the films; his signature
was sold for $1,600; a Texas town was named for him, a
thirteen-hundred-foot Lindbergh tower was proposed for the
city of Chicago, "the largest dinner ever tendered to an individual in modern history" was consumed in his honor, and a
staggering number of streets, schools, restaurants, and corporations sought to share the glory of his name.

Nor was there any noticeable group of dissenters from all
this hullabaloo. Whatever else people might disagree about,
they joined in praise of him.

To appreciate how extraordinary was this universal outpour-
ing of admiration and love—for the word love is hardly too
strong—one must remind oneself of two or three facts.

Lindbergh's flight was not the first crossing of the Atlantic
by air. Alcock and Brown had flown direct from Newfoundland to Ireland in 1919. That same year the N-C 4, with
five men aboard, had crossed by way of the Azores, and the
British dirigible R-34 had flown from Scotland to Long Island
with 31 men aboard, and then had turned about and made a
return flight to England. The German dirigible ZR-3 (later
known as the *Los Angeles*) had flown from Friedrichshafen to
Lakehurst, New Jersey, in 1924 with 32 people aboard. Two
Round-the-World American army planes had crossed the North
Atlantic by way of Iceland, Greenland, and Newfoundland in
1924. The novelty of Lindbergh's flight lay only in the fact that
he went all the way from New York to Paris instead of jumping off from Newfoundland, that he reached his precise objective, and that he went alone.

Furthermore, there was little practical advantage in such an
exploit. It brought about a boom in aviation, to be sure, but a
not altogether healthy one, and it led many a flyer to hop off

blindly for foreign shores in emulation of Lindbergh and be drowned. Looking back on the event after a lapse of years, and stripping it of its emotional connotations, one sees it simply as a daring stunt flight—the longest up to that time—by a man who did not claim to be anything but a stunt flyer. Why, then, this idolization of Lindbergh?

The explanation is simple. A disillusioned nation fed on cheap heroics and scandal and crime was revolting against the low estimate of human nature which it had allowed itself to entertain. For years the American people had been spiritually starved. They had seen their early ideals and illusions and hopes one by one worn away by the corrosive influence of events and ideas—by the disappointing aftermath of the war, by scientific doctrines and psychological theories which undermined their religion and ridiculed their sentimental notions, by the spectacle of graft in politics and crime on the city streets, and finally by their recent newspaper diet of smut and murder. Romance, chivalry and self-dedication had been debunked; the heroes of history had been shown to have feet of clay, and the saints of history had been revealed as people with queer complexes. There was the god of business to worship—but a suspicion lingered that he was made of brass. Ballyhoo had given the public contemporary heroes to bow down before—but these contemporary heroes, with their fat profits from moving-picture contracts and ghost-written syndicated articles, were not wholly convincing. Something that people needed, if they were to live at peace with themselves and with the world, was missing from their lives. And all at once Lindbergh provided it. Romance, chivalry, self-dedication—here they were, embodied in a modern Galahad for a generation which had foresworn Galahads. Lindbergh did not accept the moving-picture offers that came his way, he did not sell testimonials, did not boast, did not get himself involved in scandal, conducted himself with unerring taste—and was handsome and brave withal. The machinery of ballyhoo was ready and waiting to lift him up where every eye could see him. Is it any wonder that the public's reception of him took on the aspects of a vast religious revival?

Lindbergh did not go back on his admirers. He undertook a series of exhibition flights and good-will flights—successfully and with quiet dignity. He married a daughter of the ambassa-

dor to Mexico, and in so doing delighted the country by turning the tables on ballyhoo itself—by slipping away with his
bride on a motor-boat and remaining hidden for days despite
the efforts of hundreds of newspaper men to spy upon his honeymoon. Wherever he went, crowds fought for a chance to be
near him, medals were pinned upon him, tributes were showered upon him, his coming and going was news. He packed
away a good-sized fortune earned chiefly as consultant for
aviation companies, but few people grudged him that. Incred-
ibly, he kept his head and his instinct for fine conduct.

And he remained a national idol.

Even three and four years after his flight, the roads about his
New Jersey farm were blocked on week-ends with the cars of
admirers who wanted to catch a glimpse of him, and it was
said that he could not even send his shirts to a laundry because
they did not come back—they were too valuable as souvenirs.
His picture hung in hundreds of schoolrooms and in thousands
of houses. No living American—no dead American, one might
almost say, save perhaps Abraham Lincoln—commanded such
unswerving fealty. You might criticize Coolidge or Hoover o
Ford or Edison or Bobby Jones or any other headline hero; but
if you decried anything that Lindbergh did, you knew that you
had wounded your auditors. For Lindbergh was a god.

Pretty good, one reflects, for a stunt flyer. But also, one must
add, pretty good for the American people. They had shown
that they had better taste in heroes than anyone would have
dared to predict during the years which immediately preceded
the 20th of May, 1927.

[8]

After Lindbergh's flight the profits of heroism were so apparent that a horde of seekers after cash and glory appeared,
not all of whom seemed to realize that one of the things which
had endeared Lindbergh to his admirers had been his in-
difference both to easy money and to applause. The formula
was simple. You got an airplane, some financial backing, and a
press agent, and made the first non-stop flight from one place
to another place (there were still plenty of places that nobody
had flown between). You arranged in advance to sell your
personal story to a syndicate if you were successful. If neces-

sary you could get a good deal of your equipment without paying for it, on condition that the purveyors of your oil or your flying suit or your five-foot shelf might say how useful you had found it. Having landed at your destination—and on the front pages—you promptly sold your book, your testimonials, your appearance in vaudeville, your appearance in the movies, or whatever else there was demand for. If you did not know how to pilot a plane you could still be a passenger; a woman passenger, in fact, had better news value than a male pilot. And if flying seemed a little hazardous for your personal taste, you could get useful publicity by giving a prize for other people to fly after.

When Chamberlin followed Lindbergh across the Atlantic, Charles A. Levine, the owner of the plane, was an extremely interested passenger. He got an official welcome at New York. Everybody was getting official welcomes at New York. Grover Whalen, the well-dressed Police Commissioner, was taking incessant advantage of what Alva Johnston called the great discovery that anybody riding up Broadway at noon with a motorcycle escort would find thousands of people gathered there in honor of luncheon. British open golf champions, Channel swimmers, and the Italian soccer team were greeted by Mr. Whalen as deferentially as the Persian Minister of Finance and the Mayor of Leipzig, and it was always fun for the citizenry to have an excuse to throw ticker tape and fragments of the Bronx telephone directory out the window.

Byrd and his men hopped off from Roosevelt Field a few weeks after Chamberlin and Levine, and came down in the sea —but so close to the French coast that they waded ashore. Brock and Schlee not only crossed the Atlantic, but continued on in a series of flights till they reached Japan. And then a good-looking dentist's assistant from Lakeland, Florida, named Ruth Elder, who had been taking flying lessons from George Haldeman, got a citrus-grower and a real-estate man to back her, and Haldeman to pilot her, and set out to become the first woman transatlantic airplane rider. She dropped into the sea much too far out to wade ashore, as it happened; but what matter? She and Haldeman were picked up providentially by a tanker; her manager did good business for her; and she got her welcome—though the City of New York spent only $333.90 on greeting her, as compared with more than $1,000 for Levine, $12,000 for the President of the Irish Free State, $26,000 for Byrd, and $71,000 for Lindbergh.

After Ruth Elder there were so many flights, successful or disastrous, that one could hardly keep track of them. They were always front-page news, but they were less exciting than the unveiling of the new Ford (in December, 1927) and the sinking of the steamship *Vestris*, which (late in 1928) was so hysterically reported that one might have imagined it to be the greatest marine disaster in history. There were no more Lindberghs.

The procession of sporting heroes continued. Bobby Jones went on from triumph to triumph, until no one could doubt that he was the greatest golfer of all time. Babe Ruth remained the home-run king. Cagle and Booth gave the football writers a chance to be the romantic fellows they longed to be. Tilden was slipping, but could still beat almost anybody but a Frenchman. Prize-fighting, however, languished, and there were signs that the public taste in sporting exhibitions was becoming a little jaded. The efforts to find something novel enough to arouse the masters of ballyhoo became almost pathological: Marathon dancers clung to one another by the hour and day and week, shuffling about the floor in an agony of weariness, and the unhappy participants in C. C. Pyle's "Bunion Derby" ran across the continent with results painful both to their feet and to Mr. Pyle's fortunes as a promoter. Thousands stood and gaped while Alvin Shipwreck Kelly sat on a flagpole. There was still money in breaking records, even if your achievement was that of perching on a flagpole in Baltimore for 23 days and 7 hours, having your food and drink hoisted to you in a bucket, and hiring a man to shout at you if you showed signs of dozing for more than twenty minutes at a time. But nobody seemed to be persuaded that there was anything epic about Mr. Kelly. Flagpole sitting and Marathon dancing were just freak shows to watch in an idle moment.

Perhaps the bloom of youth was departing from ballyhoo: the technic was becoming a little too obvious. Perhaps Lindbergh had spoiled the public for lesser heroes. Perhaps the grim execution of Sacco and Vanzetti in 1927 and the presidential campaign of 1928 reminded a well-fed people that there were such things as public issues, after all. But perhaps, too, there was some significance in the fact that in March,

1928, only a few months after the new Ford appeared and less than a year after Lindbergh's flight, the Big Bull Market went into its sensational phase. A ten-point gain in Radio common in a single day promised more immediate benefits than all the non-stop flyers and heavyweight champions in the world.

IX

The Revolt of the Highbrows

"Here was a new generation . . . grown up to find all Gods dead, all wars fought, all faiths in man shaken."
—F. Scott Fitzgerald's *This Side of Paradise.*

By the end of the war with Germany, social compulsion had become a national habit. The typical American of the old stock had never had more than a half-hearted enthusiasm for the rights of the minority; bred in a pioneer tradition, he had been accustomed to set his community in order by the first means that came to hand—a sumptuary law, a vigilance committee, or if necessary a shotgun. Declarations of Independence and Bills of Rights were all very well in the history books, but when he was running things himself he had usually been open to the suggestion that liberty was another name for license and that the Bill of Rights was the last resort of scoundrels. During the war he had discovered how easy it was to legislate and propagandize and intimidate his neighbors into what seemed to him acceptable conduct, and after peace was declared he went on using the same sort of methods to see that they continued to conform.

From Liberty-loan campaigns—with a quota for everybody and often a threat for those who were slow to contribute—he turned to community-chest drives and college-endowment-fund drives and church-membership drives and town-boosting drives and a multitude of other public campaigns: committees and subcommittees were organized, press agents distributed their canned releases, orators bellowed, and the man who kept a tight grip on his pocketbook felt the uncomfortable pressure of mass opinion. From the coercion of alien enemies and supposed pro-Germans it was a short step, as we have seen, to the coercion of racial minorities and supposed Bolsheviks. From war-time censorship it was a short step to peace-time censorship of newspapers and books and public speech. And from legislating sobriety in war-time it was a short step to imbedding prohibition permanently in the Constitution and trying to write the moral code of the majority into the statute-books. Business, to be sure, was freed of most of the shackles which had bound it in 1917 and 1918, for the average American now identified his own interests with those of business. But outside of business he thought he knew how people ought to behave, and he would stand for no nonsense.

After the early days of the Big Red Scare, the American middle-class majority met with little resistance in its stern measures against radicalism and its insistence upon *laissez faire* for business. While labor was being cowed by the police or lured into compliance by stock ownership and the hope of riches, the educated liberals who a few years before had been ready to die at the barricades for minimum-wage laws and equal suffrage and the right to collective bargaining were sinking into hopeless discouragement. Politics, they were deciding, was a vulgar mess; the morons always outnumbered the enlightened, the tobacco-spitting district leaders held the morons in a firm grip, and the right to vote was a joke. Welfare work was equally futile: it was stuffy, sentimental, and presumptuous. The bright young college graduate who in 1915 would have risked disinheritance to march in a Socialist parade yawned at Socialism in 1925, called it old stuff, and cared not at all whether the employees of the Steel Corporation were underpaid or overpaid. Fashions had changed: now the young insurgent enraged his father by arguing against monogamy and God.

When, however, the middle-class majority turned from persecuting political radicals to regulating personal conduct, they met with bitter opposition not only from the bright young college graduate but from the whole of a newly class-conscious group. The intellectuals of the country—the "civilized minority," as the *American Mercury* liked to call them—rose in loud and bitter revolt.

They were never an organized group, these embattled highbrows. They differed vehemently among themselves, and even if they had agreed, the idea of organizing would have been repugnant to them as individualists. They were widely dispersed; New York was their chief rallying-point, but groups of them were to be found in all the other urban centers. They consisted mostly of artists and writers, professional people, the intellectually restless element in the college towns, and such members of the college-educated business class as could digest more complicated literature than was to be found in the *Saturday Evening Post* and *McCall's Magazine;* and they were followed by an ill-assorted mob of faddists who were ready to take up with the latest idea. They may be roughly and inclusively defined as the men and women who had heard of James Joyce, Proust, Cézanne, Jung, Bertrand Russell, John Dewey, Petronius, Eugene O'Neill, and Eddington; who looked down on the movies but revered Charlie Chaplin as a great artist, could talk about relativity even if they could not understand it, knew a few of the leading complexes by name, collected Early American furniture, had ideas about progressive education, and doubted the divinity of Henry Ford and Calvin Coolidge. Few in numbers though they were, they were highly vocal, and their influence not merely dominated American literature but filtered down to affect by slow degrees the thought of the entire country.

These intellectuals felt the full disenchantment of the Peace of Versailles while the returning heroes of Armageddon were still parading past the reviewing-stands. The dreary story of a brutal war and a sordid settlement was spread before their resentful eyes in books like Sir Philip Gibbs's *Now It Can Be Told,* John Dos Passos's *Three Soldiers,* E. E. Cummings's *The Enormous Room,* and John Maynard Keynes's *Economic Consequences of the Peace.* They were early converts to the devastating new psychology; the more youthful of them, in fact, were petting according to Freud while their less tutored contemporaries were petting simply because they liked it and could get away with it. Many of the intellectuals had felt the loss of certainty which resulted from new scientific knowledge long before the word Fundamentalism had even been coined or the Einstein theory had reached the research laboratories.

Their revolt against the frock-coated respectability and decorous formality of American literature had been under way for several years; Theodore Dreiser, Willa Cather, Carl Sandburg, Edgar Lee Masters, Robert Frost, Vachel Lindsay, Amy Lowell, and the Imagists and exponents of free verse had been breaking new ground since before the war. When twenty of the intellectuals collaborated in the writing of *Civilization in the United States* (published in 1922 under the editorship of Harold Stearns) they summed up the opinion of thousands of their class in their agreement that "the most amusing and pathetic fact in the social life of America today is its emotional and æsthetic starvation." But the revolt of the highbrows against this emotional and æsthetic starvation, and against "the mania for petty regulation" to which it led, would hardly have gathered imposing force as soon as it did had Sinclair Lewis not brought out *Main Street* in October, 1920, and *Babbitt* some two years later.

The effect of these two books was overwhelming. In two volumes of merciless literary photography and searing satire, Lewis revealed the ugliness of the American small town, the cultural poverty of its life, the tyranny of its mass prejudices, and the blatant vulgarity and insularity of the booster. There were other things which he failed to reveal—such as the friendly sentiment and easy generosity of the Gopher Prairies and Zeniths of America—but his books were all the more widely devoured for their very one-sidedness. By the end of 1922 the sale of *Main Street* had reached 390,000 copies. The intellectuals had only to read Lewis's books to realize that the qualities in American life which they most despised and feared were precisely the ones which he put under the microscope for cold-blooded examination. It was George F. Babbitt who was the arch enemy of the enlightened, and it was the Main Street state of mind which stood in the way of American civilization.

After *Babbitt*, a flood of books reflected the dissatisfaction of the highbrows with the rule of America by the business man and their growing disillusionment. The keynoter of this revolt, its chief tomtom beater, was H. L. Mencken.

[2]

For several years Mencken, a Baltimorean trained in newspaper work on the *Baltimore Sun*, had been editing the *Smart*

Set in company with George Jean Nathan. The *Smart Set* did not prosper; its name and its somewhat dubious previous reputation were against it. When it was languishing Alfred A. Knopf, the book-publisher, engaged Mencken and Nathan to conduct a new monthly magazine addressed to the intellectual left wing, and the first issue of the *American Mercury* appeared at the close of 1923. This—if you are uncertain about dates—was a few weeks before Woodrow Wilson's death; it was at the moment when Senator Walsh was trying to find out who had bestowed money upon Secretary Fall, when Richard Simon was about to hatch the *Cross-Word Puzzle Book* idea, and the Bok Peace Prize was about to be awarded to Charles H. Levermore.

The green cover of the *Mercury* and its format were as sedate as the marble-trimmed façade of Mencken's house in Baltimore, but its contents were explosive. It carried over from the *Smart Set* as regular features Mencken's literary notes, Nathan's theatrical criticisms, a series of editorial jottings which had been called Répétition Generale and now became Clinical Notes, and a museum of American absurdities known as Americana. Every month Mencken occupied several pages with a polemic against the lowbrow majority and its works. The magazine lustily championed writers such as Dreiser, Cabell, Sherwood Anderson, Willa Cather, and Sinclair Lewis, who defied the polite traditions represented by the American Academy of Arts and Letters; it poured critical acid upon sentimentality and evasion and academic pomposity in books and in life; it lambasted Babbitts, Rotarians, Methodists, and reformers, ridiculed both the religion of Coolidge Prosperity and what Mencken called the "bilge of idealism," and looked upon the American scene in general with raucous and profane laughter.

The *Mercury* made an immediate hit. It was new, startling, and delightfully destructive. It crystallized the misgivings of thousands. Soon its green cover was clasped under the arms of the young iconoclasts of a score of college campuses. Staid small-town executives, happening upon it, were shocked and bewildered; this man Mencken, they decided, must be a debauched and shameless monster if not a latter-day emissary of the devil. When Mencken visited Dayton to report the Scopes trial and called the Daytonians yokels, hillbillies, and peasants, the Reverend A. C. Stribling replied that Mencken was a "cheap blatherskite of a pen-pusher"; and to such retorts there was a large section of outraged public opinion ready to cry Amen. After a few years so much abuse had been heaped upon the editor of the *Mercury* that it was possible to publish for the delectation of his admirers a *Schimpflexicon*—a book made up entirely of highly uncomplimentary references to him. Meanwhile the circulation of his magazine climbed to more than 77,-000 by 1927; and in that same year Walter Lippmann called him, without exaggeration, "the most powerful personal influence on this whole generation of educated people."

To many readers it seemed as if Mencken were against everything. This was not true, but certainly rebellion was the breath of his life. He was "against all theologians, professors, editorial-writers, right thinkers, and reformers" (to quote his own words). He was "against patriotism because it demands the acceptance of propositions that are obviously imbecile—*e.g.*, that an American Presbyterian is the equal of Anatole France, Brahms, or Ludendorff." He did not believe that "civilized life was possible under a democracy." He spoke of socialists and anarchists as fools. He was against prohibition, censorship, and all other interferences with personal liberty. He scoffed at morality and Christian marriage. There was an apparent inconsistency in this formidable collection of prejudices: how, some of his critics asked, could one expect an aristocracy of intellect, such as he preferred, to permit such liberties as he insisted upon, unless it happened to be made up entirely of Menckens—a rather unlikely premise? Inconsistencies, however, bothered Mencken not at all, and at first bothered few of his followers. For it was not easy to be coolly analytical in the face of such a prose style as he commanded.

He brought to his offensive against the lowbrows an unparalleled vocabulary of invective. He pelted his enemies with words and phrases like mountebank, charlatan, swindler, numskull, swine, witch-burner, *homo boobiens,* and imbecile; he said of sentimentalists that they squirted rosewater about, of Bryan that "he was born with a roaring voice and it had a trick of inflaming half-wits," of books which he disliked that they were garbage; he referred to the guileless farmers of Tennessee as "gaping primates" and "the anthropoid rabble." On occasion—as in his scholarly book on *The American Language*—Mencken could write measured and precise English, but when his blood was up, his weapons were gross exaggeration and gross metaphors. The moment he appeared the air was full of flying brick-bats; and to read him for the first time gave one, if not blind rage, the sort of intense visceral delight which comes from heaving baseballs at crockery in an amusement park.

The years when Mencken's wholesale idol-smashing first attracted wide attention, be it remembered, were the very years when the prosperity chorus was in full voice, Bruce Barton was revising Christian doctrine for the glorification of the higher salesmanship, the Fundamentalists were on the rampage against evolution, and the Methodist Board of Temperance, Prohibition, and Public Morals was trying to mold the country into sober conformity. Up to this time the intellectuals had been generally on the defensive. But now, with Mencken's noisy tub-thumping to give them assurance, they changed their tone. Other magazines joined, though less stridently, in the cry of dissent: *Harper's* put on an orange cover in 1925 and doubled its circulation by examining American life with a new critical boldness, *The Forum* debated subjects which Main Street considered undebatable, the *Atlantic* published the strictures of James Truslow Adams, and by the end of the decade even *Scribner's* was banned from the newsstands of Boston for printing a Hemingway serial. Books reflecting the intellectual minority's views of the United States and of life gushed from the presses. Slowly the volume of protest grew, until by 1926 or 1927 anybody who uttered a good word for Rotary or Bryan in any house upon whose walls hung a reproduction of Picasso or Marie Laurencin, or upon whose shelves stood *The Sun Also Rises* or *Notes on Democracy*, was likely to be set down as an incurable moron.

[3]

What was the credo of the intellectuals during these years of revolt? Not many of them accepted all the propositions in the following rough summary; yet it suggests, perhaps, the general drift of their collective opinion:

1. They believed in a greater degree of sex freedom than had been permitted by the strict American code; and as for discussion of sex, not only did they believe it should be free, but some of them appeared to believe it should be continuous. They formed the spearhead of the revolution in manners and morals which has been described in Chapter V. From the early

days of the decade, when they thrilled at the lackadaisical petting of F. Scott Fitzgerald's young thinkers and at the boldness of Edna St. Vincent Millay's announcement that her candle burned at both ends and could not last the night, to the latter days when they were all agog over the literature of homosexuality and went by the thousand to take Eugene O'Neill's five-hour lesson in psychopathology, *Strange Interlude,* they read about sex, talked about sex, thought about sex, and defied anybody to say No.

2. In particular, they defied the enforcement of propriety by legislation and detested all the influences to which they attributed it. They hated the Methodist lobby, John S. Sumner, and all other defenders of censorship; they pictured the Puritan, even of Colonial days, as a blue-nosed, cracked-voiced hypocrite; and they looked at Victorianism as half indecent and half funny. The literary reputations of Thackeray, Tennyson, Longfellow, and the Boston *literati* of the last century sank in their estimation to new lows for all time. Convinced that the era of short skirts and literary dalliance had brought a new enlightenment, the younger intellectuals laughed at the "Gay Nineties" as depicted in *Life* and joined Thomas Beer in condescending scrutiny of the voluminous dresses and fictional indirections of the Mauve Decade. Some of them, in fact, seemed to be persuaded that all periods prior to the coming of modernity had been ridiculous—with the exception of Greek civilization, Italy at the time of Casanova, France at the time of the great courtesans, and eighteenth-century England.

3. Most of them were passionate anti-prohibitionists, and this fact, together with their dislike of censorship and their skepticism about political and social regeneration, made them dubious about all reform movements and distrustful of all reformers. They emphatically did not believe that they were their brothers' keepers; anybody who did not regard tolerance as one of the supreme virtues was to them intolerable. If one heard at a single dinner party of advanced thinkers that there were "too many laws" and that people ought to be let alone, one heard it at a hundred. In 1915 the word reformer had been generally a complimentary term; in 1925 it had become— among the intellectuals, at least—a term of contempt.

4. They were mostly, though not all, religious skeptics. If there was less shouting agnosticism and atheism in the nineteen-twenties than in the eighteen-nineties it was chiefly

because disbelief was no longer considered sensational and because the irreligious intellectuals, feeling no evangelical urge to make over others in their own image, were content quietly to stay away from church. It is doubtful if any college undergraduate of the 'nineties or of any other previous period in the United States could have said "No intelligent person believes in God any more" as blandly as undergraduates said it during the discussions of compulsory college chapel which raged during the 'twenties. Never before had so many books addressed to the thinking public assumed at the outset that their readers had rejected the old theology.

5. They were united in a scorn of the great bourgeois majority which they held responsible for prohibition, censorship, Fundamentalism, and other repressions. They emulated Mencken in their disgust at Babbitts, Rotarians, the Ku-Klux Klan, Service-with-a-Smile, boosters, and super-salesmen. Those of them who lived in the urban centers prided themselves on their superiority to the denizens of the benighted outlying cities and towns where Babbittry flourished; witness, for example, the motto of the *New Yorker* when it was first established in the middle of the decade: "Not for the old lady from Dubuque." Particularly did they despise the mobs of prosperous American tourists which surged through Europe; one could hardly occupy a steamer chair next to anybody who had Aldous Huxley's latest novel on his lap without being told of a delightful little restaurant somewhere in France which was quite "unspoiled by Americans."

6. They took a particular pleasure in overturning the idols of the majority; hence the vogue among them of the practice for which W. E. Woodward, in a novel published in 1923, invented the word "debunking." Lytton Strachey's *Queen Victoria*, which had been a best seller in the United States in 1922, was followed by a deluge of debunking biographies. Rupert Hughes removed a few coats of whitewash from George Washington and nearly caused a riot when he declared in a speech that "Washington was a great card-player, a distiller of whisky, and a champion curser, and he danced for three hours without stopping with the wife of his principal general." Other American worthies were portrayed in all their erring humanity, and the notorious rascals of history were rediscovered as picturesque and glamorous fellows; until for a

time it was almost taken for granted that a biographer, if he were to be successful, must turn conventional white into black and *vice versa*.

7. They feared the effect upon themselves and upon American culture of mass production and the machine, and saw themselves as fighting at the last ditch for the right to be themselves in a civilization which was being leveled into monotony by Fordismus and the chain-store mind. Their hatred of regimentation gave impetus to the progressive school movement and nourished such innovations in higher education as Antioch, Rollins, Meiklejohn's Experimental College at Wisconsin, and the honors plan at Swarthmore and elsewhere. It gave equal impetus to the little-theater movement, which made remarkable headway from coast to coast, especially in the schools. The heroes of current novels were depicted as being stifled in the air of the home town, and as fleeing for their cultural lives either to Manhattan or, better yet, to Montparnasse or the Riviera. In any café in Paris one might find an American expatriate thanking his stars that he was free from standardization at last, oblivious of the fact that there was no more standardized institution even in the land of automobiles and radio than the French sidewalk café. The intellectuals lapped up the criticisms of American culture offered them by foreign lecturers imported in record-breaking numbers, and felt no resentment when the best magazines flaunted before their eyes, month after month, titles like "Our American Stupidity" and "Childish Americans." They quite expected to be told that America was sinking into barbarism and was an altogether impossible place for a civilized person to live in—as when James Truslow Adams lamented in the *Atlantic Monthly*, "I am wondering, as a personal but practical question, just how and where a man of moderate means who prefers simple living, simple pleasures, and the things of the mind is going to be able to live any longer in his native country."

Few of the American intellectuals of the nineteen-twenties, let it be repeated, subscribed to all the propositions in this credo; but he or she who accepted none of them was suspect among the enlightened. He was not truly civilized, he was not modern. The prosperity band-wagon rolled on, but by the wayside stood the highbrows with voices upraised in derision and dismay.

[4]

Mencken enjoyed his battle enormously, cynic though he was. He went on to meet the armed men, and said among the trumpets, Ha-ha. Everything might be wrong with American civilization, but at least it made a lovely target for his blunder-buss. "If you find so much that is unworthy of reverence in the United States, then why do you live here?" he asked himself in the Fifth Series of his *Prejudices,* only to answer, "Why do men go to zoos?" Nobody had such a good time in the American zoo as Mencken; he even got a good laugh out of the Tennessee anthropoids.

Not so, however, with most of his *confrères* in the camp of the intellectuals. The word disillusionment has been frequently employed in this history, for in a sense disillusionment (except about business and the physical luxuries and improvements which business would bring) was the keynote of the nineteen-twenties. With the majority of Americans its workings were perhaps unconscious; they felt a queer disappointment after the war, they felt that life was not giving them all they had hoped it would, they knew that some of the values which had once meant much to them were melting away, but they remained cheerful and full of gusto, quite unaware of the change which was taking place beneath the surface of their own minds. Most of the intellectuals, however, in America as else-where, knew all too well that they were disillusioned. Few of them, unfortunately, had grown up with as low expectations for humanity as Mencken. You cannot fully enjoy a zoo if you have been led to think of it as the home of an enlightened citizenry.

The intellectuals believed in a greater degree of sex freedom —and many of them found it disappointing when they got it, either in person or vicariously through books and plays. They were discovering that the transmutation of love into what Krutch called a "carefully catalogued psychosis" had robbed the loveliest passages of life of their poetry and their meaning. "Emotions," as Krutch said, "cannot be dignified unless they are first respected," and love was becoming too easy and too biological to be an object of respect. Elmer Davis referred in one of his essays to the heroine of a post-war novel who "indulged in 259 amours, if I remember correctly, without getting the emotional wallop out of any of them, or out of all of them together, that the lady of Victorian literature would have derived from a single competently conducted seduction." This busy heroine had many a literary counterpart and doubtless some in real life; and if one thing became clear to them, it was that romance cannot be put into quantity production, that the moment love becomes casual, it becomes commonplace as well. Even their less promiscuous contemporaries felt something of the sense of futility which came when romantic love was marked down.

As enemies of standardization and repression, the intellectuals believed in freedom—but freedom for what? Uncomfortable as it was to be harassed by prohibition agents and dictated to by chambers of commerce, it was hardly less comfortable in the long run to have their freedom and not know what to do with it. In all the nineteen-twenties there was no more dismal sight than that described by Richmond Barrett in an article in *Harper's* entitled "Babes in the Bois"—the sight of young Americans dashing to Paris to be free to do what Buffalo or Iowa City would not permit, and after being excessively rude to everybody they met and tasting a few short and tasteless love-affairs and soaking themselves in gin, finally passing out undecoratively under a table in the Café du Dôme. Mr. Barrett, to be sure, was portraying merely the lunatic fringe of the younger generation of intellectuals; but who during the nineteen-twenties did not recognize the type characterized in the title of one of Scott Fitzgerald's books as "All the Sad Young Men"? Wrote Walter Lippmann, "What most distinguishes the generation who have approached maturity since the débâcle of idealism at the end of the war is not their rebellion against the religion and the moral code of their parents, but their disillusionment with their own rebellion. It is common for young men and women to rebel, but that they should rebel sadly and without faith in their rebellion, and that they should distrust the new freedom no less than the old certainties—that is something of a novelty." It may be added that there were older and wiser heads than these who, in quite different ways, felt the unanswerability of the question, After freedom, what next?

They believed also, these intellectuals, in scientific truth and the scientific method—and science not only took their God away from them entirely, or reduced Him to a principle of order in the universe or a figment of the mind conjured up to meet a psychological need, but also reduced man, as Krutch pointed out in *The Modern Temper*, to a creature for whose ideas of right and wrong there was no transcendental authority. No longer was it possible to say with any positiveness, This is right, or, This is wrong; an act which was considered right in Wisconsin might be (according to the ethnologists) considered wrong in Borneo, and even in Wisconsin its merits seemed to be a matter of highly fallible human opinion. The certainty had departed from life. And what was worse still, it had departed from science itself. In earlier days those who denied the divine order had still been able to rely on a secure order of nature, but now even this was wabbling. Einstein and the quantum theory introduced new uncertainties and new doubts. Nothing, then, was sure; the purpose of life was undiscoverable, the ends of life were less discoverable still; in all this fog there was no solid thing on which a man could lay hold and say, This is real; this will abide.

[5]

Yet in all this uncertainty there was new promise for the intellectual life of the country. With the collapse of fixed values went a collapse of the old water-tight critical standards in the arts, opening the way for fresh and independent work to win recognition. Better still, the idea was gaining ground that this fresh and independent work might as well be genuinely native, that the time had come when the most powerful nation in the world might rid itself of its cultural subjection to Europe.

It was still hard to persuade the *cognoscenti* that first-class painting or music might come out of America. Rejecting scornfully the pretty confections of the Academicians, art collectors went in so wholeheartedly for the work of the French moderns and their imitators that the United States became almost—from the artistic point of view—a French colony. American orchestras remained under the domination of foreign conductors, played foreign compositions almost exclusively, and gave scant opportunity to the native composer. Even in art and music, however, there were signs of change. Artists were beginning to open their eyes to the pictorial possibilities of the skyscraper and the machine, and collectors waited only for George Bellows to die to bid up his rugged oils and lithographs of the American prize-ring. Music-lovers recognized at last the glory of the Negro spirituals, dabbled with the idea that George Gershwin might bridge the gap between popular jazz and vital music, permitted singers with such un-European names as Marion Talley and Lawrence Tibbett to become stars at the Metropolitan, and listened approvingly to an American opera (without, to be sure, an American subject) composed by Deems Taylor.

In architecture there was a somewhat more eager welcome for the indigenous product. Though the usual American country house was still a Georgian manor-house or a French farmhouse or a Spanish villa fitted out with bathrooms and a two-car garage, but trying to recapture, even in Lake Forest, what the real-estate agents called "Old World charm"; though the American bank was still a classical temple and there were still architects who tried to force the life of a modern American university into a medieval Gothic frame; nevertheless there was an increasing agreement with Lewis Mumford that new materials and new uses for them called for new treatment without benefit of the Beaux Arts. The *Chicago Tribune*'s competition early in the decade, and particularly the startling design by Saarinen which won second prize, suggested new possibilities for the skyscraper—possibilities at which Louis Sullivan and Frank Lloyd Wright and Cass Gilbert's Woolworth Building had already hinted. The skyscraper was peculiarly American—why not solve this problem of steel construction in a novel and American way? Gradually an American architecture began to evolve. Goodhue's Public Library in Los Angeles, his Nebraska State Capitol, Arthur Loomis Harmon's Shelton Hotel in New York, the Barclay-Vesey Telephone Building (by McKenzie, Voorhees & Gmelin and Ralph Thomas Loamas), and other fine achievements at least paved the way for something which might be the logical and beautiful expression of an American need.

Finally, in literature the foreign yoke was almost completely thrown off. Even if the intellectuals bought more foreign books than ever before and migrated by the thousands to Montparnasse and Antibes, they expected to write and to appreciate American literature. Their writing and their appreciation were both stimulated by Mencken's strenuous praise of uncompromisingly native work, by the establishment of good critical journals (such as the *Saturday Review of Literature*),

and by researches into the American background which disclosed such native literary material as the Paul Bunyan legends
and the cowboy ballads and such potential material as the
desperadoes of the frontier and the show-boats of the rivers.
There was a new ferment working, and at last there was an
audience quite unconvinced that American literature must be
forever inferior or imitative. Certainly a decade which produced Sinclair Lewis's *Arrowsmith,* Dreiser's *An American
Tragedy,* Hemingway's *A Farewell to Arms,* Willa Cather's
novels, Benet's *John Brown's Body,* some of the plays of Eugene O'Neill, and such short stories as Ring Lardner's "Golden
Honeymoon"—to make invidious mention of only a few per-
formances—could lay claim to something better than mere
promise for the future.

[6]

Gradually the offensive against Babbittry spent itself, if only
because the novelty of rebellion wore off. The circulation of
the *Mercury* (and with it, perhaps, the influence of its editor)
reached its peak in 1927 and thereafter slowly declined. The
New Yorker forgot the old lady from Dubuque and developed
a casual and altogether charming humor with malice toward
none; the other magazines consumed by the urban intelligentsia tired somewhat of viewing the American scene with alarm.
Sex fiction began to seem a little less adventurous and the
debunking fad ran its course. And similarly there began to be
signs, here and there, that the mental depression of the intellectuals might have seen its worst days.

In 1929—the very year which produced Krutch's *The Modern Temper,* a dismally complete statement of the philosophical disillusionment of the times—Walter Lippmann tried to lay
the foundations for a new system of belief and of ethics which
might satisfy even the disillusioned. The success of *A Preface
to Morals* suggested that many people were tired of toboggan-
ing into mental chaos. That same year there was a great hue
and cry among the highbrows over humanism. The humanist
fad was not without its comic aspect, since very few of those
who diligently talked about it were clear as to which of three or
four varieties of humanism they had in mind, and such clois-
tered beings as Paul Elmer More and Irving Babbitt were
hardly the leaders to rally a popular movement of any

dimensions; but it gave further evidence of a disposition among the doubters to dig in and face confusion along a new line of defense. There was also a widespread effort to find in the scientific philosophizing of Whitehead and Eddington and Jeans some basis for a belief that life might be worth living, after all. Perhaps the values which had been swept away during the post-war years had departed never to return, but at least there was a groping for new ones to take their place.

If there was, it came none too soon. For to many men and women the new day so sonorously heralded by the optimists and propagandists of war-time had turned into night before it ever arrived, and in the uncertain blackness they did not know which way to turn. They could revolt against stupidity and mediocrity, they could derive a meager pleasure from regarding themselves with pity as members of a lost generation, but they could not find peace.

X

Alcohol and Al Capone

If in the year 1919—when the Peace Treaty still hung in the balance, and Woodrow Wilson was chanting the praises of the League, and the Bolshevist bogey stalked across the land, and fathers and mothers were only beginning to worry about the Younger Generation—you had informed the average American citizen that prohibition was destined to furnish the most violently explosive public issue of the nineteen-twenties, he would probably have told you that you were crazy. If you had been able to sketch for him a picture of conditions as they were actually to be—rum-ships rolling in the sea outside the twelve-mile limit and transferring their cargoes of whisky by night to fast cabin cruisers, beer-running trucks being hijacked on the interurban boulevards by bandits with Thompson sub-machine guns, illicit stills turning out alcohol by the carload, the fashionable dinner party beginning with contraband cocktails as a matter of course, ladies and gentlemen undergoing scrutiny from behind the curtained grill of the speakeasy, and Alphonse Capone, multi-millionaire master of the Chicago bootleggers, driving through the streets in an armor-plated car with bullet-proof windows—the innocent citizen's jaw would have dropped. The Eighteenth Amendment had been ratified, to go into effect on January 16, 1920; and the Eighteenth Amendment, he had been assured and he firmly believed, had settled the prohibition issue. You might like it or not, but the country was going dry.

Nothing in recent American history is more extraordinary, as one looks back from the nineteen-thirties, than the ease with which—after generations of uphill fighting by the drys—prohibition was finally written upon the statute-books. The country accepted it not only willingly, but almost absent-mindedly. When the Eighteenth Amendment came before the Senate in 1917, it was passed by a one-sided vote after only thirteen hours of debate, part of which was conducted under the ten-minute rule. When the House of Representatives accepted it a few months later, the debate upon the Amendment as a whole occupied only a single day. The state legislatures ratified it in short order; by January, 1919, some two months after the Armistice, the necessary three-quarters of the states had fallen into line and the Amendment was a part of the Constitution. (All the rest of the states but two subsequently added their ratifications—only Connecticut and Rhode Island remained outside the pale.) The Volstead Act for the enforcement of the Amendment, drafted after a pattern laid down by the Anti-Saloon League, slipped through with even greater ease and dispatch. Woodrow Wilson momentarily surprised the country by vetoing it, but it was promptly repassed over his veto. There were scattered protests—a mass-meeting in New York, a parade in Baltimore, a resolution passed by the American Federation of Labor demanding modification in order that the workman might not be deprived of his beer, a noisy demonstration before the Capitol in Washington—but so half-hearted and ineffective were the forces of the opposition and so completely did the country as a whole take for granted the inevitability of a dry régime, that few of the arguments in the press or about the dinner table raised the question whether the law would or would not prove enforceable; the burning question was what a really dry country would be like, what effect enforced national sobriety would have upon industry, the social order, and the next generation.

How did it happen? Why this overwhelming, this almost casual acceptance of a measure of such huge importance?

As Charles Merz has clearly shown in his excellent history of the first ten years of the prohibition experiment, the forces behind the Amendment were closely organized; the forces

opposed to the Amendment were hardly organized at all. Until
the United States entered the war, the prospect of national
prohibition had seemed remote, and it is always hard to mobilize an unimaginative public against a vague threat. Furthermore, the wet leadership was discredited; for it was furnished
by the dispensers of liquor, whose reputation had been unsavory and who had obstinately refused to clean house even in
the face of a growing agitation for temperance.

The entrance of the United States into the war gave the dry
leaders their great opportunity. The war diverted the attention
of those who might have objected to the bone-dry program:
with the very existence of the nation at stake, the future status
of alcohol seemed a trifling matter. The war accustomed the
country to drastic legislation conferring new and wide powers
upon the Federal Government. It necessitated the saving of
food and thus commended prohibition to the patriotic as a
grain-saving measure. It turned public opinion against everything German—and many of the big brewers and distillers
were of German origin. The war also brought with it a mood
of Spartan idealism of which the Eighteenth Amendment was a
natural expression. Everything was sacrificed to efficiency,
production, and health. If a sober soldier was a good soldier
and a sober factory hand was a productive factory hand, the
argument for prohibition was for the moment unanswerable.
Meanwhile the American people were seeing Utopian visions;
if it seemed possible to them that the war should end all wars
and that victory should bring a new and shining world order,
how much easier to imagine that America might enter an
endless era of efficient sobriety! And finally, the war made
them impatient for immediate results. In 1917 and 1918,
whatever was worth doing at all was worth doing at once,
regardless of red tape, counter-arguments, comfort, or convenience. The combination of these various forces was irresistible.
Fervently and with headlong haste the nation took the short
cut to a dry Utopia.

Almost nobody, even after the war had ended, seemed to
have any idea that the Amendment would be really difficult to
enforce. Certainly the first Prohibition Commissioner, John F.
Kramer, displayed no doubts. "This law," he declared in a
burst of somewhat Scriptural rhetoric, "will be obeyed in cities,
large and small, and in villages, and where it is not obeyed it
will be enforced. . . . The law says that liquor to be used as a

beverage must not be manufactured. We shall see that it is not manufactured. Nor sold, nor given away, nor hauled in anything on the surface of the earth or under the earth or in the air." The Anti-Saloon League estimated that an appropriation by Congress of five million dollars a year would be ample to secure compliance with the law (including, presumably, the prevention of liquor-hauling "under the earth"). Congress voted not much more than that, heaved a long sigh of relief at having finally disposed of an inconvenient and vexatious issue, and turned to other matters of more pressing importance. The morning of January 16, 1920, arrived and the era of promised aridity began. Only gradually did the dry leaders, or Congress, or the public at large begin to perceive that the problem with which they had so light-heartedly grappled was a problem of gigantic proportions.

[2]

Obviously the surest method of enforcement was to shut off the supply of liquor at its source. But consider what this meant.

The coast lines and land borders of the United States offered an 18,700-mile invitation to smugglers. Thousands of druggists were permitted to sell alcohol on doctors' prescriptions, and this sale could not be controlled without close and constant inspection. Near-beer was still within the law, and the only way to manufacture near-beer was to brew real beer and then remove the alcohol from it—and it was excessively easy to fail to remove it from the entire product. The manufacture of industrial alcohol opened up inviting opportunities for diversion which could be prevented only by watchful and intelligent inspection—and after the alcohol left the plant where it was produced, there was no possible way of following it down the line from purchaser to purchaser and making sure that the ingredients which had been thoughtfully added at the behest of the Government to make it undrinkable were not extracted by ingenious chemists. Illicit distilling could be undertaken almost anywhere, even in the householder's own cellar; a commercial still could be set up for five hundred dollars which would produce fifty or a hundred highly remunerative gallons a day, and a one-gallon portable still could be bought for only six or seven dollars.

To meet all these potential threats against the Volstead Act,

the Government appropriations provided a force of prohibition agents which in 1920 numbered only 1,520 men and
as late as 1930 numbered only 2,836; even with the sometimes unenthusiastic aid of the Coast Guard and the Cus-
toms Service and the Immigration Service, the force was
meager. Mr. Merz puts it graphically: if the whole army of
agents in 1920 had been mustered along the coasts and borders
—paying no attention for the moment to medicinal alcohol,
breweries, industrial alcohol, or illicit stills—there would have
been one man to patrol every twelve miles of beach, harbor,
headland, forest, and river-front. The agents' salaries in 1920
mostly ranged between $1,200 and $2,000; by 1930 they had
been munificently raised to range between $2,300 and $2,800.
Anybody who believed that men employable at thirty-five or
forty or fifty dollars a week would surely have the expert
technical knowledge and the diligence to supervise successfully
the complicated chemical operations of industrial-alcohol
plants or to outwit the craftiest devices of smugglers and bootleggers, and that they would surely have the force of character
to resist corruption by men whose pockets were bulging with
money, would be ready to believe also in Santa Claus, perpetual
motion, and pixies.

Yet even this body of prohibition agents, small and underpaid as it was in view of the size and complexity of its task and
the terrific pressure of temptation, might conceivably have
choked off the supply of alcohol if it had had the concerted
backing of public opinion. But public opinion was changing.
The war was over; by 1920 normalcy was on the way. The dry
cause confronted the same emotional let-down which defeated
Woodrow Wilson and hastened the Revolution in Manners and
Morals. Spartan idealism was collapsing. People were tired of
girding up their loins to serve noble causes. They were tired of
making the United States a land fit for heroes to live in. They
wanted to relax and be themselves. The change of feeling
toward prohibition was bewilderingly rapid. Within a few short
months it was apparent that the Volstead Act was being
smashed right and left and that the formerly inconsiderable
body of wet opinion was growing to sizable proportions. The
law was on the statute-books, the Prohibition Bureau was
busily plying its broom against the tide of alcohol, and the
corner saloon had become a memory; but the liquorless millen-
nium had nevertheless been indefinitely postponed.

[3]

The events of the next few years present one of those paradoxes which fascinate the observer of democratic government. Obviously there were large sections of the country in which prohibition was not prohibiting. A rational observer would have supposed that the obvious way out of this situation would be either to double or treble or quadruple the enforcement squad or to change the law. But nothing of the sort was done. The dry leaders, being unwilling to admit that the task of mopping up the United States was bigger than they had expected, did not storm the Capitol to recommend huge increases in the appropriations for enforcement; it was easier to denounce the opponents of the law as Bolshevists and destroyers of civilization and to hope that the tide of opinion would turn again. Congress was equally unwilling to face the music; there was a comfortable dry majority in both Houses, but it was one thing to be a dry and quite another to insist on enforcement at whatever cost and whatever inconvenience to some of one's influential constituents. The Executive was as wary of the prohibition issue as of a large stick of dynamite; the contribution of Presidents Harding and Coolidge to the problem—aside from negotiating treaties which increased the three-mile limit to twelve miles, and trying to improve the efficiency of enforcement without calling for too much money from Congress—consisted chiefly of uttering resounding platitudes on the virtues of law observance. The state governments were supposed to help the Prohibition Bureau, but by 1927 their financial contribution to the cause was about one-eighth of the sum they spent enforcing their own fish and game laws. Some legislatures withdrew their aid entirely, and even the driest states were inclined to let Uncle Sam bear the brunt of the Volstead job. Local governments were supposed to war against the speakeasy, but did it with scant relish except where local opinion was insistent. Nor could the wets, for their part, agree upon any practical program. It seemed almost hopeless to try to repeal or modify the Amendment, and for the time being they contented themselves chiefly with loud and indignant lamentation. The law was not working as it had been intended to, but nobody seemed willing or able to do anything positive about it one way or the other.

Rum-ships plied from Bimini or Belize or St. Pierre, entering American ports under innocent disguises or transferring their cargoes to fast motor-boats which could land in any protected cove. Launches sped across the river at Detroit with good Canadian whisky aboard. Freighters brought in cases of contraband gin mixed among cases of other perfectly legal and properly labeled commodities. Liquor was hidden in freightcars crossing the Canadian border; whole carfuls of whisky were sometimes smuggled in by judicious manipulation of seals. These diverse forms of smuggling were conducted with such success that in 1925 General Lincoln C. Andrews, Assistant Secretary of the Treasury in charge of enforcement, hazarded the statement that his agents succeeded in intercepting only about 5 per cent of the liquor smuggled into the country; and the value of the liquor which filtered in during the single year 1924 was estimated by the Department of Commerce at $40,000,000! Beer leaked profusely from the breweries; alley breweries unknown to the dry agents flourished and coined money. The amount of industrial alcohol illegally diverted was variously estimated in the middle years of the decade at from thirteen to fifteen million gallons a year; and even in 1930, after the Government had improved its technic of dealing with this particular source of supply (by careful control of the permit system and otherwise), the Director of Prohibition admitted that the annual diversion still amounted to nine million gallons, and other estimates ran as high as fifteen. (Bear in mind that one gallon of diverted alcohol, watered down and flavored, was enough to furnish three gallons of bogus liquor, bottled with lovely Scotch labels and described by the bootlegger at the leading citizen's door as "just off the boat.")

As for illicit distilling, as time went on this proved the most copious of all sources of supply. At the end of the decade it furnished, on the testimony of Doctor Doran of the prohibition staff, perhaps seven or eight times as much alcohol as even the process of diversion. If anything was needed to suggest how ubiquitous was the illicit still in America, the figures for the production of corn sugar provided it. Between 1919 and 1929 the output of this commodity increased *sixfold*, despite the fact that, as the Wickersham Report put it, the legitimate uses of corn sugar "are few and not easy to ascertain." Undoubtedly corn whisky was chiefly responsible for the vast increase.

This overwhelming flood of outlaw liquor introduced into the American scene a series of picturesque if unedifying phenomena: hip flasks uptilted above faces both masculine and feminine at the big football games; the speakeasy, equipped with a regular old-fashioned bar, serving cocktails made of gin turned out, perhaps, by a gang of Sicilian alky-cookers (seventy-five cents for patrons, free to the police); well-born damsels with one foot on the brass rail, tossing off Martinis; the keg of grape juice simmering hopefully in the young couple's bedroom closet, subject to periodical inspection by a young man sent from a "service station"; the business executive departing for the trade convention with two bottles of gin in his bag; the sales manager serving lavish drinks to the visiting buyer as in former days he had handed out lavish boxes of cigars; the hotel bellhop running to Room 417 with another order of ginger ale and cracked ice, provided by the management on the ironical understanding that they were "not to be mixed with spirituous liquors"; federal attorneys padlocking nightclubs and speakeasies, only to find them opening shortly at another address under a different name; Izzy Einstein and Moe Smith, prohibition agents extraordinary, putting on a series of comic-opera disguises to effect miraculous captures of bootleggers; General Smedley Butler of the Marines advancing in military formation upon the rum-sellers of Philadelphia, and retiring in disorder after a few strenuous months with the admission that politics made it impossible to dry up the city; the Government putting wood alcohol and other poisons into industrial alcohol to prevent its diversion, and the wets thereupon charging the Government with murder; Government agents, infuriated by their failure to prevent liquor-running by polite methods, finally shooting to kill—and sometimes picking off an innocent by-stander; the good ship *I'm Alone*, of Canadian registry, being pursued by a revenue boat for two and a half days and sunk at a distance of 215 miles from the American coast, to the official dismay of the Canadian Government; the federal courts jammed with prohibition cases, jurymen in wet districts refusing to pronounce bootleggers guilty, and the coin of corruption sifting through the hands of all manner of public servants.

Whatever the contribution of the prohibition régime to temperance, at least it produced intemperate propaganda and counter-propaganda. Almost any dry could tell you that prohi-

bition was the basis of American prosperity, as attested by the
mounting volume of saving-banks deposits and by what some
big manufacturer had said about the men returning to work on
Monday morning with clear eyes and steady hands. Or that
prohibition had reduced the deaths from alcoholism, emptied
the jails, and diverted the workman's dollar to the purchase of
automobiles, radios, and homes. Almost any wet could tell you
that prohibition had nothing to do with prosperity but had
caused the crime wave, the increase of immorality and of the
divorce rate, and a disrespect for all law which imperiled the
very foundations of free government. The wets said the drys
fostered Bolshevism by their fanatical zeal for laws which were
inevitably flouted; the drys said the wets fostered Bolshevism
by their cynical lawbreaking. Even in matters of supposed fact
you could find, if you only read and listened, any sort of am-
munition that you wanted. One never saw drunkards on the
streets any more; one saw more drunkards than ever. Drinking
in the colleges was hardly a problem now; drinking in the
colleges was at its worst. There was a still in every other home
in the mining districts of Pennsylvania; drinking in the mining
districts of Pennsylvania was a thing of the past. Cases of
poverty as a result of drunkenness were only a fraction of what
they used to be; the menace of drink in the slums was three
times as great as in pre-Volstead days. Bishop A and Doctor B
and Governor C were much encouraged by the situation;
Bishop X and Doctor Y and Governor Z were appalled by it.
And so the battle raged, endlessly and loudly, back and forth.

The mass of statistics dragged to light by professional drys
and professional wets and hurled at the public need not detain
us here. Many of them were grossly unreliable, and the use of
most of them would have furnished an instructor in logic with
perfect specimens of the *post hoc* fallacy. It is perhaps enough
to point out a single anomaly—that with the Eighteenth
Amendment and the Volstead Act in force, there should
actually have been constant and vociferous argument throughout the nineteen-twenties over the question whether there was
more drinking or less in the United States than before the war.
Presumably there was a good deal less except among the prosperous; but the fact that it was not transparently obvious that
there was less, showed how signal was the failure of the law to
accomplish what almost everyone in 1919 had supposed it
would accomplish.

[4]

By 1928 the argument over prohibition had reached such intensity that it could no longer be kept out of presidential politics. Governor Smith of New York was accepted as the Democratic nominee despite his unterrified wetness, and campaigned lustily for two modifications: first, an amendment to the Volstead law giving a "scientific definition of the alcoholic content of an intoxicating beverage" (a rather large order for science), each state being allowed to fix its own standard if this did not exceed the standard fixed by Congress; and second, "an amendment in the Eighteenth Amendment which would give to each individual state itself, only after approval by a referendum popular vote of its people, the right wholly within its borders to import, manufacture, or cause to be manufactured and sell alcoholic beverages, the sale to be made only by the state itself and not for consumption in any public place." The Republican candidate, in reply, stepped somewhat definitely off the fence on the dry side. Herbert Hoover's dry declaration, to be sure, left much unsaid; he called prohibition "a great social and economic experiment, noble in motive and far-reaching in purpose," but he did not claim nobility for its results. The omission, however, was hardly noticed by an electorate which regarded indorsement of motives as virtually equivalent to indorsement of performance. Hoover was considered a dry.

The Republican candidate was elected in a landslide, and the drys took cheer. Despite the somewhat equivocal results of various state referenda and straw ballots, they had always claimed that they had a substantial majority in the country as well as in Congress; now they were sure of it. Still the result of the election left room for haunting doubts. Who could tell whether the happy warrior from the East Side had been defeated because he was a wet, or because he was a Roman Catholic, or because he was considered a threat to the indefinite continuance of the delights of Coolidge Prosperity, or because he was a Democrat?

But Herbert Hoover had done more than endorse the motives of the prohibitionists. He had promised a study of the enforcement problem by a governmental commission. Two and a half months after his arrival at the White House, the commission, consisting of eleven members under the chairmanship of George W. Wickersham of New York, was appointed and immersed itself in its prodigious task.

By the time the Wickersham Commission emerged from the sea of fact and theory and contention in which it had been delving, and handed its report to the President, the Post-war Decade was dead and done with. Not until January, 1931, nineteen months after his appointment, did Mr. Wickersham lay the bulky findings of the eleven investigators upon the presidential desk. Yet the report calls for mention here, if only because it represented the findings of a group of intelligent and presumably impartial people with regard to one of the critical problems of the nineteen-twenties.

It was a paradoxical document. In the first place, the complete text revealed very clearly the sorry inability of the enforcement staff to dry up the country. In the second place, each of the eleven commissioners submitted a personal report giving his individual views, and only five of the eleven—a minority—favored further trial for the prohibition experiment without substantial change; four of them favored modification of the Amendment, and two were for outright repeal. But the commission *as a whole* cast its vote for further trial, contenting itself with suggesting a method of modification if time proved that the experiment was a failure. The confusing effect of the report was neatly satirized in Flaccus's summary of it in F. P. A.'s column in the *New York World*:

> Prohibition is an awful flop.
>   We like it.
> It can't stop what it's meant to stop.
>   We like it.
> It's left a trail of graft and slime,
> It's filled our land with vice and crime,
> It don't prohibit worth a dime,
>   Nevertheless we're for it.

Yet if the Wickersham report was confusing, this was highly appropriate; for so also was the situation with which it dealt. Although it seemed reasonably clear to an impartial observer that the country had chosen the wrong road in 1917-20, legislating with a sublime disregard for elementary chemistry—which might have taught it how easily alcohol may be manufactured—and for elementary psychology—which might have suggested that common human impulses are not easily suppressed by fiat—it was nevertheless very far from clear how the country could best extricate itself from the morass into which it had so blithely plunged. How could people who had become gin-drinkers be expected to content themselves with light wines and beers, as some of the modificationists suggested? How could any less drastic system of governmental regulation or governmental sale of liquor operate without continued transgression and corruption, now that a large element had learned how to live with impunity on the fruits of lawbreaking? To what sinister occupations might not the bootlegging gentry turn if outright repeal took their accustomed means of livelihood away from them? How could any new national policy toward alcohol be successfully put into effect when there was still violent disagreement, even among those who wanted the law changed, as to whether alcohol should be regarded as a curse, as a blessing to be used in moderation, or as a matter of personal rather than public concern? Even if a clear majority of the American people were able to decide to their own satisfaction what was the best way out of the morass, what chance was there of putting through their program when thirteen dry states could block any change in the Amendment? No problem which had ever faced the United States had seemed more nearly insoluble.

[5]

In 1920, when prohibition was very young, Johnny Torrio of Chicago had an inspiration. Torrio was a formidable figure in the Chicago underworld. He had discovered that there was big money in the newly outlawed liquor business. He was fired with the hope of getting control of the dispensation of booze to the whole city of Chicago. At the moment there was a great deal too much competition; but possibly a well-disciplined gang of men handy with their fists and their guns could take care of that, by intimidating rival bootleggers and persuading speakeasy proprietors that life might not be wholly comfortable for them unless they bought Torrio liquor. What Torrio needed was a lieutenant who could mobilize and lead his shock troops.

Being a graduate of the notorious Five Points gang in New York and a disciple of such genial fellows as Lefty Louie and Gyp the Blood (he himself had been questioned about the murder of Herman Rosenthal in the famous Becker case in 1912), he naturally turned to his *alma mater* for his man. He picked for the job a bullet-headed twenty-three-year-old Neapolitan roughneck of the Five Points gang, and offered him a generous income and half the profits of the bootleg trade if he would come to Chicago and take care of the competition. The young hoodlum came, established himself at Torrio's gambling-place, the Four Deuces, opened by way of plausible stage setting an innocent-looking office which contained among its properties a family Bible, and had a set of business cards printed:

ALPHONSE CAPONE

Second Hand Furniture Dealer   2220 South Wabash Avenue

Torrio had guessed right—in fact, he had guessed right three times. The profits of bootlegging in Chicago proved to be prodigious, allowing an ample margin for the mollification of the forces of the law. The competition proved to be exacting: every now and then Torrio would discover that his rivals had approached a speakeasy proprietor with the suggestion that he buy their beer instead of the Torrio-Capone brand, and on receipt of an unfavorable answer had beaten the proprietor senseless and smashed up his place of business. But Al Capone had been an excellent choice as leader of the Torrio offensives; Capone was learning how to deal with such emergencies.

Within three years it was said that the boy from the Five Points had seven hundred men at his disposal, many of them adept in the use of the sawed-off shotgun and the Thompson sub-machine gun. As the profits from beer and "alky-cooking" (illicit distilling) rolled in, young Capone acquired more finesse —particularly finesse in the management of politics and politicians. By the middle of the decade he had gained complete control of the suburb of Cicero, had installed his own mayor in office, had posted his agents in the wide-open gambling-resorts and in each of the 161 bars, and had established his personal headquarters in the Hawthorne Hotel. He was taking in millions now. Torrio was fading into the background; Capone was becoming the Big Shot. But his conquest of power did not come without bloodshed. As the rival gangs—the O'Banions, the Gennas, the Aiellos—disputed his growing domination, Chicago was afflicted with such an epidemic of killings as no civilized modern city had ever before seen, and a new technic of wholesale murder was developed.

One of the standard methods of disposing of a rival in this warfare of the gangs was to pursue his car with a stolen automobile full of men armed with sawed-off shotguns and submachine guns; to draw up beside it, forcing it to the curb, open fire upon it—and then disappear into the traffic, later abandoning the stolen car at a safe distance. Another favorite method was to take the victim "for a ride": in other words, to lure him into a supposedly friendly car, shoot him at leisure, drive to some distant and deserted part of the city, and quietly throw his body overboard. Still another was to lease an apartment or a room overlooking his front door, station a couple of hired assassins at the window, and as the victim emerged from the house some sunny afternoon, to spray him with a few dozen machine-gun bullets from behind drawn curtains. But there were also more ingenious and refined methods of slaughter.

Take, for example, the killing of Dion O'Banion, leader of the gang which for a time most seriously menaced Capone's reign in Chicago. The preparation of this particular murder was reminiscent of the kiss of Judas. O'Banion was a bootlegger and a gangster by night, but a florist by day: a strange and complex character, a connoisseur of orchids and of manslaughter. One morning a sedan drew up outside his flower shop and three men got out, leaving the fourth at the wheel. The three men had apparently taken good care to win O'Banion's trust, for although he always carried three guns, now for the moment he was off his guard as he advanced among the flowers to meet his visitors. The middle man of the three cordially shook hands with O'Banion—*and then held on* while his two companions put six bullets into the gangster-florist. The three conspirators walked out, climbed into the sedan, and departed. They were never brought to justice, and it is not recorded that any of them hung themselves to trees in remorse. O'Banion had a first-class funeral, gangster style: a ten-thousand-dollar casket, twenty-six truckloads of flowers, and among them a basket of flowers which bore the touching inscription, "From Al."

In 1926 the O'Banions, still unrepentant despite the loss of their leader, introduced another novelty in gang warfare. In broad daylight, while the streets of Cicero were alive with

traffic, they raked Al Capone's headquarters with machine-gun
fire from eight touring cars. The cars proceeded down the
crowded street outside the Hawthorne Hotel in solemn line, the
first one firing blank cartridges to disperse the innocent citizenry and to draw the Capone forces to the doors and windows, while from the succeeding cars, which followed a block
behind, flowed a steady rattle of bullets, spraying the hotel and
the adjoining buildings up and down. One gunman even got
out of his car, knelt carefully upon the sidewalk at the door of
the Hawthorne, and played one hundred bullets into the lobby
—back and forth, as one might play the hose upon one's garden. The casualties were miraculously light, and Scarface Al
himself remained in safety, flat on the floor of the Hotel Hawthorne restaurant; nevertheless, the bombardment quite
naturally attracted public attention. Even in a day when bul-
lion was transported in armored cars, the transformation of a
suburban street into a shooting-gallery seemed a little unorthodox.

The war continued, one gangster after another crumpling
under a rain of bullets; not until St. Valentine's Day of 1929
did it reach its climax in a massacre which outdid all that had
preceded it in ingenuity and brutality. At half-past ten on the
morning of February 14, 1929, seven of the O'Banions were
sitting in the garage which went by the name of the S. M. C.
Cartage Company, on North Clark Street, waiting for a promised consignment of hijacked liquor. A Cadillac touring-car
slid to the curb, and three men dressed as policemen got out,
followed by two others in civilian dress. The three supposed
policemen entered the garage alone, disarmed the seven O'Banions, and told them to stand in a row against the wall. The
victims readily submitted; they were used to police raids and
thought nothing of them; they would get off easily enough,
they expected. But thereupon the two men in civilian clothes
emerged from the corridor and calmly mowed down all seven
O'Banions with sub-machine gun fire as they stood with hands
upraised against the wall. The little drama was completed when
the three supposed policemen solemnly marched the two plain-
clothes killers across the sidewalk to the waiting car, and all
five got in and drove off—having given to those in the wintry
street a perfect tableau of an arrest satisfactorily made by the
forces of the law!

These killings—together with that of "Jake" Lingle, who led

a double life as reporter for the *Chicago Tribune* and as associate of gangsters, and who was shot to death in a crowded subway leading to the Illinois Central suburban railway station in 1930—were perhaps the most spectacular of the decade in Chicago. But there were over five hundred gang murders in all. Few of the murderers were apprehended; careful planning, money, influence, the intimidation of witnesses, and the refusal of any gangster to testify against any other, no matter how treacherous the murder, met that danger. The city of Chicago was giving the whole country, and indeed the whole world, an astonishing object lesson in violent and unpunished crime. How and why could such a thing happen?

To say that prohibition—or, if you prefer, the refusal of the public to abide by prohibition—caused the rise of the gangs to lawless power would be altogether too easy an explanation. There were other causes: the automobile, which made escape easy, as the officers of robbed banks had discovered; the adaptation to peace-time use of a new arsenal of handy and deadly weapons; the murderous traditions of the Mafia, imported by Sicilian gangsters; the inclination of a wet community to wink at the by-products of a trade which provided them with beer and gin; the sheer size and unwieldiness of the modern metropolitan community, which prevented the focusing of public opinion upon any depredation which did not immediately concern the average individual citizen; and, of course, the easy-going political apathy of the times. But the immediate occasion of the rise of gangs was undoubtedly prohibition—or, to be more precise, beer-running. (Beer rather than whisky on account of its bulk; to carry on a profitable trade in beer one must transport it in trucks, and trucks are so difficult to disguise that the traffic must be protected by bribery of the prohibition staff and the police and by gunfire against bandits.) There was vast profit in the manufacture, transportation, and sale of beer. In 1927, according to Fred D. Pasley, Al Capone's biographer, federal agents estimated that the Capone gang controlled the sources of a revenue from booze of something like sixty million dollars a year, and much of this—perhaps most of it—came from beer. Fill a man's pockets with money, give him a chance at a huge profit, put him into an illegal business and thus deny him recourse to the law if he is attacked, and you have made it easy for him to bribe and shoot. There have always been gangs and gangsters in American life and doubtless always will be; there has always been corruption of city officials and doubtless always will be; yet it is ironically true, none the less, that the outburst of corruption and crime in Chicago in the nineteen-twenties was immediately occasioned by the attempt to banish the temptations of liquor from the American home.

The young thug from the Five Points, New York, had traveled fast and far since 1920. By the end of the decade he had become as widely renowned as Charles Evans Hughes or Gene Tunney. He had become an American portent. Not only did he largely control the sale of liquor to Chicago's ten thousand speakeasies; he controlled the sources of supply, it was said, as far as Canada and the Florida coast. He had amassed, and concealed, a fortune the extent of which nobody knew; it was said by federal agents to amount to twenty millions. He was arrested and imprisoned once in Philadelphia for carrying a gun, but otherwise he seemed above the law. He rode about Chicago in an armored car, a traveling fortress, with another car to patrol the way ahead and a third car full of his armed henchmen following behind; he went to the theater attended by a body-guard of eighteen young men in dinner coats, with guns doubtless slung under their left armpits in approved gangster fashion; when his sister was married, thousands milled about the church in the snow, and he presented the bride with a nine-foot wedding cake and a special honeymoon car; he had a fine estate at Miami where he sometimes entertained seventy-five guests at a time; and even, it has been said, judges—took orders from him over the telephone from his headquarters in a downtown Chicago hotel. And still he was only thirty-two years old. What was Napoleon doing at thirty-two?

Meanwhile gang rule and gang violence were quickly penetrating other American cities. Toledo had felt them, and Detroit, and New York, and many another. Chicago was not alone. Chicago had merely led the way.

[6]

By the middle of the decade it was apparent that the gangs were expanding their enterprises. In Mr. Pasley's analysis of the gross income of the Capone crew in 1927, as estimated by federal agents, the item of $60,000,000 from beer and liquor, including alky-cooking, and the items of $25,000,000 from gambling-establishments and dog-tracks, and of $10,000,000 from vice, dance-halls, roadhouses, and other resorts, were followed by this entry: Rackets, $10,000,000. The bootlegging underworld was venturing into fresh fields and pastures new.

The word "racket," in the general sense of an occupation which produces easy money, is of venerable age: it was employed over fifty years ago in Tammany circles in New York. But it was not widely used in its present meaning until the middle nineteen-twenties, and the derived term "racketeering" did not enter the American vocabulary until the year when Sacco and Vanzetti were executed and Lindbergh flew the Atlantic and Calvin Coolidge did not choose to run—the year 1927. The name was a product of the Post-war Decade; and so was the activity to which it was attached.

Like the murderous activities of the bootlegging gangs, racketeering grew out of a complex of causes. One of these was violent labor unionism. Since the days of the Molly Maguires, organized labor had now and again fought for its rights with brass knuckles and bombs. During the Big Red Scare the labor unions had lost the backing of public opinion, and Coolidge Prosperity was making things still more difficult for them by persuading thousands of their members that a union card was not the only ticket to good fortune. More than one fighting labor leader thereupon turned once more to dynamite in the effort to maintain his job and his power. Gone was the ardent radicalism of 1919, the hope of a new industrial order; the labor leader now found himself simply a man who hoped to get his when others were getting theirs, a man tempted to smash the scab's face or to blow the roof off the anti-union factory to show that he meant business and could deliver the goods. In many cases he turned for aid to the hired thug, the killer; he protected himself from the law by bribery or at least by political influence; he connived with business men who were ready to play his game for their own protection or for profit. These unholy alliances were now the more easily achieved because the illicit liquor trade was making the underworld rich and confident and quick on the trigger and was accustoming many politicians and business men to large-scale graft and conspiracy. Gangsters and other crafty fellows learned of the labor leader's tricks and went out to organize rackets on their own account. Thus by 1927 the city which had nourished Al Capone was nourishing also a remarkable assortment of these curious enterprises.

Some of them were labor unions perverted to criminal ends; some were merely conspiracies for extortion masquerading as labor unions; others were conspiracies masquerading as trade associations, or were combinations of these different forms. But the basic principle was fairly uniform: the racket was a scheme for collecting cash from business men to protect them from damage, and it prospered because the victim soon learned that if he did not pay, his shop would be bombed, or his trucks wrecked, or he himself might be shot in cold blood—and never a chance to appeal to the authorities for aid, because the authorities were frightened or fixed.

There was the cleaners' and dyers' racket, which collected heavy dues from the proprietors of retail cleaning shops and from master cleaners, and for a time so completely controlled the industry in Chicago that it could raise the price which the ordinary citizen paid for having his suit cleaned from $1.25 to $1.75. A cleaner and dyer who defied this racket might have his place of business bombed, or his delivery truck drenched with gasoline and set on fire, or he might be disciplined in a more devilish way: explosive chemicals might be sewn into the seams of trousers sent to him to be cleaned. There was the garage racket, product of the master mind of David Ablin, alias "Cockeye" Mulligan: if a garage owner chose not to join in the Mid-West Garage Association, as this enterprise was formally entitled, his garage would be bombed, or his mechanics would be slugged, or thugs would enter at night and smash windshields or lay about among the sedans with sledgehammers, or tires would be flattened by the expert use of an ice-pick. There was the window-washing racket; when Max Wilner, who had been a window-washing contractor in Cleveland, moved to Chicago and tried to do business there, and was told that he could not unless he bought out some contractor already established, and refused to do so, he was not merely slugged or cajoled with explosives—he was shot dead. The list of rackets and of crimes could be extended for pages; in 1929, according to the State Attorney's office, there were ninety-one rackets in Chicago, seventy-five of them in active operation, and the Employers' Association figured the total cost to the citizenry at $136,000,000 a year.

As the favorite weapon of the bootlegging gangster was the machine gun, so the favorite weapon of the racketeer was the bomb. He could hire a bomber to do an ordinary routine job with a black-powder bomb for $100, but a risky job with a dynamite bomb might cost him all of $1,000. In the course of a little over fifteen months—from October 11, 1927, to January 15, 1929—no less than 157 bombs were set or exploded in the Chicago district, and according to Gordon L. Hostetter and Thomas Quinn Beesley, who made a careful compilation of these outrages in *It's a Racket*, there was no evidence that the perpetrators of *any of them* were brought to book.

A merry industry, and reasonably safe, it seemed—for the racketeers. Indeed, before the end of the decade racketeering had made such strides in Chicago that business men were turning in desperation to Al Capone for protection; Capone's henchmen were quietly attending union meetings to make sure that all proceeded according to the Big Shot's desires, and it was said that there were few more powerful figures in the councils of organized labor than the lord of the bootleggers had come to be. Racketeering, like gang warfare, had invaded other American cities, too. New York had laughed at Chicago's lawlessness, had it? New York was acquiring a handsome crop of rackets of its own—a laundry racket, a slot-machine racket, a fish racket, a flour racket, an artichoke racket, and others too numerous to mention. In every large urban community the racketeer was now at least a potential menace. In the course of a few short years he had become a national institution.

[7]

The prohibition problem, the gangster problem, the racket problem: as the Post-war Decade bowed itself out, all of them remained unsolved, to challenge the statesmanship of the nineteen-thirties. Still the rum-running launch slipped across the river, the alky-cooker's hidden apparatus poured forth alcohol, *entrepreneurs* of the contraband liquor industry put one another "on the spot," "typewriters" rattled in the Chicago streets, automobiles laden with roses followed the gangster to his grave, professional sluggers swung on non-union workmen, bull-necked gentlemen with shifty eyes called on the tradesman to suggest that he do business with them or they could not be responsible for what might happen, bombs reduced little shops to splintered wreckage; and tabloid-readers, poring over the stories of gangster killings, found in them adventure and splendor and romance.

XI

Home, Sweet Florida

. . ."Go to Florida—

"Where enterprise is enthroned—

"Where you sit and watch at twilight the fronds of the graceful palm, latticed against the fading gold of the sun-kissed sky—

"Where sun, moon and stars, at eventide, stage a welcome constituting the glorious galaxy of the firmament—

"Where the whispering breeze springs fresh from the lap of Caribbean and woos with elusive cadence like unto a mother's lullaby—

"Where the silver cycle is heaven's lavalier, and the full orbit [*sic*] its glorious pendant."

This outburst of unbuttoned rhetoric was written in the autumn of 1925, when the Scopes trial was receding into memory, Santa Barbara was steadying itself from the shock of earthquake, Red Grange was plunging to fame, the cornerstone of Bishop Manning's house of prayer for all people was about to be laid, Brigadier-General Smedley Butler was wishing he had never undertaken to mop up Philadelphia, *The Man Nobody Knows* was selling its ten thousands—and the Florida boom was at its height. The quotation is not, as you might imagine, from the collected lyrics of an enraptured schoolgirl, but from the conclusion of an article written for the *Miamian* by the vice-president of a bank. It faintly suggests what hap-

pened to the mental processes of supposedly hard-headed men
and women when they were exposed to the most delirious fever
of real-estate speculation which had attacked the United States
in ninety years.

There was nothing languorous about the atmosphere of
tropical Miami during that memorable summer and autumn of
1925. The whole city had become one frenzied real-estate
exchange. There were said to be 2,000 real-estate offices and
25,000 agents marketing house-lots or acreage. The shirt-
sleeved crowds hurrying to and fro under the widely advertised
Florida sun talked of binders and options and water-frontages
and hundred-thousand-dollar profits; the city fathers had been
forced to pass an ordinance forbidding the sale of property in
the street, or even the showing of a map, to prevent inordinate
traffic congestion. The warm air vibrated with the clatter of
riveters, for the steel skeletons of skyscrapers were rising to
give Miami a skyline appropriate to its metropolitan destiny.
Motor-busses roared down Flagler Street, carrying "prospects"
on free trips to watch dredges and steam-shovels converting
the outlying mangrove swamps and the sandbars of the Bay of
Biscayne into gorgeous Venetian cities for the American home-
makers and pleasure-seekers of the future. The Dixie Highway
was clogged with automobiles from every part of the country;
a traveler caught in a traffic jam counted the license-plates of
eighteen states among the sedans and flivvers waiting in line.
Hotels were overcrowded. People were sleeping wherever they
could lay their heads, in station waiting-rooms or in automobiles. The railroads had been forced to place an embargo on
imperishable freight in order to avert the danger of famine;
building materials were now being imported by water and the
harbor bristled with shipping. Fresh vegetables were a rarity,
the public utilities of the city were trying desperately to meet
the suddenly multiplied demand for electricity and gas and
telephone service, and there were recurrent shortages of ice.

How Miami grew! In 1920 its population had been only 30,-
000. According to the state census of 1925 it had jumped to
75,000—and probably if one had counted the newcomers of
the succeeding months and Miami's share of the visitors who
swarmed down to Florida from the North in one of the might-
iest popular migrations of all time, the figure would have been
nearer 150,000. And this, one was told, was only a beginning.
Had not S. Davies Warfield, president of the Seaboard Air

Line Railway, been quoted as predicting for Miami a population of a million within the next ten years? Did not the Governor of Florida, the Honorable John W. Martin, assert that "marvelous as is the wonder-story of Florida's recent achievements, these are but heralds of the dawn"?

Everybody was making money on land, prices were climbing to incredible heights, and those who came to scoff remained to speculate.

Nor was Miami alone booming. The whole strip of coast line from Palm Beach southward was being developed into an American Riviera; for sixty-odd miles it was being rapidly staked out into fifty-foot lots. The fever had spread to Tampa, Sarasota, St. Petersburg, and other cities and towns on the West Coast. People were scrambling for lots along Lake Okeechobee, about Sanford, all through the state; even in Jacksonville, near its northern limit, the "Believers in Jacksonville" were planning a campaign which would bring their city its due in growth and riches.

[2]

For this amazing boom, which had gradually been gathering headway for several years but had not become sensational until 1924, there were a number of causes. Let us list them categorically.

1. First of all, of course, the climate—Florida's unanswerable argument.

2. The accessibility of the state to the populous cities of the Northeast—an advantage which Southern California could not well deny.

3. The automobile, which was rapidly making America into a nation of nomads; teaching all manner of men and women to explore their country, and enabling even the small farmer, the summer-boarding-house keeper, and the garage man to pack their families into flivvers and tour southward from auto-camp to auto-camp for a winter of sunny leisure.

4. The abounding confidence engendered by Coolidge Prosperity, which persuaded the four-thousand-dollar-a-year salesman that in some magical way he too might tomorrow be able to buy a fine house and all the good things of earth.

5. A paradoxical, widespread, but only half-acknowledged revolt against the very urbanization and industrialization of the

country, the very concentration upon work, the very routine
and smoke and congestion and twentieth-century standardization of living upon which Coolidge Prosperity was based.
These things might bring the American business man money,
but to spend it he longed to escape from them—into the free
sunshine of the remembered countryside, into the easy-going
life and beauty of the European past, into some never-never
land which combined American sport and comfort with Latin
glamour—a Venice equipped with bathtubs and electric ice-
boxes, a Seville provided with three eighteen-hole golf courses.

6. The example of Southern California, which had advertised its climate at the top of its lungs and had prospered by so
doing: why, argued the Floridians, couldn't Florida do likewise?

7. And finally, another result of Coolidge Prosperity: not
only did John Jones expect that presently he might be able to
afford a house at Boca Raton and a vacation-time of tarpon-
fishing or polo, but he also was fed on stories of bold business
enterprise and sudden wealth until he was ready to believe that
the craziest real-estate development might be the gold-mine
which would work this miracle for him.

Crazy real-estate developments? But were they crazy? By
1925 few of them looked so any longer. The men whose fantastic projects had seemed in 1923 to be evidences of megalomania were now coining millions: by the pragmatic test they
were not madmen but—as the advertisements put it—inspired
dreamers. Coral Gables, Hollywood-by-the-Sea, Miami Beach,
Davis Islands—there they stood: mere patterns on a blue-print
no longer, but actual cities of brick and concrete and stucco;
unfinished, to be sure, but growing with amazing speed, while
prospects stood in line to buy and every square foot within
their limits leaped in price.

Long years before, a retired Congregational minister named
Merrick had bought cheap land outside Miami, built a many-
gabled house out of coral rock, and called it "Coral Gables."
Now his son, George Edgar Merrick, had added to this parcel
of land and was building what the advertisements called
"America's Most Beautiful Suburb." The plan was enticing, for
Merrick had had sense enough to insist upon a uniform type of
architecture—what he called a "modified Mediterranean"
style. By 1926 his development, which had incorporated itself
as the City of Coral Gables, contained more than two thousand

houses built or building, with "a bustling business center, schools, banks, hotels, apartment houses and club houses"; with shady streets, lagoons, and anchorages. Merrick advertised boldly and in original ways: at one time he engaged William Jennings Bryan to sit under a sun-umbrella on a raft in a lagoon and lecture (at a handsome price) to the crowds on the shore—not upon the Prince of Peace or the Cross of Gold, but upon the Florida climate. (Bryan's tribute to sunshine was followed with dancing by Gilda Gray.) Merrick also knew how to make a romantic virtue of necessity: having low-lying land to drain and build on, he dug canals and imported real gondolas and gondoliers from Venice. The Miami-Biltmore Hotel at Coral Gables rose to a height of twenty-six stories, the country club had two eighteen-hole golf courses, and Merrick was making further audacious plans for a great casino, a yacht club, and a University of Miami. "Ten years of hard work, a hundred millions of hard money, is what George Merrick plans to spend before he rests," wrote Rex Beach in a brochure on Coral Gables. "Who can envisage what ten years will bring to that wonderland of Ponce de Leon's? Not you nor I. Nor Mr. Merrick, with all his soaring vision." (Alas for soaring vision! Among the things which ten years were to bring was an advertisement in the *New York Times* reminding the holders of nine series of bonds of the City of Coral Gables that the city had been "in default of the payment of principal and interest of a greater part of the above bonds since July 1, 1930.")

There were other miracle-workers besides Merrick. Miami Beach had been a mangrove swamp until Carl G. Fisher cut down the trees, buried their stumps under five feet of sand, fashioned lagoons and islands, built villas and hotels, and—so it was said—made nearly forty million dollars selling lots. Joseph W. Young built Hollywood-by-the-Sea on the same grand scale, and when the freight embargo cut off his supply of building materials, bought his own seagoing fleet to fetch them to his growing "city." Over on the West Coast, D. P. Davis bought two small islets in the bay at Tampa—"two small marshy clumps of mangrove, almost submerged at high tide" —and by dredging and piling sand, raised up an island on which he built paved streets, hotels, houses. On the first day when Davis offered his lots to the public he sold three million dollars' worth—though at that time it is said that not a single dredge had begun to scoop up sand!

Yes, the public bought. By 1925 they were buying anything, anywhere, so long as it was in Florida. One had only to announce a new development, be it honest or fraudulent, be it on the Atlantic Ocean or deep in the wasteland of the interior, to set people scrambling for house lots. "Manhattan Estates" was advertised as being "not more than three-fourths of a mile from the prosperous and fast-growing city of Nettie"; there was no such city as Nettie, the name being that of an abandoned turpentine camp, yet people bought. Investigators of the claims made for "Melbourne Gardens" tried to find the place, found themselves driving along a trail "through prairie muck land, with a few trees and small clumps of palmetto," and were hopelessly mired in the mud three miles short of their destination. But still the public bought, here and elsewhere, blindly, trustingly,—natives of Florida, visitors to Florida, and good citizens of Ohio and Massachusetts and Wisconsin who had never been near Florida but made out their checks for lots in what they were told was to be "another Coral Gables" or was "next to the right of way of the new railroad" or was to be a "twenty-million-dollar city." The stories of prodigious profits made in Florida land were sufficient bait. A lot in the business center of Miami Beach had sold for $800 in the early days of the development and had resold for $150,000 in 1924. For a strip of land in Palm Beach a New York lawyer had been offered $240,000 some eight or ten years before the boom; in 1923 he finally accepted $800,000 for it; the next year the strip of land was broken up into building lots and disposed of at an aggregate price of $1,500,000; and in 1925 there were those who claimed that its value had risen to $4,000,000. A poor woman who had bought a piece of land near Miami in 1896 for $25 was able to sell it in 1925 for $150,000. Such tales were legion; every visitor to the Gold Coast could pick them up by the dozen; and many if not most of them were quite true —though the profits were largely on paper. No wonder the rush for Florida land justified the current anecdote of a native saying to a visitor, "Want to buy a lot?" and the visitor at once replying, "Sold."

Speculation was easy—and quick. No long delays while titles were being investigated and deeds recorded; such tiresome formalities were postponed. The prevalent method of sale was thus described by Walter C. Hill of the Retail Credit Company of Atlanta in the Inspection Report issued by his concern: "Lots are bought from blueprints. They look better that way. . . . Around Miami, subdivisions, except the very large ones, are often sold out the first day of sale. Advertisements appear describing the location, extent; special features, and approximate price of the lots. Reservations are accepted. This requires a check for 10 per cent of the price of the lot the buyer expects to select. On the first day of sale, at the promoter's office in town, the reservations are called out in order, and the buyer steps up and, from a beautifully drawn blueprint, with lots and dimensions and prices clearly shown, selects a lot or lots, gets a receipt in the form of a 'binder' describing it, and has the thrill of seeing 'Sold' stamped in the blue-lined square which represents his lot, a space usually fifty by a hundred feet of Florida soil or swamp. There are instances where these first-day sales have gone into several millions of dollars. And the prices! . . . Inside lots from $8,000 to $20,000. Water-front lots from $15,000 to $25,000. Seashore lots from $20,000 to $75,000. And these are not in Miami. They are miles out—ten miles out, fifteen miles out, and thirty miles out."

The binder, of course, did not complete the transaction. But few people worried much about the further payments which were to come. Nine buyers out of ten bought their lots with only one idea, to resell, and hoped to pass along their binders to other people at a neat profit before even the first payment fell due at the end of thirty days. There was an immense traffic in binders—immense and profitable.

Steadily, during that feverish summer and autumn of 1925, the hatching of new plans for vast developments continued. A great many of them, apparently, were intended to be occupied by what the advertisers of Miami Beach called "America's wealthiest sportsmen, devotees of yachting and the other expensive sports," and the advertisers of Boca Raton called "the world of international wealth that dominates finance and industry . . . that sets fashions . . . the world of large affairs, smart society and leisured ease." Few of those in the land-rush seemed to question whether there would be enough devotees of yachting and men and women of leisured ease to go round.

Everywhere vast new hotels, apartment houses, casinos were being projected. At the height of the fury of building a visitor to West Palm Beach noticed a large vacant lot almost

completely covered with bathtubs. The tubs had apparently
been there some time; the crates which surrounded them were
well weathered. The lot, he was informed, was to be the site of
"one of the most magnificent apartment buildings in the
South"—but the freight embargo had held up the contractor's
building material and only the bathtubs had arrived! Throughout Florida resounded the slogans and hyperboles of boundless
confidence. The advertising columns shrieked with them, those
swollen advertising columns which enabled the *Miami Daily
News,* one day in the summer of 1925, to print an issue of 504
pages, the largest in newspaper history, and enabled the *Miami
Herald* to carry a larger volume of advertising in 1925 than
any paper anywhere had ever before carried in a year. Miami
was not only "The Wonder City," it was also "The Fair White
Goddess of Cities," "The World's Playground," and "The City
Invincible." Fort Lauderdale became "The Tropical Wonderland," Orlando "The City Beautiful," and Sanford "The City
Substantial."

Daily the turgid stream of rhetoric poured forth to the glory
of Florida. It reached its climax, perhaps, in the joint
Proclamation issued by the mayors of Miami, Miami Beach,
Hialeah, and Coral Gables (who modestly referred to their
county as "the most Richly Blessed Community of the most
Bountifully Endowed State of the most Highly Enterprising
People of the Universe"), setting forth the last day of 1925
and the first two days of 1926 as "The Fiesta of the American
Tropics"—"our Season of Fiesta when Love, Good
Fellowship, Merrymaking, and Wholesome Sport shall prevail
throughout Our Domains." The mayors promised that there
would be dancing: "that our Broad Boulevards, our Beautiful
Plazas and Ballroom Floors, our Patios, Clubs and Hostelries
shall be the scenes where Radiant Terpsichore and her Sparkling Devotees shall follow with Graceful Tread the Measure
of the Dance." They promised much more, to the extent of a
page of flatulent text sprinkled with capitals; but especially
they promised "that through our Streets and Avenues shall
wind a glorious Pageantry of Sublime Beauty Depicting in
Floral Loveliness the Blessing Bestowed upon us by Friendly
Sun, Gracious Rain, and Soothing Tropic Wind."

Presumably the fiesta was successful, with its full quota of
Sparkling Devotees and Sublime Beauty. But by New Year's
Day of 1926 the suspicion was beginning to insinuate itself into

the minds of the merrymakers that new buyers of land were no longer so plentiful as they had been in September and October, that a good many of those who held binders were exceedingly anxious to dispose of their stake in the most Richly Blessed Community, and that Friendly Sun and Gracious Rain were not going to be able, unassisted, to complete the payments on lots. The influx of winter visitors had not been quite up to expectations. Perhaps the boom was due for a "healthy breathing-time."

[3]

As a matter of fact, it was due for a good deal more than that. It began obviously to collapse in the spring and summer of 1926. People who held binders and had failed to get rid of them were defaulting right and left on their payments. One man who had sold acreage early in 1925 for twelve dollars an acre, and had cursed himself for his stupidity when it was resold later in the year for seventeen dollars, and then thirty dollars, and finally sixty dollars an acre, was surprised a year or two afterward to find that the entire series of subsequent purchases was in default, that he could not recover the money still due him, and that his only redress was to take his land back again. There were cases in which the land not only came back to the original owner, but came back burdened with taxes and assessments which amounted to more than the cash he had received for it; and furthermore he found his land blighted with a half-completed development.

Just as it began to be clear that a wholesale deflation was inevitable, two hurricanes showed what a Soothing Tropic Wind could do when it got a running start from the West Indies.

No malevolent Providence bent upon the teaching of humility could have struck with a more precise aim than the second and worst of these Florida hurricanes. It concentrated upon the exact region where the boom had been noisiest and most hysterical—the region about Miami. Hitting the Gold Coast early in the morning of September 18, 1926, it piled the waters of Biscayne Bay into the lovely Venetian developments, deposited a five-masted steel schooner high in the street at Coral Gables, tossed big steam yachts upon the avenues of Miami, picked up trees, lumber, pipes, tiles, débris, and even small automobiles and sent them crashing into the houses, ripped the roofs off thousands of jerry-built cottages and villas, almost wiped out the town of Moore Haven on Lake Okeechobee, and left behind it some four hundred dead, sixty-three hundred injured, and fifty thousand homeless. Valiantly the Floridians insisted that the damage was not irreparable; so valiantly, in fact, that the head of the American Red Cross, John Barton Payne, was quoted as charging that the officials of the state had "practically destroyed" the national Red Cross campaign for relief of the homeless. Mayor Romfh of Miami declared that he saw no reason "why this city should not entertain her winter visitors the coming season as comfortably as in past seasons." But the Soothing Tropic Wind had had its revenge; it had destroyed the remnants of the Florida boom.

By 1927, according to Homer B. Vanderblue, most of the elaborate real-estate offices on Flagler Street in Miami were either closed or practically empty; the Davis Islands project, "bankrupt and unfinished," had been taken over by a syndicate organized by Stone & Webster; and many Florida cities, including Miami, were having difficulty collecting their taxes. By 1928 Henry S. Villard, writing in *The Nation*, thus described the approach to Miami by road: "Dead subdivisions line the highway, their pompous names half-obliterated on crumbling stucco gates. Lonely white-way lights stand guard over miles of cement sidewalks, where grass and palmetto take the place of homes that were to be. . . . Whole sections of outlying subdivisions are composed of unoccupied houses, past which one speeds on broad thoroughfares as if traversing a city in the grip of death." In 1928 there were thirty-one bank failures in Florida; in 1929 there were fifty-seven; in both of these years the liabilities of the failed banks reached greater totals than were recorded for any other state in the Union. The Mediterranean fruitfly added to the gravity of the local economic situation in 1929 by ravaging the citrus crop. Bank clearings for Miami, which had climbed sensationally to over a billion dollars in 1925, marched sadly downhill again:

1925	$1,066,528,000
1926	632,867,000
1927	260,039,000
1928	143,364,000
1929	142,316,000

And those were the very years when elsewhere in the country prosperity was triumphant! By the middle of 1930, after the general business depression had set in, no less than twenty-six Florida cities had gone into default of principal or interest on their bonds, the heaviest defaults being those of West Palm Beach, Miami, Sanford, and Lake Worth; and even Miami, which had a minor issue of bonds maturing in August, 1930, confessed its inability to redeem them and asked the bondholders for an extension.

The cheerful custom of incorporating real-estate developments as "cities" and financing the construction of all manner of improvements with "tax-free municipal bonds," as well as the custom on the part of development corporations of issuing real-estate bonds secured by new structures located in the boom territory, were showing weaknesses unimagined by the inspired dreamers of 1925. Most of the millions piled up in paper profits had melted away, many of the millions sunk in developments had been sunk for good and all, the vast inverted pyramid of credit had toppled to earth, and the lesson of the economic falsity of a scheme of land values based upon grandiose plans, preposterous expectations, and hot air had been taught in a long agony of deflation.

For comfort there were only a few saving facts to cling to. Florida still had her climate, her natural resources. The people of Florida still had energy and determination, and having recovered from their debauch of hope, were learning from the relentless discipline of events. Not all Northerners who had moved to Florida in the days of plenty had departed in the days of adversity. Far from it: the census of 1930, in fact, gave Florida an increase in population of over 50 per cent since 1920—a larger increase than that of any other state except California—and showed that in the same interval Miami had grown by nearly 400 per cent. Florida still had a future; there was no doubt of that, sharp as the pains of enforced postponement were. Nor, for that matter, were the people of Florida alone blameworthy for the insanity of 1925. They, perhaps, had done most of the shouting, but the hysteria which had centered in their state had been a national hysteria, enormously increased by the influx of outlanders intent upon making easy money.

[4]

The Florida boom, in fact, was only one—and by all odds the most spectacular—of a series of land and building booms during the Post-war Decade, each of which had its marked effect upon the national economy and the national life.

At the very outset of the decade there had been a sensational market in farm lands, caused by the phenomenal prices brought by wheat and other crops during and immediately after the war. Prices of farm property leaped, thousands of mortgages and loans were based upon these exaggerated values, and when the bottom dropped out of the agricultural markets in 1920-21, the distress of the farmers was intensified by the fact that in innumerable cases they could not get money enough from their crops to cover the interest due at the bank or to pay the taxes which were now levied on the increased valuation. Thousands of country banks, saddled with mortgages and loans in default, ultimately went to the wall. In one of the great agricultural states, the average earnings of *all* the national and state banks during the years 1924-29, a time of great prosperity for the country at large, were less than 1½ per cent; and in seven states of the country, between 40 and 50 per cent of the banks which had been in business prior to 1920 had failed before 1929. Just how many of these failures were directly attributable to the undisciplined rise and subsequent fall in real-estate prices is, of course, impossible to say; but undoubtedly many of the little country banks which suffered so acutely would never have gone down to ruin if there had been no boom in farm lands.

All through the decade, but especially during and immediately after the Florida fever, there was an epidemic of ambitious schemes hatched by promoters and boosters to bring prosperity to various American cities, towns, and resorts, by presenting each of them, in sumptuous advertisements, circulars, and press copy put out by hustling chambers of commerce, as the "center of a rising industrial empire" or as the "new playground of America's rich." Some of these ventures prospered; in California, for example, where the technic of boosting had been brought to poetic perfection long years previously, concerted campaigns brought industries, winter visitors, summer visitors, and good fortune for the business man and the hotel-keeper alike. It was estimated that a million people a year went to California "just to look and play"—and, of course, to spend money. But not all such ventures could prosper, the number of factories and of wealthy vacationists being unhappily limited. City after city, hoping to attract industries within its limits, eloquently pointed out its "advantages" and tried to "make its personality felt" and to "carry its constructive message to the American people"; but at length it began to dawn upon the boosters that attracting industries bore some resemblance to robbing Peter to pay Paul, and that if all of them were converted to boosting, each of them was as likely to find itself in the rôle of Peter as in that of Paul. And exactly as the developers of the tropical wonderlands of Florida had learned that there were more land-speculators able and willing to gamble in houses intended for the polo-playing class than there were members of this class, so also those who carved out playgrounds for the rich in North Carolina or elsewhere learned to their ultimate sorrow that the rich could not play everywhere at once. And once more the downfall of their bright hopes had financial repercussions, as bankrupt developments led to the closing of bank after bank.

Again, all through the decade, but especially during its middle years, there was a boom in suburban lands outside virtually every American city. As four million discouraged Americans left the farms, and the percentage of city-dwellers in the United States increased from 51.4 to 57.6, and the cities grew in size and in stridency, and urban traffic became more noisy and congested, and new high buildings cut off the city-dweller's light and air, the drift of families from the cities to the urban-rural compromise of the neighboring countryside became more rapid. Here again the automobile played its part in changing the conditions of American life, by bringing within easy range of the suburban railroad station, and thus of the big city, great stretches of woodland and field which a few years before had seemed remote and inaccessible. Attractive suburbs grew with amazing speed, blossoming out with brand-new Colonial farmhouses (with attached garage), Tudor cottages (with age-old sagging roofs constructed by inserting wedge-shaped blocks of wood at the ends of the roof-trees), and Spanish stucco haciendas (with built-in radios). Once more the real-estate developer had his golden opportunity. The old Jackson farm with its orchards and daisy-fields was staked out in lots and attacked by the steam-shovel and became Jacobean Heights or Colonial Terrace or Alhambra Gardens, with paved roads, twentieth-century comforts, Old World charm, and land for sale on easy payments.

On the immediate outskirts of great cities such as New York, Chicago, Los Angeles, and Detroit huge tracts were less luxuriously developed. The Borough of Queens, just across the East River from New York, grew vastly and hideously: its population more than doubled during the decade, reaching a total of over a million. Outside Detroit immense districts were subdivided and numerous lots in them were bought by people so poor that they secured permits to build "garage dwellings" —temporary one-room shacks—and lived in them for years without ever building real houses. So furious was the competition among developers that it was estimated that in a single year there were subdivided in the Chicago region enough lots to accommodate the growth of the city for twenty years to come (at the rate at which it had previously grown), and that by the end of the decade enough lots had been staked out between Patchogue, Long Island, and the New York City limits to house the entire metropolitan population of six millions.

For a time the Florida boom had a picturesque influence on suburban developments. Many of them went Venetian. There was, for example, American Venice, thirty-four miles from New York on Long Island, where the first bridge to be built was "a replica of the famous Della Paglia Bridge at Venice," and the whole scene, according to the promoters, "recalls the famous city of the Doges, only more charming—and more homelike." "To live at American Venice," chanted one of the advertisements of this proposed retreat for stockbrokers and insurance salesmen, "is to quaff the very Wine of Life. . . . A turquoise lagoon under an aquamarine sky! Lazy gondolas! Beautiful Italian gardens! . . . And, ever present, the waters of the Great South Bay lapping lazily all day upon a beach as white and fine as the soul of a little child." And there was Biltmore Shores, also developed on Long Island (by William Fox of the movies and Jacob Frankel of the clothing business) where, in 1926, "an artistic system of canals and waterways" was advertised as being "in progress of completion."

The Venetian phase of the suburban boom was of short duration: after 1926 the mention of lagoons introduced painful thoughts into the minds of prospective purchasers. But the suburban boom itself did not begin to languish in most localities until 1928 or 1929. By that time many suburbs were plainly overbuilt: as one drove out along the highways, one began to notice houses that must have stood long untenanted, shops with staring vacant windows, districts blighted with half-finished and abandoned "improvements"; one heard of suburban apartment houses which had changed hands again and again as mortgages were foreclosed, or of householders in uncompleted subdivisions who were groaning under a naïvely unexpected burden of taxes and assessments. Yet even then it was clear that, like Florida, the suburb had a future. The need of men and women for space and freedom, as well as for access to the centers of population, had not come to an end.

The final phase of the real-estate boom of the nineteen-twenties centered in the cities themselves. To picture what happened to the American sky line during those years, compare a 1920 airplane view of almost any large city with one taken in 1930. There is scarcely a city which does not show a bright new cluster of skyscrapers at its center. The tower-building mania reached its climax in New York—since towers in the metropolis are a potent advertisement—and particularly in the Grand Central district of New York. Here the building boom attained immense proportions, coming to its peak of intensity in 1928. New pinnacles shot into the air forty stories, fifty stories, and more; between 1918 and 1930 the amount of space available for office use in large modern buildings in that district was multiplied approximately by ten. In a photograph of uptown New York taken from the neighborhood of the East River early in 1931, the twenty most conspicuous structures were all products of the Post-war Decade. The tallest two of all, to be sure, were not completed until after the panic of 1929; by the time the splendid shining tower of the Empire State Building stood clear of scaffolding there were apple salesmen shivering on the curbstone below. Yet it was none the less a monument to the abounding confidence of the days in which it was conceived.

The confidence had been excessive. Skyscrapers had been over-produced. In the spring of 1931 it was reliably stated that some 17 per cent of the space in the big office buildings of the Grand Central district, and some 40 per cent of that in the big office buildings of the Plaza district farther uptown, was not bringing in a return, owners of new skyscrapers were inveigling business concerns into occupying vacant floors by offering them space rent-free for a period or by assuming their leases in other buildings; and financiers were shaking their heads over the precarious condition of many realty investments in New York. The metropolis, too, had a future, but speculative enthusiasm had carried it upward a little too fast.

[5]

After the Florida hurricane, real-estate speculation lost most of its interest for the ordinary man and woman. Few of them were much concerned, except as householders or as spectators, with the building of suburban developments or of forty-story experiments in modernist architecture. Yet the national speculative fever which had turned their eyes and their cash to the Florida Gold Coast in 1925 was not chilled; it was merely checked. Florida house-lots were a bad bet? Very well, then, said a public still enthralled by the radiant possibilities of Coolidge Prosperity: what else was there to bet on? Before long a new wave of popular speculation was accumulating momentum. Not in real-estate this time; in something quite different. The focus of speculative infection shifted from Flagler Street, Miami, to Broad and Wall Streets, New York. The Big Bull Market was getting under way.

XII

The Big Bull Market

One day in February, 1928, an investor asked an astute banker about the wisdom of buying common stocks. The banker shook his head. "Stocks look dangerously high to me," he said. "This bull market has been going on for a long time, and although prices have slipped a bit recently, they might easily slip a good deal more. Business is none too good. Of course if you buy the right stock you'll probably be all right in the long run and you may even make a profit. But if I were you I'd wait awhile and see what happens."

By all the canons of conservative finance the banker was right. That enormous confidence in Coolidge Prosperity which had lifted the business man to a new preëminence in American life and had persuaded innumerable men and women to gamble their savings away in Florida real estate had also carried the prices of common stocks far upward since 1924, until they had reached what many hard-headed financiers considered alarming levels. Throughout 1927 speculation had been increasing. The amount of money loaned to brokers to carry margin accounts for traders had risen during the year from $2,-818,561,000 to $3,558,355,000—a huge increase. During the week of December 3, 1927, more shares of stock had changed hands than in any previous week in the whole history of the New York Stock Exchange. One did not have to listen long to an after-dinner conversation, whether in New York or San Francisco or the lowliest village of the plain, to realize that all sorts of people to whom the stock ticker had been a hitherto alien mystery were carrying a hundred shares of Studebaker or Houston Oil, learning the significance of such recondite symbols as GL and X and ITT, and whipping open the early editions of afternoon papers to catch the 1:30 quotations from Wall Street.

The speculative fever had been intensified by the action of the Federal Reserve System in lowering the rediscount rate from 4 per cent to 3½ per cent in August, 1927, and purchasing Government securities in the open market. This action had been taken from the most laudable motives: several of the European nations were having difficulty in stabilizing their currencies, European exchanges were weak, and it seemed to the Reserve authorities that the easing of American money rates might prevent the further accumulation of gold in the United States and thus aid in the recovery of Europe and benefit foreign trade. Furthermore, American business was beginning to lose headway; the lowering of money rates might stimulate it. But the lowering of money rates also stimulated the stock market. The bull party in Wall Street had been still further encouraged by the remarkable solicitude of President Coolidge and Secretary Mellon, who whenever confidence showed signs of waning came out with opportunely reassuring statements which at once sent prices upward again. In January 1928, the President had actually taken the altogether unprecedented step of publicly stating that he did not consider brokers' loans too high, thus apparently giving White House sponsorship to the very inflation which was worrying the sober minds of the financial community.

While stock prices had been climbing, business activity had been undeniably subsiding. There had been such a marked recession during the latter part of 1927 that by February, 1928, the director of the Charity Organization Society in New York reported that unemployment was more serious than at any time since immediately after the war. During January and February the stock market turned ragged and unsettled, and no wonder—for with prices still near record levels and the future trend of business highly dubious, it was altogether too easy to foresee a time of reckoning ahead.

The tone of the business analysts and forecasters—a fraternity whose numbers had hugely increased in recent years and whose lightest words carried weight—was anything but exuberant. On January 5, 1928, Moody's Investors Service said that stock prices had "over-discounted anticipated progress" and wondered "how much of a readjustment may be required to place the stock market in a sound position." On March 1st this agency was still uneasy: "The public," it declared, "is not likely to change its bearish state of mind until about the time when money becomes so plethoric as to lead the banks to encourage credit expansion." Two days later the Harvard Economic Society drew from its statistical graphs the chilly conclusion that "the developments of February suggest that business is entering upon a period of temporary readjustment"; the best cheer which the Harvard prognosticators could offer was a prophecy that "intermediate declines in the stock market will not develop into such *major* movements as forecast business depression." The National City Bank looked for gradual improvement in business and the Standard Statistics Company suggested that a turn for the better had already arrived; but the latter agency also sagely predicted that the course of stocks during the coming months would depend "almost entirely upon the money situation." The financial editor of the *New York Times* described the picture of current conditions presented by the mercantile agencies as one of "hesitation." The newspaper advertisements of investment services testified to the uncomfortable temper of Wall Street with headlines like "Will You 'Overstay' This Bull Market?" and "Is the Process of Deflation Under Way?" The air was fogged with uncertainty.

Anybody who had chosen this moment to predict that the bull market was on the verge of a wild advance which would make all that had gone before seem trifling would have been quite mad—or else inspired with a genius for mass psychology. The banker who advised caution was quite right about financial conditions, and so were the forecasters. But they had not taken account of the boundless commercial romanticism of the American people, inflamed by year after plentiful year of Coolidge Prosperity. For on March 3, 1928—the very day when the Harvard prophets were talking about intermediate declines and the *Times* was talking about hesitation—the stock market entered upon its sensational phase.

[2]

Let us glance for a moment at the next morning's paper, that
arm-breaking load of reading-matter which bore the date of
Sunday, March 4, 1928. It was now many months since Calvin
Coolidge had stated, with that characteristic simplicity which
led people to suspect him of devious meanings, that he did not
"choose to run for President in 1928"; and already his Secretary of Commerce, who eight years before had been annoyed
at being called an amateur in politics, was corralling delegates
with distinctly professional efficiency against the impending
Republican convention. It was three months since Henry Ford
had unveiled Model A, but eyes still turned to stare when a
new Ford went by, and those who had blithely ordered a Sedan
in Arabian Sand were beginning to wonder if they would have
to wait until September and then have to take Dawn Gray or
leave it. Colonel Lindbergh had been a hero these nine months
but was still a bachelor: on page 21 of that Sunday paper of
March 4, 1928, he was quoted in disapproval of a bill introduced in Congress to convert the Lindbergh homestead at
Little Falls, Minnesota, into a museum. Commander Byrd was
about to announce his plans for a flight to the South Pole.
Women's skirts, as pictured in the department store advertisements, were at their briefest; they barely covered the knee-
cap. The sporting pages contained the tidings that C. C. Pyle's
lamentable Bunion Derby was about to start from Los Angeles
with 274 contestants. On another page Mrs. William Jay, Mrs.
Robert Low Bacon, and Mrs. Charles Cary Rumsey exem-
plified the principle of *noblesse oblige* by endorsing Simmons
beds. *The Bridge of San Luis Rey* was advertised as having
sold 100,000 copies in ninety days. The book section of the
newspaper also advertised *The Greene Murder Case* by S. S.
Van Dine (not yet identified as Willard Huntington Wright),
Willa Cather's *Death Comes for the Archbishop,* and Ludwig
Lewisohn's *The Island Within.* The theatrical pages disclosed
that "The Trial of Mary Dugan" had been running in New
York for seven months, Galsworthy's "Escape" for five; New
York theater-goers might also take their choice between
"Strange Interlude," "Show Boat," "Paris Bound," "Porgy,"
and "Funny Face." The talking pictures were just beginning to
rival the silent films: Al Jolson was announced in "The Jazz

Singer" on the Vitaphone, and two Fox successes "with symphonic movietone accompaniment" were advertised. The stock market—but one did not need to turn to the financial pages for that. For on page 1 appeared what was to prove a portentous piece of news.

General Motors stock, opening at 139¾ on the previous morning, had skyrocketed in two short hours to 144¼, with a gain of more than five points since the Friday closing. The trading for the day had amounted to not much more than 1,-200,000 shares, but nearly a third of it had been in Motors. The speculative spring fever of 1928 had set in.

It may interest some readers to be reminded of the prices brought at the opening on March 3rd by some of the leading stocks of that day or of subsequent days. Here they are, with the common dividend rate for each stock in parentheses:

> American Can (2), 77
> American Telephone & Telegraph (9), 179½
> Anaconda (3), 54½
> General Electric (5 including extras), 128¾
> General Motors (5), 139¾
> Montgomery Ward (5 including extras), 132¾
> New York Central (8), 160½
> Radio (no dividend), 94½
> Union Carbide & Carbon (6), 145
> United States Steel (7), 138⅛
> Westinghouse (4), 91⅝
> Woolworth (5), 180¾
> Electric Bond & Share (1), 89¾

On Monday General Motors gained 2¼ points more, on Tuesday 3½; there was great excitement as the stock "crossed 150." Other stocks were beginning to be affected by the contagion as day after day the market "made the front page": Steel and Radio and Montgomery Ward were climbing, too. After a pause on Wednesday and Thursday, General Motors astounded everybody on Friday by pushing ahead a cool 9¼ points as the announcement was made that its Managers Securities Company had bought 200,000 shares in the open market for its executives at around 150. And then on Saturday the common stock of the Radio Corporation of America threw General Motors completely into the shade by leaping upward for a net gain of 12¾ points, closing at 120½.

What on earth was happening? Wasn't business bad, and credit inflated, and the stock-price level dangerously high? Was the market going crazy? Suppose all these madmen who insisted on buying stocks at advancing prices tried to sell at the same moment! Canny investors, reading of the wild advance in Radio, felt much as did the forecasters of Moody's Investors Service a few days later: the practical question, they said, was "how long the opportunity to sell at the top will remain."

What was actually happening was that a group of powerful speculators with fortunes made in the automobile business and in the grain markets and in the earlier days of the bull market in stocks—men like W. C. Durant and Arthur Cutten and the Fisher Brothers and John J. Raskob—were buying in unparalleled volume. They thought that business was due to come out of its doldrums. They knew that with Ford production delayed, the General Motors Corporation was likely to have a big year. They knew that the Radio Corporation had been consolidating its position and was now ready to make more money than it had ever made before, and that as scientific discovery followed discovery, the future possibilities of the biggest radio company were exciting. Automobiles and radios—these were the two most characteristic products of the decade of confident mass production, the brightest flowers of Coolidge Prosperity: they held a ready-made appeal to the speculative imagination. The big bull operators knew, too, that thousands of speculators had been selling stocks short in the expectation of a collapse in the market, would continue to sell short, and could be forced to repurchase if prices were driven relentlessly up. And finally, they knew their American public. It could not resist the appeal of a surging market. It had an altogether normal desire to get rich quick, and it was ready to believe anything about the golden future of American business. If stocks started upward the public would buy, no matter what the forecasters said, no matter how obscure was the business prospect.

They were right. The public bought.

Monday the 12th of March put the stock market on the front page once more. Radio opened at 120½—and closed at 138½. Other stocks made imposing gains, the volume of trading broke every known record by totaling 3,875,910 shares, the ticker fell six minutes behind the market, and visitors to the gallery of the Stock Exchange reported that red-haired Michael Meehan, the specialist in Radio, was the center of what appeared to be a five-hour scrimmage on the floor. "It looked like a street fight," said one observer.

Tuesday the 13th was enough to give anybody chills and fever. Radio opened at 160, a full 21½ points above the closing price the night before—a staggering advance. Then came an announcement that the Stock Exchange officials were beginning an investigation to find out whether a technical corner in the stock existed, and the price cascaded to 140. It jumped again that same day to 155 and closed at 146, 7½ points above Monday's closing, to the accompaniment of rumors that one big short trader had been wiped out. This time the ticker was twelve minutes late.

And so it went on, day after day and week after week. On March 16th the ticker was thirty-three minutes late and one began to hear people saying that some day there might occur a five-million share day—which seemed almost incredible. On the 20th, Radio jumped 18 points and General Motors 5. On March 26th the record for total volume of trading was smashed again. The new mark lasted just twenty-four hours, for on the 27th—a terrifying day when a storm of unexplained selling struck the market and General Motors dropped abruptly, only to recover on enormous buying—there were 4,-790,000 shares traded. The speculative fever was infecting the whole country. Stories of fortunes made overnight were on everybody's lips. One financial commentator reported that his doctor found patients talking about the market to the exclusion of everything else and that his barber was punctuating with the hot towel more than one account of the prospects of Montgomery Ward. Wives were asking their husbands why they were so slow, why they weren't getting in on all this, only to hear that their husbands had bought a hundred shares of American Linseed that very morning. Brokers' branch offices were jammed with crowds of men and women watching the shining transparency on which the moving message of the ticker tape was written; whether or not one held so much as a share of stock, there was a thrill in seeing the news of that abrupt break and recovery in General Motors on March 27th run across the field of vision in a long string of quotations:

GM 50.85 (meaning 5,000 shares at 185) 20.80. 50.82. 14.83. 30.85. 20.86. 25.87. 40.88. 30.87. . . .

New favorites took the limelight as the weeks went by. Montgomery Ward was climbing. The aviation stocks leaped upward; in a single week in May, Wright Aeronautical gained 34¾ points to reach 190, and Curtiss gained 35½ to reach 142. Several times during the spring of 1928 the New York Stock Exchange had to remain closed on Saturday to give brokers' clerks a chance to dig themselves out from under the mass of paper work in which this unprecedented trading involved them. And of course brokers' loans were increasing; the inflation of American credit was becoming steadily intensified.

The Reserve authorities were disturbed. They had raised the rediscount rate in February from 3½ to 4 per cent, hoping that if a lowering of the rate in 1927 had encouraged speculation, a corresponding increase would discourage it—and instead they had witnessed a common-stock mania which ran counter to all logic and all economic theory. They raised the rate again in May to 4½ per cent, but after a brief shudder the market went boiling on. They sold the Government bonds they had accumulated during 1927, and the principal result of their efforts was that the Government-bond market became demoralized. Who would ever have thought the situation would thus get out of hand?

In the latter part of May, 1928, the pace of the bull market slackened. Prices fell off, gained, fell off again. The reckoning, so long expected, appeared at last to be at hand.

It came in June, after several days of declining prices. The Giannini stocks, the speculative favorites of the Pacific coast, suddenly toppled for gigantic losses. On the San Francisco Stock Exchange the shares of the Bank of Italy fell 100 points in a single day (June 11th), Bancitaly fell 86 points, Bank of America 120, and United Security 80. That same day, on the New York Curb Exchange, Bancitaly dove perpendicularly from 200 to 110, dragging with it to ruin a horde of small speculators who, despite urgent warnings from A. P. Giannini himself that the stock was overvalued, had naïvely believed that it was "going to a thousand."

The next day, June 12th, this Western tornado struck Wall Street in full force. As selling orders poured in, the prophecy that the Exchange would some day see a five-million share day was quickly fulfilled. The ticker slipped almost two hours behind in recording prices on the floor. Radio, which had marched well beyond the 200 mark in May, lost 23½ points. The day's losses for the general run of securities were not, to be sure, very large by subsequent standards; the *New York*

Times averages for fifty leading stocks dropped only a little over three points. But after the losses of the preceding days, it seemed to many observers as if the end had come at last, and one of the most conservative New York papers began its front-page account of the break with the unqualified sentence, "Wall Street's bull market collapsed yesterday with a detonation heard round the world."

(If the Secretary of Commerce had been superstitious, he might have considered that day of near-panic an omen of troubles to come; for on that same front page, streamer headlines bore the words, "HOOVER CERTAIN ON 1ST BALLOT AS CONVENTION OPENS.")

But had the bull market collapsed? On June 13th it appeared to have regained its balance. On June 14th, the day of Hoover's nomination, it extended its recovery. The promised reckoning had been only partial. Prices still stood well above their February levels. A few thousand traders had been shaken out, a few big fortunes had been lost, a great many pretty paper profits had vanished; but the Big Bull Market was still young.

[3]

A few weeks after the somewhat unenthusiastic nomination of Herbert Hoover by the Republicans, that coalition of incompatibles known as the Democratic party nominated Governor Alfred E. Smith of New York, a genial son of the East Side with a genius for governmental administration and a taste for brown derbies. Al Smith was a remarkable choice. His Tammany affiliations, his wetness, and above all the fact that he was a Roman Catholic made him repugnant to the South and to most of the West. Although the Ku-Klux Klan had recently announced the abandonment of its masks and the change of its name to "Knights of the Great Forest," anti-Catholic feeling could still take ugly forms. That the Democrats took the plunge and nominated Smith on the first ballot was eloquent testimony to the vitality of his personality, to the wide-spread respect for his ability, to the strength of the belief that any Democrat could carry the Solid South and that a wet candidate of immigrant stock would pull votes from the Republicans in the industrial North and the cities generally,—and to the lack of other available candidates.

The campaign of 1928 began.

It was a curious campaign. One great issue divided the candidates. As already recorded in Chapter Ten, Al Smith made no secret of his distaste for prohibition; Hoover, on the other hand, called it "a great social and economic experiment, noble in motive and far-reaching in purpose," which "must be worked out constructively." Although Republican spellbinders in the damply urban East seemed to be under the impression that what Hoover really meant was "worked out of constructively," and Democratic spellbinders in the South and rural West explained that Smith's wetness was just an odd personal notion which he would be powerless to impose upon his party, the division between the two candidates remained: prohibition had forced its way at last into a presidential campaign. There was also the ostensible issue of farm-relief, but on this point there was little real disagreement; instead there was a competition to see which candidate could most eloquently offer largesse to the unhappy Northwest. There was Smith's cherished water-power issue, but this aroused no flaming enthusiasm in the electorate, possibly because too many influential citizens had rosy hopes for the future of Electric Bond & Share or Cities Service. There were also, of course, many less freely advertised issues: millions of men and women turned to Hoover because they thought Smith would make the White House a branch office of the Vatican, or turned to Smith because they wished to strike at religious intolerance, or opposed Hoover because they thought he would prove to be a stubborn doctrinaire, or were activated chiefly by dislike of Smith's hats or Mrs. Smith's jewelry. But no aspect of the campaign was more interesting than the extent to which it reflected the obsession of the American people with bull-market prosperity.

To begin with, there was no formidable third party in the field in 1928 as there had been in 1924. The whispering radicals had been lulled to sleep by the prophets of the new economic era. The Socialists nominated Norman Thomas, but were out of the race from the start. So closely had the ticker tape bound the American people to Wall Street, in fact, that even the Democrats found themselves in a difficult position. In other years they had shown a certain coolness toward the rulers of the banking and industrial world; but this would never do now. To criticize the gentlemen who occupied front seats on the prosperity band-wagon, or to suggest that the ultimate destination of the band-wagon might not be the promised land, would be suicidal. Nor could they deny that good times had arrived under a Republican administration. The best they could do was to argue by word and deed that they, too, could make America safe for dividends and rising stock prices.

This they now did with painful earnestness. For the chairmanship of the Democratic National Committee, Al Smith chose no wild-eyed Congressman from the great open spaces; he chose John J. Raskob, vice-president and chairman of the finance committee of the General Motors Corporation, vice-president of the General Motors Acceptance Corporation, vice-president and member of the finance committee of the E. I. duPont de Nemours & Company, director of the Bankers Trust Company, the American Surety Company, and the County Trust Company of New York—and reputed inspirer of the bull forces behind General Motors. Mr. Raskob was new to politics; in *Who's Who* he not only gave his occupation as "capitalist," but was listed as a Republican; but what matter? All the more credit to Al Smith, thought many Democrats, for having brought him at the eleventh hour to labor in the vineyard. With John J. Raskob on the Democratic side, who could claim that a Democratic victory would prevent common stocks from selling at twenty times earnings?

Mr. Raskob moved the Democratic headquarters to the General Motors Building in New York—than which there was no more bullish address. He proudly announced the fact that Mr. Harkness, "a Standard Oil financier," and Mr. Spreckels, "a banker and sugar refiner," and Mr. James, "A New York financier whose interests embrace railroads, securities companies, real estate, and merchandising," did not consider that their interests were "in the slightest degree imperiled by the prospect of Smith's election." (Shades of a thousand Democratic orators who had once extolled the New Freedom and spoken harsh words about Standard Oil magnates and New York financiers!) And Mr. Raskob and Governor Smith both applied a careful soft pedal to the ancient Democratic low-tariff doctrine—being quite unaware that within two years many of their opponents would be wishing that the Republican high-tariff plank had fallen entirely out of the platform and been carted away.

As for the Republicans, they naturally proclaimed prosper-

ity as a peculiarly Republican product, not yet quite perfected
but ready for the finishing touches. Herbert Hoover himself
struck the keynote for them in his acceptance speech.

"One of the oldest and perhaps the noblest of human as-
pirations," said the Republican candidate, "has been the abolition of poverty. . . . We in America today are nearer to
the final triumph over poverty than ever before in the history of any land. The poorhouse is vanishing from among us.
We have not yet reached the goal, but, given a chance to go
forward with the policies of the last eight years, we shall soon,
with the help of God, be in sight of the day when poverty will
be banished from this nation. There is no guaranty against
poverty equal to a job for every man. That is the primary
purpose of the policies we advocate."

The time was to come when Mr. Hoover would perhaps
regret the cheerful confidence of that acceptance speech. It left
only one loophole for subsequent escape: it stipulated that
God must assist the Republican administration.

Mr. Hoover was hardly to be blamed, however, for his
optimism. Was not business doing far better in the summer of
1928 than it had done during the preceding winter? Was not
the Big Bull Market getting under way again after its fainting
fit in June? One drank in optimism from the very air about
one. And, after all, the first duty of a candidate is to get himself elected. However dubious the abolition of poverty might
appear to Hoover the engineer and economist seated before a
series of graphs of the business cycle, it appeared quite
differently to Hoover the politician standing before the micro-
phone. Prosperity was a sure-fire issue for a Republican in
1928.

Al Smith put up a valiant fight, swinging strenuously from
city to city, autographing brown derbies, denouncing prohibition, denouncing bigotry, and promising new salves for the
farmer's wounds; but it was no use. The odds against him
were too heavy. Election Day came and Hoover swept the
country. His popular vote was nearly twenty-one and a half
millions to Smith's fifteen; his electoral vote was 444 to Smith's
87; and he not only carried Smith's own state of New York
and the doubtful border states of Oklahoma, Tennessee, and
Kentucky, but broke the Solid South itself, winning Florida,
Texas, North Carolina, and even Virginia.

It was a famous victory, and in celebration of it the stock

market—which all through the campaign had been pushing into new high ground—went into a new frenzy. Now the bulls had a new slogan. It was "four more years of prosperity."

[4]

During that "Hoover bull market" of November, 1928, the records made earlier in the year were smashed to flinders. Had brokers once spoken with awe of the possibility of five-million-share days? Five-million-share days were now occurring with monotonous regularity; on November 23rd the volume of trading almost reached seven millions. Had they been amazed at the rising prices of seats on the Stock Exchange? In November a new mark of $580,000 was set. Had they been disturbed that Radio should sell at such an exorbitant price as 150? Late in November it was bringing 400. Ten-point gains and new highs for all time were commonplaces now. Montgomery Ward, which the previous spring had been climbing toward 200, touched 439⅞ on November 30. The copper stocks were skyrocketing; Packard climbed to 145; Wright Aeronautical flew as high as 263. Brokers' loans? Of course they were higher than ever; but this, one was confidently told, was merely a sign of prosperity—a sign that the American people were buying on the part-payment plan a partnership in the future progress of the country. Call money rates? They ranged around 8 and 9 per cent; a little high, perhaps, admitted the bulls, but what was the harm if people chose to pay them? Business was not suffering from high money rates; business was doing better than ever. The new era had arrived, and the abolition of poverty was just around the corner.

In December the market broke again, and more sharply than in June. There was one fearful day—Saturday, December 7th —when the weary ticker, dragging far behind the trading on the floor, hammered out the story of a 72-point decline in Radio. Horrified tape-watchers in the brokers' offices saw the stock open at 361, struggle weakly up to 363, and then take the bumps, point by point, all the way down to 296—which at that moment seemed like a fire-sale figure. (The earnings of the Radio Corporation during the first nine months of 1928 had been $7.54 per share, which on the time-honored basis of "ten times earnings" would have suggested the appropriateness of a price of not much over 100; but the ten-times-earnings basis for prices had long since been discarded. The market, as Max Winkler said, was discounting not only the future but the hereafter.) Montgomery Ward lost 29 points that same nerve-racking Saturday morning, and International Harvester slipped from 368½ to 307. But just as in June, the market righted itself at the moment when demoralization seemed to be setting in. A few uneasy weeks of ragged prices went by, and then the advance began once more.

The Federal Reserve authorities found themselves in an unhappy predicament. Speculation was clearly absorbing more and more of the surplus funds of the country. The inflation of credit was becoming more and more dangerous. The normal course for the Reserve banks at such a juncture would have been to raise the rediscount rate, thus forcing up the price of money for speculative purposes, rendering speculation less attractive, liquidating speculative loans, and reducing the volume of credit outstanding. But the Reserve banks had already raised the rate (in July) to 5 per cent, and speculation had been affected only momentarily. Apparently speculators were ready to pay any amount for money if only prices kept on climbing. The Reserve authorities had waited patiently for the speculative fever to cure itself and it had only become more violent. Things had now come to such a pass that if they raised the rate still further, they not only ran the risk of bringing about a terrific smash in the market—and of appearing to do so deliberately and wantonly—but also of seriously handicapping business by forcing it to pay a high rate for funds. Furthermore, they feared the further accumulation of gold in the United States and the effect which this might have upon world trade. And the Treasury had a final special concern about interest rates—it had its own financing to do, and Secretary Mellon was naturally not enthusiastic about forcing the Government to pay a fancy rate for money for its own current use. It almost seemed as if there were no way to deflation except through disaster.

The Reserve Board finally met the dilemma by thinking up a new and ingenious scheme. They tried to prevent the reloaning of Reserve funds to brokers without raising the rediscount rate.

On February 2, 1929, they issued a statement in which they said: "The Federal Reserve Act does not, in the opinion of the Federal Reserve Board, contemplate the use of the resources of the Federal Reserve Banks for the creation or extension of speculative credit. A member bank is not within its reasonable claims for rediscount facilities at its Federal Reserve Bank when it borrows either for the purpose of making speculative loans or for the purpose of maintaining speculative loans." A little less than a fortnight later the Board wrote to the various Reserve Banks asking them to "prevent as far as possible the diversion of Federal Reserve funds for the purpose of carrying loans based on securities." Meanwhile the Reserve Banks drastically reduced their holdings of securities purchased in the open market. But no increases in rediscount rates were permitted. Again and again, from February on, the directors of the New York Reserve Bank asked Washington for permission to lift the New York rate, and each time the permission was denied. The Board preferred to rely on their new policy.

The immediate result of the statement of February 2, 1929, was a brief overnight collapse in stock prices. The subsequent result, as the Reserve Banks proceeded to bring pressure on their member banks to borrow only for what were termed legitimate business purposes, was naturally a further increase in call-money rates. Late in March—after Herbert Hoover had entered the White House and the previous patron saint of prosperity had retired to Northampton to explore the delights of autobiography—the pinch in money came to a sudden and alarming climax. Stock prices had been falling for several days when on March 26th the rate for call money jumped from 12 per cent to 15, and then to 17, and finally to 20 per cent—the highest rate since the dismal days of 1921. Another dizzy drop in prices took place. The turnover in stocks on the Exchange broke the November record, reaching 8,246,740 shares. Once again thousands of requests for more margin found their way into speculators' mail-boxes, and thousands of participators in the future prosperity of the country were sold out with the loss of everything they owned. Once again the Big Bull Market appeared to be on its last legs.

That afternoon several of the New York banks decided to come to the rescue. Whatever they thought of the new policy of the Federal Reserve Board, they saw a possible panic brewing—and anything, they decided, was better than a panic. The next day Charles E. Mitchell, president of the National City Bank, announced that his bank was prepared to lend twenty million dollars on call, of which five million would be available at 15 per cent, five million more at 16 per cent, and so on up to

20 per cent. Mr. Mitchell's action—which was described by Senator Carter Glass as a slap in the face of the Reserve Board —served to peg the call money rate at 15 per cent and the threatened panic was averted.

Whereupon stocks not only ceased their precipitous fall, but cheerfully recovered!

The lesson was plain: the public simply would not be shaken out of the market by anything short of a major disaster.

During the next month or two stocks rose and fell uncertainly, sinking dismally for a time in May, and the level of brokers' loans dipped a little, but no general liquidation took place. Gradually money began to find its way more plentifully into speculative use despite the barriers raised by the Federal Reserve Board. A corporation could easily find plenty of ways to put its surplus cash out on call at 8 or 9 per cent without doing it through a member bank of the Federal Reserve System; corporations were eager to put their funds to such remunerative use, as the increase in loans "for others" showed; and the member banks themselves, realizing this, were showing signs of restiveness. When June came, the advance in prices began once more, almost as if nothing had happened. The Reserve authorities were beaten.

[5]

By the summer of 1929, prices had soared far above the stormy levels of the preceding winter into the blue and cloudless empyrean. All the old markers by which the price of a promising common stock could be measured had long since been passed; if a stock once valued at 100 went to 300, what on earth was to prevent it from sailing on to 400? And why not ride with it for fifty or a hundred points, with Easy Street at the end of the journey?

By every rule of logic the situation had now become more perilous than ever. If inflation had been serious in 1927, it was far more serious in 1929, as the total of brokers' loans climbed toward six billions (it had been only three and a half billions at the end of 1927). If the price level had been extravagant in 1927 it was preposterous now; and in economics, as in physics, there is no gainsaying the ancient principle that the higher they go, the harder they fall. But the speculative memory is short. As people in the summer of 1929 looked back for precedents, they were comforted by the recollection that every crash of the past few years had been followed by a recovery, and that every recovery had ultimately brought prices to a new high point. Two steps up, one step down, two steps up again—that was how the market went. If you sold, you had only to wait for the next crash (they came every few months) and buy in again. And there was really no reason to sell at all: you were bound to win in the end if your stock was sound. The really wise man, it appeared, was he who "bought and held on."

Time and again the economists and forecasters had cried wolf, wolf, and the wolf had made only the most fleeting of visits. Time and again the Reserve Board had expressed fear of inflation, and inflation had failed to bring hard times. Business in danger? Why, nonsense! Factories were running at full blast and the statistical indices registered first-class industrial health. Was there a threat of overproduction? Nonsense again! Were not business concerns committed to hand-to-mouth buying, were not commodity prices holding to reasonable levels? Where were the overloaded shelves of goods, the heavy inventories, which business analysts universally accepted as storm signals? And look at the character of the stocks which were now leading the advance! At a moment when many of the high-flyers of earlier months were losing ground, the really sensational advances were being made by the shares of such solid and conservatively managed companies as United States Steel, General Electric, and American Telephone—which were precisely those which the most cautious investor would select with an eye to the long future. Their advance, it appeared, was simply a sign that they were beginning to have a scarcity value. As General George R. Dyer of Dyer, Hudson & Company was quoted as saying in the *Boston News Bureau,* "Anyone who buys our highest-class rails and industrials, including the steels, coppers, and utilities, and holds them, will make a great deal of money, *as these securities will gradually be taken out of the market.*" What the bull operators had long been saying must be true, after all. This was a new era. Prosperity was coming into full and perfect flower.

Still there remained doubters. Yet so cogent were the arguments against them that at last the great majority of even the sober financial leaders of the country were won over in some degree. They recognized that inflation might ultimately be a menace, but the fears of immediate and serious trouble which had gripped them during the preceding winter were being dissipated. This bull market had survived some terrific shocks; perhaps it was destined for a long life, after all.

On every side one heard the new wisdom sagely expressed. "Prosperity due for a decline? Why, man, we've scarcely started!" "Be a bull on America." "Never sell the United States short." "I tell you, some of these prices will look ridiculously low in another year or two." "Just watch that stock—it's going to five hundred." "The possibilities of that company are *unlimited*." "Never give up your position in a good stock." Everybody heard how many millions a man would have made if he had bought a hundred shares of General Motors in 1919 and held on. Everybody was reminded at some time or another that George F. Baker never sold anything. As for the menace of speculation, one was glibly assured that—as Ex-Governor Stokes of New Jersey had proclaimed in an eloquent speech— Columbus, Washington, Franklin, and Edison had all been speculators. "The way to wealth," wrote John J. Raskob in an article in the *Ladies Home Journal* alluringly entitled "Everybody Ought to be Rich," "is to get into the profit end of wealth production in this country," and he pointed out that if one saved but fifteen dollars a month and invested it in good common stocks, allowing the dividends and rights to accumulate, at the end of twenty years one would have at least eighty thousand dollars and an income from investments of at least four hundred dollars a month. It was all so easy. The gateway to fortune stood wide open.

Meanwhile, one heard, the future of American industry was to be assured by the application of a distinctly modern principle. Increased consumption, as Waddill Catchings and William T. Foster had pointed out, was the road to plenty. If we all would only spend more and more freely, the smoke would belch from every factory chimney, and dividends would mount. Already the old economic order was giving way to the new. As Dr. Charles Amos Dice, professor of the somewhat unacademic subject of business organization at Ohio State University, wrote in a book called *New Levels in the Stock Market,* there was taking place "a mighty revolution in industry, in trade, and in finance." The stock market was but "registering the tremendous changes that were in progress."

When Professor Dice spoke of changes in finance, he certainly was right. The public no longer wanted anything so stale and profitless as bonds, it wanted securities which would return profits. Company after company was taking shrewd advantage of this new appetite to retire its bonds and issue new common stock in their place. If new bonds were issued, it became fashionable to give them a palatably speculative flavor by making them convertible into stock or by attaching to them warrants for the purchase of stock at some time in the rosy future. The public also seemed to prefer holding a hundred shares of stock priced at $50 to holding twenty shares priced at $250—it made one feel so much richer to be able to buy and sell in quantity! —and an increasing number of corporations therefore split up their common shares to make them attractive to a wide circle of buyers, whether or not any increase in the dividend was in immediate prospect. Many concerns had long made a practice of securing new capital by issuing to their shareholders the rights to buy new stock at a concession in price; this practice now became widely epidemic. Mergers of industrial corporations and of banks were taking place with greater frequency than ever before, prompted not merely by the desire to reduce overhead expenses and avoid the rigors of cut-throat competition, but often by sheer corporate megalomania. And every rumor of a merger or a split-up or an issue of rights was the automatic signal for a leap in the prices of the stocks affected —until it became altogether too tempting to the managers of many a concern to arrange a split-up or a merger or an issue of rights not without a canny eye to their own speculative fortunes.

For many years rival capitalistic interests, imitating the brilliant methods of Sidney Z. Mitchell, had sought to secure control of local electric light and power and gas companies and water companies and weld them into chains; and as the future possibilities of the utilities seized upon the speculative imagination, the battle between these groups led to an amazing proliferation of utility holding companies. By the summer of 1929 the competing systems had become so elaborate, and their interrelations had become so complicated, that it was difficult to arrive at even the vaguest idea of the actual worth of their soaring stocks. Even the professional analyst of financial properties was sometimes bewildered when he found Company A holding a 20-per-cent interest in Company B, and B an interest in C, while C in turn invested in A, and D held shares in each of the others. But few investors seemed to care about actual worth. Utilities had a future and prices were going up—that was enough.

Meanwhile investment trusts multiplied like locusts. There were now said to be nearly five hundred of them, with a total paid-in capital of some three billions and with holdings of stocks—many of them purchased at the current high prices—amounting to something like two billions. These trusts ranged all the way from honestly and intelligently managed companies to wildly speculative concerns launched by ignorant or venal promoters. Some of them, it has been said, were so capitalized that they could not even pay their preferred dividends out of the income from the securities which they held, but must rely almost completely upon the hope of profits. Other investment trusts, it must be admitted, served from time to time the convenient purpose of absorbing securities which the bankers who controlled them might have difficulty in selling in the open market. Reprehensible, you say? Of course; but it was so easy! One could indulge in all manner of dubious financial practices with an unruffled conscience so long as prices rose. The Big Bull Market covered a multitude of sins. It was a golden day for the promoter, and his name was legion.

Gradually the huge pyramid of capital rose. While supersalesmen of automobiles and radios and a hundred other gadgets were loading the ultimate consumer with new and shining wares, supersalesmen of securities were selling him shares of investment trusts which held stock in holding companies which owned the stock of banks which had affiliates which in turn controlled holding companies—and so on *ad infinitum*. Though the shelves of manufacturing companies and jobbers and retailers were not overloaded, the shelves of the ultimate consumer and the shelves of the distributors of securities were groaning. Trouble was brewing—not the same sort of trouble which had visited the country in 1921, but trouble none the less. Still, however, the cloud in the summer sky looked no bigger than a man's hand.

How many Americans actually held stock on margin during the fabulous summer of 1929 there seems to be no way of computing, but it is probably safe to put the figure at more than a million. (George Buchan Robinson estimated that three hundred million shares of stock were being carried on margin.) The additional number of those who held common stock outright and followed the daily quotations with an interest nearly as absorbed as that of the margin trader was, of course, considerably larger. As one walked up the aisle of the 5:27 local, or found one's seat in the trolley car, two out of three newspapers that one saw were open to the page of stock-market quotations. Branch offices of the big Wall Street houses blossomed in every city and in numerous suburban villages. In 1919 there had been five hundred such offices; by October, 1928, there were 1,192; and throughout most of 1929 they appeared in increasing numbers. The broker found himself regarded with a new wonder and esteem. Ordinary people, less intimate with the mysteries of Wall Street than he was supposed to be, hung upon his every word. Let him but drop a hint of a possible split-up in General Industries Associates and his neighbor was off hot-foot the next morning to place a buying order.

The rich man's chauffeur drove with his ear laid back to catch the news of an impending move in Bethlehem Steel; he held fifty shares himself on a twenty-point margin. The window-cleaner at the broker's office paused to watch the ticker, for he was thinking of converting his laboriously accumulated savings into a few shares of Simmons. Edwin Lefèvre told of a broker's valet who had made nearly a quarter of a million in the market, of a trained nurse who cleaned up thirty thousand following the tips given her by grateful patients; and of a Wyoming cattleman, thirty miles from the nearest railroad, who bought or sold a thousand shares a day,—getting his market returns by radio and telephoning his orders to the nearest large town to be transmitted to New York by telegram. An ex-actress in New York fitted up her Park Avenue apartment as an office and surrounded herself with charts, graphs, and financial reports, playing the market by telephone on an increasing scale and with increasing abandon. Across the dinner table one heard fantastic stories of sudden fortunes: a young banker had put every dollar of his small capital into Niles-Bement-Pond and now was fixed for life; a widow had been able to buy a large country house with her winnings in Kennecott. Thousands speculated—and won, too—without the slightest knowledge of the nature of the company upon whose fortunes they were relying, like the people who bought Seaboard Air Line under the impression that it was an aviation stock. Grocers, motormen, plumbers, seamstresses, and speakeasy waiters were in the market. Even the revolting intellectuals were there: loudly as they might lament the depressing effects of standardization and mass production upon American life, they found themselves quite ready to reap the fruits thereof. Literary editors whose hopes were wrapped about American Cyanamid B lunched with poets who swore by Cities Service, and as they left the table, stopped for a moment in the crowd at the broker's branch office to catch the latest quotations; and the artist who had once been eloquent only about Gauguin laid aside his brushes to proclaim the merits of National Bellas Hess. The Big Bull Market had become a national mania.

[6]

In September the market reached its ultimate glittering peak.

It was six months, now, since Herbert Hoover had driven down Pennsylvania Avenue in the rain to take the oath of office as President of the United States. He had appointed the Wickersham Commission to investigate law enforcement in general and prohibition in particular. At the President's instance Congress had passed the Agricultural Marketing Act; and Alexander Legge had assumed, among his duties as chairman of the new Federal Farm Board, the task of "preventing and controlling surpluses in any agricultural commodity." The Kellogg-Briand Treaty had been proclaimed in effect, and Ramsay MacDonald was preparing to sail for the United States to discuss a new treaty for the reduction of naval armaments. The long wrangle over the Harding oil scandals was at last producing definite results: Colonel Stewart, buried under a mountain of Rockefeller proxies, had left the chairmanship of the Standard Oil Company of Indiana, and Harry F. Sinclair was sitting in jail. Colonel Lindbergh, true to his rôle as the national super-hero, had married Miss Anne Morrow. Commander Byrd, the man who put heroism into quantity production, was waiting in the Antarctic darkness of "Little America" for his chance to fly to the South Pole. Non-stop flyers were zooming about over the American countryside, and emulation of the heroes of the air had reached its climax of absurdity in the exploit of a twenty-two-year-old boy who had climbed into the cabin of the *Yellow Bird* and had been carried as a stowaway by Assolant and Lefèvre from Old Orchard, Maine, to the Spanish coast. And on the sands of a thousand American beaches, girls pulled down the shoulder-straps of their bathing suits to acquire fashionably tanned backs, and wondered whether it would be all right to leave their stockings off when they drove to town, and whether it was true, as the journals of fashion declared, that every evening dress must soon reach all the way to the ground.

This was the season when Tilden won his seventh and last American amateur tennis championship. It was Bobby Jones's penultimate year as monarch of amateur golfers—his seventh successive year as winner of either the amateur or the open championship of the United States. Babe Ruth was still hammering out home runs as successfully as in 1920, but he too was getting older: a sporting cycle was drawing to its close. Dempsey had lost his crown to Tunney, Tunney had hung it on the wall to go and foregather with the *literati*, and there was no one to follow them as a magnet for two-million-dollar crowds.

Everybody was reading *All Quiet on the Western Front* and singing the songs which Rudy Vallee crooned over the radio. The literary journals were making a great fuss over humanism. But even sun-tan and Ramsay MacDonald's proposed good-will voyage and humanism and *All Quiet* were dull subjects for talk compared with the Big Bull Market. Had not Goldman, Sachs & Company just expressed its confidence in the present level of prices by sponsoring the Blue Ridge Corporation, an investment trust which offered to exchange its stock for those of the leading "blue chips" at the current figures—324 for Allied Chemical and Dye, 293 for American Telephone, 179 for Consolidated Gas, 395 for General Electric, and so on down the list?

Stop for a moment to glance at a few of the prices recorded on the overworked ticker on September 3, 1929, the day when the Dow-Jones averages reached their high point for the year; and compare them with the opening prices of March 3, 1928, when, as you may recall, it had seemed as if the bull market had already climbed to a perilous altitude. Here they are, side by side—first the figures for March, 1928; then the figures for September, 1929; and finally the latter figures translated into 1928 terms—or in other words revised to make allowance for intervening split-ups and issues of rights. (Only thus can you properly judge the extent of the advance during those eighteen confident months.)

	Opening price March 3 1928	High price Sept. 3 1929	Adjusted high price Sept. 3 1929
American Can	77	181⅞	181⅞
American Telephone & Telegraph .	179½	304	335⅝
Anaconda Copper	54½	131½	162
General Electric	128¾	396¼	396¼
General Motors	139¾	72¾	181⅞
Montgomery Ward	132¾	137⅞	466½
New York Central	160½	256⅜	256⅜
Radio	94½	101	505
Union Carbide & Carbon	145	137⅞	413⅝
United States Steel	138⅛	261¾	279⅛
Westinghouse E. & M.	91⅝	289⅞	313
Woolworth	180¾	100⅜	251
Electric Bond & Share	89¾	186¾	203⅝

Note—The prices of General Electric, Radio, Union Carbide, and Woolworth are here adjusted to take account of split-ups occurring subsequent to March 3, 1928. The prices of American Telephone, Anaconda, Montgomery Ward, United States Steel, Westinghouse, and Electric Bond & Share are adjusted to take account of intervening issues of rights; they represent the value per share on September 3, 1929, of a holding acquired on March 3, 1928, the adjustment being based on the assumption that rights offered in the interval were exercised.

One thing more: as you look at the high prices recorded on September 3, 1929, remember that on that day few people imagined that the peak had actually been reached. The enormous majority fully expected the Big Bull Market to go on and on.

For the blood of the pioneers still ran in American veins; and if there was no longer something lost behind the ranges, still the habit of seeing visions persisted. What if bright hopes had been wrecked by the sordid disappointments of 1919, the collapse of Wilsonian idealism, the spread of political cynicism, the slow decay of religious certainty, and the debunking of love? In the Big Bull Market there was compensation. Still the American could spin wonderful dreams—of a romantic day when he would sell his Westinghouse common at a fabulous price and live in a great house and have a fleet of shining cars and loll at ease on the sands of Palm Beach. And when he looked toward the future of his country, he could vision an

America set free—not from graft, nor from crime, nor from war, nor from control by Wall Street, nor from irreligion, nor from lust, for the utopias of an earlier day left him for the most part skeptical or indifferent; he visioned an America set free from poverty and toil. He saw a magical order built on the new science and the new prosperity: roads swarming with millions upon millions of automobiles, airplanes darkening the skies, lines of high-tension wire carrying from hilltop to hilltop the power to give life to a thousand labor-saving machines, skyscrapers thrusting above one-time villages, vast cities rising in great geometrical masses of stone and concrete and roaring with perfectly mechanized traffic—and smartly dressed men and women spending, spending, spending with the money they had won by being far-sighted enough to foresee, way back in 1929, what was going to happen.

XIII

Crash!

Early in September the stock market broke. It quickly recovered, however; indeed, on September 19th the averages as compiled by the *New York Times* reached an even higher level than that of September 3rd. Once more it slipped, farther and faster, until by October 4th the prices of a good many stocks had coasted to what seemed first-class bargain levels. Steel, for example, after having touched 261¾ a few weeks earlier, had dropped as low as 204; American Can, at the closing on October 4th, was nearly twenty points below its high for the year; General Electric was over fifty points below its high; Radio had gone down from 114¾ to 82½.

A bad break, to be sure, but there had been other bad breaks, and the speculators who escaped unscathed proceeded to take advantage of the lessons they had learned in June and December of 1928 and March and May of 1929: when there was a break it was a good time to buy. In the face of all this tremendous liquidation, brokers' loans as compiled by the Federal Reserve Bank of New York mounted to a new high record on October 2nd, reaching $6,804,000,000—a sure sign that margin buyers were not deserting the market but coming into it in numbers at least undiminished. (Part of the increase in the loan figure was probably due to the piling up of unsold securities in dealers' hands, as the spawning of investment trusts and the issue of new common stock by every manner of business concern continued unabated.) History, it seemed, was about to repeat itself, and those who picked up Anaconda at 109¾ or American Telephone at 281 would count themselves wise investors. And sure enough, prices once more began to climb. They had already turned upward before that Sunday in early October when Ramsay MacDonald sat on a log with Herbert Hoover at the Rapidan camp and talked over the prospects for naval limitation and peace.

Something was wrong, however. The decline began once more. The wiseacres of Wall Street, looking about for causes, fixed upon the collapse of the Hatry financial group in England (which had led to much forced selling among foreign investors and speculators), and upon the bold refusal of the Massachusetts Department of Public Utilities to allow the Edison Company of Boston to split up its stock. They pointed, too, to the fact that the steel industry was undoubtedly slipping, and to the accumulation of "undigested" securities. But there was little real alarm until the week of October 21st. The consensus of opinion, in the meantime, was merely that the equinoctial storm of September had not quite blown over. The market was readjusting itself into a "more secure technical position."

[2]

In view of what was about to happen, it is enlightening to recall how things looked at this juncture to the financial prophets, those gentlemen whose wizardly reputations were based upon their supposed ability to examine a set of graphs brought to them by a statistician and discover, from the relation of curve to curve and index to index, whether things were going to get better or worse. Their opinions differed, of course; there never has been a moment when the best financial opinion was unanimous. In examining these opinions, and the outgivings of eminent bankers, it must furthermore be acknowledged that a bullish statement cannot always be taken at its face value: few men like to assume the responsibility of spreading alarm by making dire predictions, nor is a banker with unsold securities on his hands likely to say anything which will make it more difficult to dispose of them, unquiet as his private mind may be. Finally, one must admit that prophecy is at best the most hazardous of occupations. Nevertheless, the general state of financial opinion in October, 1929, makes an instructive contrast with that in February and March, 1928, when, as we have seen, the skies had not appeared any too bright.

Some forecasters, to be sure, were so unconventional as to counsel caution. Roger W. Babson, an investment adviser who had not always been highly regarded in the inner circles of Wall Street, especially since he had for a long time been warning his clients of future trouble, predicted early in September a decline of sixty or eighty points in the averages. On October 7th the Standard Trade and Securities Service of the Standard Statistics Company advised its clients to pursue an "ultraconservative policy," and ventured this prediction: "We remain of the opinion that, over the next few months, the trend of common-stock prices will be toward lower levels." Poor's *Weekly Business and Investment Letter* spoke its mind on the "great common-stock delusion" and predicted "further liquidation in stocks." Among the big bankers, Paul M. Warburg had shown months before this that he was alive to the dangers of the situation. These commentators—along with others such as the editor of the *Commercial and Financial Chronicle* and the financial editor of the *New York Times*—would appear to deserve the 1929 gold medals for foresight.

But if ever such medals were actually awarded, a goodly number of leather ones would have to be distributed at the same time. Not necessarily to the Harvard Economic Society, although on October 19th, after having explained that business was "facing another period of readjustment," it predicted that "if recession should threaten serious consequences for business (as is not indicated at present) there is little doubt that the Reserve System would take steps to ease the money market and so check the movement." The Harvard soothsayers proved themselves quite fallible: as late as October 26th, after the first wide-open crack in the stock market, they delivered the cheerful judgment that "despite its severity, we believe that the slump in stock prices will prove an intermediate movement and not the precursor of a business depression such as would entail prolonged further liquidation." This judgment turned out, of course, to be ludicrously wrong; but on the other hand the Harvard Economic Society was far from being really bullish. Nor would Colonel Leonard P. Ayres of the Cleveland Trust Company get one of the leather medals. He almost qualified when, on October 15th, he delivered himself of the judgment

that "there does not seem to be as yet much real evidence that
the decline in stock prices is likely to forecast a serious recession in general business. Despite the slowing down in iron
and steel production, in automobile output, and in building,
the conditions which result in serious business depressions are
not present." But the skies, as Colonel Ayres saw them, were at
least partly cloudy. "It seems probable," he said, "that stocks
have been passing not so much from the strong to the weak as
from the smart to the dumb."

Professor Irving Fisher, however, was more optimistic. In
the newspapers of October 17th he was reported as telling the
Purchasing Agents Association that stock prices had reached
"what looks like a permanently high plateau." He expected to
see the stock market, within a few months, "a good deal higher
than it is today." On the very eve of the panic of October 24th
he was further quoted as expecting a recovery in prices. Only
two days before the panic, the *Boston News Bureau* quoted R.
W. McNeel, director of McNeel's Financial Service, as sus-
pecting "that some pretty intelligent people are now buying
stocks." "Unless we are to have a panic—which no one seriously believes—stocks have hit bottom," said Mr. McNeel.
And as for Charles E. Mitchell, chairman of the great National
City Bank of New York, he continuously and enthusiastically
radiated sunshine. Early in October Mr. Mitchell was positive
that, despite the stock-market break, "The industrial situation
of the United States is absolutely sound and our credit situation is in no way critical. . . . The interest given by the
public to brokers' loans is always exaggerated," he added.
"Altogether too much attention is paid to it." A few days later
Mr. Mitchell spoke again: "Although in some cases speculation has gone too far in the United States, the markets generally are now in a healthy condition. The last six weeks have
done an immense amount of good by shaking down prices.
. . . The market values have a sound basis in the general
prosperity of our country." Finally, on October 22nd, two days
before the panic, he arrived in the United States from a short
trip to Europe with these reassuring words: "I know of nothing
fundamentally wrong with the stock market or with the
underlying business and credit structure. . . . The public is
suffering from 'brokers' loanitis.' "

Nor was Mr. Mitchell by any means alone in his opinions.
To tell the truth, the chief difference between him and the rest

of the financial community was that he made more noise. One of the most distinguished bankers in the United States, in closing a deal in the early autumn of 1929, said privately that he saw not a cloud in the sky. Habitual bulls like Arthur Cutten were, of course, insisting that they were "still bullish." And the general run of traders presumably endorsed the view attributed to "one large house" in mid-October in the *Boston News Bureau's* "Broad Street Gossip," that "the recent break makes a firm foundation for a big bull market in the last quarter of the year." There is no doubt that a great many speculators who had looked upon the midsummer prices as too high were now deciding that deflation had been effected and were buying again. Presumably most financial opinion agreed also with the further statement which appeared in the "Broad Street Gossip" column on October 16th, that "business is now too big and diversified, and the country too rich, to be influenced by stock-market fluctuations"; and with the editorial opinion of the *News Bureau,* on October 19th, that "whatever recessions (in business) are noted, are those of the runner catching his breath. . . . The general condition is satisfactory and fundamentally sound."

The disaster which was impending was destined to be as bewildering and frightening to the rich and the powerful and the customarily sagacious as to the foolish and unwary holder of fifty shares of margin stock.

[3]

The expected recovery in the stock market did not come. It seemed to be beginning on Tuesday, October 22nd, but the gains made during the day were largely lost during the last hour. And on Wednesday, the 23rd, there was a perfect Niagara of liquidation. The volume of trading was over six million shares, the tape was 104 minutes late when the three-o'clock gong ended trading for the day, and the *New York Times* averages for fifty leading railroad and industrial stocks lost 18.24 points—a loss which made the most abrupt declines in previous breaks look small. Everybody realized that an unprecedented number of margin calls must be on their way to insecurely margined traders, and that the situation at last was getting serious. But perhaps the turn would come tomorrow. Already the break had carried prices down a good deal farther than the previous breaks of the past two years. Surely it could not go on much longer.

The next day was Thursday, October 24th.

On that momentous day stocks opened moderately steady in price, but in enormous volume. Kennecott appeared on the tape in a block of 20,000 shares, General Motors in another of the same amount. Almost at once the ticker tape began to lag behind the trading on the floor. The pressure of selling orders was disconcertingly heavy. Prices were going down. . . . Presently they were going down with some rapidity. . . . Before the first hour of trading was over, it was already apparent that they were going down with an altogether unprecedented and amazing violence. In brokers' offices all over the country, tape-watchers looked at one another in astonishment and perplexity. Where on earth was this torrent of selling orders coming from?

The exact answer to this question will probably never be known. But it seems probable that the principal cause of the break in prices during that first hour on October 24th was not fear. Nor was it short selling. It was forced selling. It was the dumping on the market of hundreds of thousands of shares of stock held in the name of miserable traders whose margins were exhausted or about to be exhausted. The gigantic edifice of prices was honeycombed with speculative credit and was now breaking under its own weight.

Fear, however, did not long delay its coming. As the price structure crumbled there was a sudden stampede to get out from under. By eleven o'clock traders on the floor of the Stock Exchange were in a wild scramble to "sell at the market." Long before the lagging ticker could tell what was happening, word had gone out by telephone and telegraph that the bottom was dropping out of things, and the selling orders redoubled in volume. The leading stocks were going down two, three, and even five points between sales. Down, down, down. . . . Where were the bargain-hunters who were supposed to come to the rescue at times like this? Where were the investment trusts, which were expected to provide a cushion for the market by making new purchases at low prices? Where were the big operators who had declared that they were still bullish? Where were the powerful bankers who were supposed to be able at any moment to support prices? There seemed to be no support whatever. Down, down, down. The roar of voices which rose from the floor of the Exchange had become a roar of panic.

United States Steel had opened at 205½. It crashed through 200 and presently was at 193½. General Electric, which only a few weeks before had been selling above 400, had opened this morning at 315—now it had slid to 283. Things were even worse with Radio: opening at 68¾, it had gone dismally down through the sixties and the fifties and forties to the abysmal price of 44½. And as for Montgomery Ward, vehicle of the hopes of thousands who saw the chain store as the harbinger of the new economic era, it had dropped headlong from 83 to 50. In the space of two short hours, dozens of stocks lost ground which it had required many months of the bull market to gain.

Even this sudden decline in values might not have been utterly terrifying if people could have known precisely what was happening at any moment. It is the unknown which causes real panic.

Suppose a man walked into a broker's branch office between twelve and one o'clock on October 24th to see how things were faring. First he glanced at the big board, covering one wall of the room, on which the day's prices for the leading stocks were supposed to be recorded. The LOW and LAST figures written there took his breath away, but soon he was aware that they were unreliable: even with the wildest scrambling, the boys who slapped into place the cards which recorded the last prices shown on the ticker could not keep up with the changes: they were too numerous and abrupt. He turned to the shining screen across which ran an uninterrupted procession of figures from the ticker. Ordinarily the practiced tape-watcher could tell from a moment's glance at the screen how things were faring, even though the Exchange now omitted all but the final digit of each quotation. A glance at the board, if not his own memory, supplied the missing digits. But today, when he saw a run of symbols and figures like

R   WX
6.5½.5.4.   9.8⅞.¾.½.¼.8.7½.7.

he could not be sure whether the price of "6" shown for Radio meant 66 or 56 or 46; whether Westinghouse was sliding from 189 to 187 or from 179 to 177. And presently he heard that the ticker was an hour and a half late; at one o'clock it was recording the prices of half-past eleven! All this that he saw was ancient history. What was happening on the floor now?

At ten-minute intervals the bond ticker over in the corner would hammer off a list of selected prices direct from the floor, and a broker's clerk would grab the uncoiling sheet of paper and shear it off with a pair of scissors and read the figures aloud in a mumbling expressionless monotone to the white-faced men who occupied every seat on the floor and stood packed at the rear of the room. The prices which he read out were *ten or a dozen or more points below those recorded on the ticker*. What about the stocks not included in that select list? There was no way of finding out. The telephone lines were clogged as inquiries and orders from all over the country converged upon the Stock Exchange. Once in a while a voice would come barking out of the broker's rear office where a frantic clerk was struggling for a telephone connection: "Steel at ninety-six!" Small comfort, however, to know what Steel was doing; the men outside were desperately involved in many another stock than Steel; they were almost completely in the dark, and their imaginations had free play. If they put in an order to buy or to sell, it was impossible to find out what became of it. The Exchange's whole system for the recording of current prices and for communicating orders was hopelessly unable to cope with the emergency, and the sequel was an epidemic of fright.

In that broker's office, as in hundreds of other offices from one end of the land to the other, one saw men looking defeat in the face. One of them was slowly walking up and down, mechanically tearing a piece of paper into tiny and still tinier fragments. Another was grinning shamefacedly, as a small boy giggles at a funeral. Another was abjectly beseeching a clerk for the latest news of American & Foreign Power. And still another was sitting motionless, as if stunned, his eyes fixed blindly upon the moving figures on the screen, those innocent-looking figures that meant the smash-up of the hopes of years. . . .

GL.	AWW.	JMP.
8.7.5.2.1.90.89.7.6.	3.2½.2.	6.5.3.2½.

A few minutes after noon, some of the more alert members of a crowd which had collected on the street outside the Stock Exchange, expecting they knew not what, recognized Charles

E. Mitchell, erstwhile defender of the bull market, slipping quietly into the offices of J. P. Morgan & Company on the opposite corner. It was scarcely more than nine years since the House of Morgan had been pitted with the shrapnel-fire of the Wall Street explosion; now its occupants faced a different sort of calamity equally near at hand. Mr. Mitchell was followed shortly by Albert H. Wiggin, head of the Chase National Bank; William Potter, head of the Guaranty Trust Company; and Seward Prosser, head of the Bankers Trust Company. They had come to confer with Thomas W. Lamont of the Morgan firm. In the space of a few minutes these five men, with George F. Baker, Jr., of the First National Bank, agreed in behalf of their respective institutions to put up forty millions apiece to shore up the stock market. The object of the two-hundred-and-forty-million-dollar pool thus formed, as explained subsequently by Mr. Lamont, was not to hold prices at any given level, but simply to make such purchases as were necessary to keep trading on an orderly basis. Their first action, they decided, would be to try to steady the prices of the leading securities which served as bellwethers for the list as a whole. It was a dangerous plan, for with hysteria spreading there was no telling what sort of *débâcle* might be impending. But this was no time for any action but the boldest.

The bankers separated. Mr. Lamont faced a gathering of reporters in the Morgan offices. His face was grave, but his words were soothing. His first sentence alone was one of the most remarkable understatements of all time. "There has been a little distress selling on the Stock Exchange," said he, "and we have held a meeting of the heads of several financial institutions to discuss the situation. We have found that there are no houses in difficulty and reports from brokers indicate that margins are being maintained satisfactorily." He went on to explain that what had happened was due to a "technical condition of the market" rather than to any fundamental cause.

As the news that the bankers were meeting circulated on the floor of the Exchange, prices began to steady. Soon a brisk rally set in. Steel jumped back to the level at which it had opened that morning. But the bankers had more to offer the dying bull market than a Morgan partner's best bedside manner.

At about half-past one o'clock Richard Whitney, vice-presi-

dent of the Exchange, who usually acted as floor broker for the
Morgan interests, went into the "steel crowd" and put in a bid
of 205—the price of the last previous sale—for 10,000 shares
of Steel. He bought only 200 shares and left the remainder of
the order with the specialist. Mr. Whitney then went to various
other points on the floor, and offered the price of the last
previous sale for 10,000 shares of each of fifteen or twenty
other stocks, reporting what was sold to him at that price and
leaving the remainder of the order with the specialist. In short,
within the space of a few minutes Mr. Whitney offered to
purchase something in the neighborhood of twenty or thirty
million dollars' worth of stock. Purchases of this magnitude
are not undertaken by Tom, Dick, and Harry; it was clear that
Mr. Whitney represented the bankers' pool.

The desperate remedy worked. The semblance of confidence
returned. Prices held steady for a while; and though many of
them slid off once more in the final hour, the net results for the
day might well have been worse. Steel actually closed two
points higher than on Wednesday, and the net losses of most of
the other leading securities amounted to less than ten points
apiece for the whole day's trading.

All the same, it had been a frightful day. At seven o'clock
that night the tickers in a thousand brokers' offices were still
chattering; not till after 7:08 did they finally record the last
sale made on the floor at three o'clock. The volume of trading
had set a new record—12,894,650 shares. ("The time may
come when we shall see a five-million-share day," the wise men
of the Street had been saying twenty months before!) Incredible rumors had spread wildly during the early afternoon—that
eleven speculators had committed suicide, that the Buffalo and
Chicago exchanges had been closed, that troops were guarding
the New York Stock Exchange against an angry mob. The
country had known the bitter taste of panic. And although the
bankers' pool had prevented for the moment an utter collapse,
there was no gainsaying the fact that the economic structure
had cracked wide open.

[4]

Things looked somewhat better on Friday and Saturday.
Trading was still on an enormous scale, but prices for the most
part held. At the very moment when the bankers' pool was

cautiously disposing of as much as possible of the stock which
it had accumulated on Thursday and was thus preparing for
future emergencies, traders who had sold out higher up were
coming back into the market again with new purchases, in the
hope that the bottom had been reached. (Hadn't they often
been told that "the time to buy is when things look blackest"?)
The newspapers carried a very pretty series of reassuring
statements from the occupants of the seats of the mighty;
Herbert Hoover himself, in a White House statement, pointed
out that "the fundamental business of the country, that is,
production and distribution of commodities, is on a sound and
prosperous basis." But toward the close of Saturday's session
prices began to slip again. And on Monday the rout was under
way once more.

The losses registered on Monday were terrific—17½ points
for Steel, 47½ for General Electric, 36 for Allied Chemical,
34½ for Westinghouse, and so on down a long and dismal list.
All Saturday afternoon and Saturday night and Sunday the
brokers had been struggling to post their records and go over
their customers' accounts and sent out calls for further margin,
and another avalanche of forced selling resulted. The prices at
which Mr. Whitney's purchases had steadied the leading stocks
on Thursday were so readily broken through that it was immediately clear that the bankers' pool had made a strategic
retreat. As a matter of fact, the brokers who represented the
pool were having their hands full plugging up the "air-holes" in
the list—in other words, buying stocks which were offered for
sale without any bids at all in sight. Nothing more than this
could have been accomplished, even if it could have been
wisely attempted. Even six great banks could hardly stem the
flow of liquidation from the entire United States. They could
only guide it a little, check it momentarily here and there.

Once more the ticker dropped ridiculously far behind, the
lights in the brokers' offices and the banks burned till dawn,
and the telegraph companies distributed thousands of margin
calls and requests for more collateral to back up loans at the
banks. Bankers, brokers, clerks, messengers were almost at the
end of their strength; for days and nights they had been driving
themselves to keep pace with the most terrific volume of business that had ever descended upon them. It did not seem as if

they could stand it much longer. But the worst was still ahead. It came the next day, Tuesday, October 29th.

The big gong had hardly sounded in the great hall of the Exchange at ten o'clock Tuesday morning before the storm broke in full force. Huge blocks of stock were thrown upon the market for what they would bring. Five thousand shares, ten thousand shares appeared at a time on the laboring ticker at fearful recessions in price. Not only were innumerable small traders being sold out, but big ones, too, protagonists of the new economic era who a few weeks before had counted themselves millionaires. Again and again the specialist in a stock would find himself surrounded by brokers fighting to sell—and nobody at all even thinking of buying. To give one single example: during the bull market the common stock of the White Sewing Machine Company had gone as high as 48; on Monday, October 28th, it had closed at 11⅛. On that black Tuesday, somebody—a clever messenger boy for the Exchange, it was rumored—had the bright idea of putting in an order to buy at 1—and in the temporarily complete absence of other bids he actually got his stock for a dollar a share! The scene on the floor was chaotic. Despite the jamming of the communication system, orders to buy and sell—mostly to sell —came in faster than human beings could possibly handle them; it was on that day that an exhausted broker, at the close of the session, found a large waste-basket which he had stuffed with orders to be executed and had carefully set aside for safe-keeping—and then had completely forgotten. Within half an hour of the opening the volume of trading had passed three million shares, by twelve o'clock it had passed eight million, by half-past one it had passed twelve million, and when the closing gong brought the day's madness to an end the gigantic record of 16,410,030 shares had been set. Toward the close there was a rally, but by that time the average prices of fifty leading stocks, as compiled by the *New York Times,* had fallen nearly forty points. Meanwhile there was a near-panic in other markets—the foreign stock exchanges, the lesser American exchanges, the grain market.

So complete was the demoralization of the stock market and so exhausted were the brokers and their staffs and the Stock Exchange employees, that at noon that day, when the panic was at its worst, the Governing Committee met quietly to

decide whether or not to close the Exchange. To quote from an
address made some months later by Richard Whitney: "In
order not to give occasion for alarming rumors, this meeting
was not held in the Governing Committee Room, but in the
office of the president of the Stock Clearing Corporation
directly beneath the Stock Exchange floor. . . . The forty
governors came to the meeting in groups of two and three as
unobtrusively as possible. The office they met in was never
designed for large meetings of this sort, with the result that
most of the governors were compelled to stand, or to sit on
tables. As the meeting progressed, panic was raging overhead
on the floor. . . . The feeling of those present was revealed
by their habit of continually lighting cigarettes, taking a puff or
two, putting them out and lighting new ones—a practice which
soon made the narrow room blue with smoke. . . ." Two of
the Morgan partners were invited to the meeting and, attempt-
ing to slip into the building unnoticed so as not to start a new
flock of rumors, were refused admittance by one of the guards
and had to remain outside until rescued by a member of the
Governing Committee. After some deliberation, the governors
finally decided not to close the Exchange.

It was a critical day for the banks, that Tuesday the 29th.
Many of the corporations which had so cheerfully loaned
money to brokers through the banks in order to obtain interest
at 8 or 9 per cent were now clamoring to have these loans
called—and the banks were faced with a choice between taking
over the loans themselves and running the risk of precipitating
further ruin. It was no laughing matter to assume the responsibility of millions of dollars' worth of loans secured by collateral which by the end of the day might prove to have dropped
to a fraction of its former value. That the call money rate
never rose above 6 per cent that day, that a money panic was
not added to the stock panic, and that several Wall Street
institutions did not go down into immediate bankruptcy, was
due largely to the nerve shown by a few bankers in stepping
into the breach. The story is told of one banker who went
grimly on authorizing the taking over of loan after loan until
one of his subordinate officers came in with a white face and
told him that the bank was insolvent. "I dare say," said the
banker, and went ahead unmoved. He knew that if he did not,
more than one concern would face insolvency.

The next day—Wednesday, October 30th—the outlook suddenly and providentially brightened. The directors of the Steel Corporation had declared an extra dividend; the directors of the American Can Company had not only declared an extra dividend, but had raised the regular dividend. There was another flood of reassuring statements—though by this time a cheerful statement from a financier fell upon somewhat skeptical ears. Julius Klein, Mr. Hoover's Assistant Secretary of Commerce, composed a rhapsody on continued prosperity. John J. Raskob declared that stocks were at bargain prices and that he and his friends were buying. John D. Rockefeller poured Standard Oil upon the waters: "Believing that fundamental conditions of the country are sound and that there is nothing in the business situation to warrant the destruction of values that has taken place on the exchanges during the past week, my son and I have for some days been purchasing sound common stocks." Better still, prices rose—steadily and buoyantly. Now at last the time had come when the strain on the Exchange could be relieved without causing undue alarm. At 1:40 o'clock Vice-President Whitney announced from the rostrum that the Exchange would not open until noon the following day and would remain closed all day Friday and Saturday—and to his immense relief the announcement was greeted, not with renewed panic, but with a cheer.

Throughout Thursday's short session the recovery continued. Prices gyrated wildly—for who could arrive at a reasonable idea of what a given stock was worth, now that all settled standards of value had been upset?—but the worst of the storm seemed to have blown over. The financial community breathed more easily; now they could have a chance to set their houses in order.

It was true that the worst of the panic was past. But not the worst prices. There was too much forced liquidation still to come as brokers' accounts were gradually straightened out, as banks called for more collateral, and terror was renewed. The next week, in a series of short sessions, the tide of prices receded once more—until at last on November 13th the bottom prices for the year 1929 were reached. Beside the figures hung up in the sunny days of September they made a tragic showing:

	High price Sept. 3, 1929	Low price Nov. 13, 1929
American Can	181⅞	86
American Telephone & Telegraph	304	197¼
Anaconda Copper	131½	70
General Electric	396¼	168⅛
General Motors	72¾	36
Montgomery Ward	137⅞	49¼
New York Central	256⅜	160
Radio	101	28
Union Carbide & Carbon	137⅞	59
United States Steel	261¾	150
Westinghouse E. & M.	289⅞	102⅝
Woolworth	100⅜	52¼
Electric Bond & Share	186¾	50¼

The *New York Times* averages for fifty leading stocks had been almost cut in half, falling from a high of 311.90 in September to a low of 164.43 on November 13th; and the *Times* averages for twenty-five leading industrials had fared still worse, diving from 469.49 to 220.95.

The Big Bull Market was dead. Billions of dollars' worth of profits—and paper profits—had disappeared. The grocer, the window-cleaner, and the seamstress had lost their capital. In every town there were families which had suddenly dropped from showy affluence into debt. Investors who had dreamed of retiring to live on their fortunes now found themselves back once more at the very beginning of the long road to riches. Day by day the newspapers printed the grim reports of suicides.

Coolidge-Hoover Prosperity was not yet dead, but it was dying. Under the impact of the shock of panic, a multitude of ills which hitherto had passed unnoticed or had been offset by stock-market optimism began to beset the body economic, as poisons seep through the human system when a vital organ has ceased to function normally. Although the liquidation of nearly three billion dollars of brokers' loans contracted credit, and the Reserve Banks lowered the rediscount rate, and the way in which the larger banks and corporations of the country had survived the emergency without a single failure of large proportions offered real encouragement, nevertheless the poisons were there: overproduction of capital; overambitious expansion of business concerns; overproduction of commodities under the stimulus of installment buying and buying with stock-market profits; the maintenance of an artificial price level for many commodities; the depressed condition of European trade. No matter how many soothsayers of high finance proclaimed that all was well, no matter how earnestly the President set to work to repair the damage with soft words and White House conferences, a major depression was inevitably under way.

Nor was that all. Prosperity is more than an economic condition; it is a state of mind. The Big Bull Market had been more than the climax of a business cycle; it had been the climax of a cycle in American mass thinking and mass emotion. There was hardly a man or woman in the country whose attitude toward life had not been affected by it in some degree and was not now affected by the sudden and brutal shattering of hope. With the Big Bull Market gone and prosperity going, Americans were soon to find themselves living in an altered world which called for new adjustments, new ideas, new habits of thought, and a new order of values. The psychological climate was changing; the ever-shifting currents of American life were turning into new channels.

The Post-war Decade had come to its close. An era had ended.

XIV

Aftermath: 1930-31

Not without long and unhappy protest did the country accept as an inevitable fact the breakdown of Coolidge-Hoover Prosperity. It was a bitter draught to swallow; especially bitter for the Republican party, which had so far forgotten the business cycle's independence of political policies as to persuade itself that prosperity was a Republican invention; and bitterest of all for Herbert Hoover, who had uttered such confident words about the abolition of poverty.

When the stock market went over the edge of Niagara in October and November, 1929, and the decline in business became alarming, the country turned to the President for action. Something must be done immediately to restore public confidence and prevent the damage from spreading too far. Mr. Hoover was a student of business, a superlative organizer, and no novice in the art of directing public opinion; whatever his deficiencies might be in dealing with politicians and meeting purely political issues, the country felt that in a public emergency of this sort he would know what to do and how to do it if anybody on earth did.

The President acted promptly. He promised a reduction in taxes. He called a series of conferences of business leaders who expressed public disapproval of the idea of lowering wages. He recommended the building of public works to take up the impending slack in employment. And he and his associates resolutely set themselves to build up the shaken morale of business by proclaiming that everything was all right and presently would be still better; that "conditions"—as the ever-lasting reiterated phrase of the day went—were "fundamentally sound." "I am convinced that through these measures we have reëstablished confidence," said the President in his annual message in December. When the year 1930 opened, Secretary Mellon predicted "a revival of activity in the spring." "There is nothing in the situation to be disturbed about," said Secretary of Commerce Lamont in February. . . . "There are grounds for assuming that this is about a normal year." In March Mr. Lamont was more specific: he predicted that business would be normal in two months. A few days later the President himself set a definite date for the promised recovery: unemployment would be ended in sixty days. On March 16th the indefatigable cheer-leader of the Presidential optimists, Julius H. Barnes, the head of Mr. Hoover's new National Business Survey Conference, spoke as if trouble were already a thing of the past. "The spring of 1930," said he, "marks the end of a period of grave concern. . . . American business is steadily coming back to a normal level of prosperity."

At first it seemed as if the Administration would succeed not only in preventing drastic and immediate wage cuts, but in restoring economic health by applying the formula of Doctor Coué. After sinking to a low level at the end of 1929 and throwing something like three million men upon the streets, the industrial indices showed measurable signs of improvement. The stock market collected itself and began a new advance. Common stocks had not lost their lure; every speculator who had not been utterly cleaned out in the panic sought eagerly for the hair of the dog that bit him. During the first three months of 1930 a Little Bull Market gave a very plausible imitation of the Big Bull Market. Trading became as heavy as in the golden summer of 1929, and the prices of the leading stocks actually regained more than half the ground they had lost during the *débâcle*. For a time it seemed as if perhaps the hopeful prophets at Washington were right and prosperity was coming once more and it would be well to get in on the ground floor and make up those dismal losses of 1929.

But in April this brief illusion began to sicken and die. Business reaction had set in again. By the end of the sixty-day period set for recovery by the President and his Secretary of Commerce, commodity prices were going down, production indices were going down, the stock market was taking a series of painful tumbles, and hope deferred was making the American heartsick. The Coué formula was failing; for the economic disease was more than a temporary case of nervous prostration, it was organic and deep-seated.

Grimly but with a set smile on their faces, the physicians at Washington continued to recite their lesson from *Self-Mastery Through Conscious Auto-Suggestion.* They had begun their course of treatment with plentiful publicity and could not well change the prescription now without embarrassment. Early in May Mr. Hoover said he was convinced that "we have now passed the worst and with continued unity of effort we shall rapidly recover." On May 8th the governor of the Federal Reserve Board admitted that the country was in "what appears to be a business depression" (*"appears to be"*—with factories shutting down, stocks skidding, and bread-lines stretching down the streets!), but that was as far as anybody at Washington seemed willing to go in facing the grim reality. On May 28th Mr. Hoover was reported as predicting that business would be normal by fall. The grim farce went on, the physicians uttering soothing words to the patient and the patient daily sinking lower and lower—until for a time it seemed as if every cheerful pronouncement was followed by a fresh collapse. Only when the failure of the treatment became obvious to the point of humiliation did the Administration lapse into temporary silence.

What were the economic diseases from which business was suffering? A few of them may be listed categorically.

1. Overproduction of capital and goods. During the nineteen-twenties, industry had become more mechanized, and thus more capable of producing on a huge scale than ever before. In the bullish days of 1928 and 1929, when installment buying and stock profits were temporarily increasing the buying power of the American people, innumerable concerns had cheerfully overexpanded; the capitalization of the nation's industry had become inflated, along with bank credit. When stock profits vanished and new installment buyers became harder to find and men and women were wondering how they could meet the next payment on the car or the radio or the furniture, manufacturers were forced to operate their enlarged

and all-too-productive factories on a reduced and unprofitable basis as they waited for buying power to recover.

2. Artificial commodity prices. During 1929, as David Friday has pointed out, the prices of many products had been stabilized at high levels by pools. There were pools, for example, in copper and cotton; there was a wheat pool in Canada, a coffee pool in Brazil, a sugar pool in Cuba, a wool pool in Australia. The prices artificially maintained by these pools had led to overproduction, which became the more dangerous the longer it remained concealed. Stocks of these commodities accumulated at a rate out of all proportion to consumption; eventually the pools could no longer support the markets, and when the inevitable day of reckoning came, prices fell disastrously.

3. A collapse in the price of silver, due partly to the efforts of several governments to put themselves on a gold basis—with a resulting paralysis to the purchasing power of the Orient.

4. The international financial derangement caused by the shifting of gold in huge quantities to France and particularly to the United States.

5. Unrest in foreign countries. As the international depression deepened, the political and economic dislocation caused by the war became newly apparent; the chickens of 1914-18 were coming home to roost. Revolutions and the threat of revolutions in various parts of the world added to the general uncertainty and fear, and incidentally jeopardized American investments abroad.

6. The self-generating effect of the depression itself. Each bankruptcy, each suspension of payments, and each reduction of operating schedules affected other concerns, until it seemed almost as if the business world were a set of tenpins ready to knock one another over as they fell; each employee thrown out of work decreased the potential buying power of the country. And finally—

7. The profound psychological reaction from the exuberance of 1929. Fundamentally, perhaps, the business cycle is a psychological phenomenon. Only when the memory of hard times has dimmed can confidence fully establish itself; only when confidence has led to outrageous excesses can it be checked. It was as difficult for Mr. Hoover to stop the psychological pendulum on its down-swing as it had been for the Reserve Board to stop it on its up-swing.

What happened after the failure of the Hoover campaign of optimism makes sad reading. Commodity prices plunged to shocking depths. Wheat, for instance: during the last few days of 1929, December wheat had brought $1.35 at Chicago; a year later it brought only 76 cents. July wheat fell during the same interval from $1.37 to 61 cents. Mr. Legge's Federal Farm Board was not unmindful of the distress throughout the wheat belt caused by this frightful decline; having been empowered by law to undertake the task of "preventing and controlling surpluses in any agricultural commodity," it tried to stabilize prices by buying wheat during the most discouraging stages of the collapse. But it succeeded chiefly in accumulating surpluses; for it came into conflict with a law older than the Agricultural Marketing Act—the law of supply and demand. When the dust cleared away the Farm Board had upward of two hundred million bushels of wheat on its hands, yet prices had nevertheless fallen all the way to the cellar; and although Mr. Legge's successor claimed that the Board's purchases had saved from failure hundreds of banks which had loaned money on the wheat crop, that was scant comfort to the agonized farmers. A terrific drought during the summer of 1930 intensified the prostration of many communities. Once more the farm population seemed pursued by a malignant fate. They had benefited little from Coolidge Prosperity, and now they were the worst sufferers of all from the nightmare of 1930-31.

Meanwhile industrial production was declining steadily. By the end of 1930 business had sunk to 28 per cent below normal. Stock prices, after rallying slightly during the summer of 1930, turned downward once more in September, and by December a long series of shudders of liquidation had brought the price-level well below the post-panic level of the year before. Alas! the poor Bull Market! Radio common, which had climbed to such dizzy heights in 1928 and 1929, retraced its steps down to—yes, and past—the point at which it had begun its sensational advance less than three years before; and in many another stock the retreat was even longer and less orderly. The drastic shrinkage in brokers' loans testified to the number of trading accounts closed out unhappily. The broker had ceased to be a man of wonderful mystery in the eyes of his acquaintances; he was approached nowadays with friendly

tact, as one who must not be upset by unfortunate references
to the market. Several brokerage houses tumbled; blue-sky
investment companies formed during the happy bull-market
days went to smash, disclosing miserable tales of rascality; over
a thousand banks caved in during 1930, as a result of the
marking down both of real estate and of securities; and in
December occurred the largest bank failure in American
financial history, the fall of the ill-named Bank of the United
States in New York. Unemployment grew steadily, until by the
end of 1930 the number of jobless was figured at somewhere in
the neighborhood of six million; apple salesmen stood on the
street corner, executives and clerks and factory hands lay
awake wondering when they, too, would be thrown off, and
contributed anxiously to funds for the workless; and a stroller
on Broadway, seeing a queue forming outside a theater where
Charlie Chaplin was opening in "City Lights," asked in some
concern, "What's that—a bread-line or a bank?"

Early in 1931 there were faint signs of improvement and the
deflated stock market took cheer, but by March the uncertain
dawn was seen to have been false, and throughout the spring
months the decline was renewed. Production ebbed once more;
commodity prices fell; stock prices faded until the panic levels
of November, 1929, looked lofty by comparison; and discouragement deepened as dividends were reduced or omitted and
failures multiplied. Would the bottom never be reached?

The rosy visions of 1929 had not been utterly effaced: it was
significant that the numbers of holders of common stock in
most of the large corporations increased during 1930. Investors stubbornly expected the tide to turn some day, and they
wanted to be there when it happened. Yet the shock of the
drop into the apparently bottomless pit of depression was
telling on their nerves. "There are far too many people, from
business men to laborers," declared an advertisement inserted
in the New York papers by the *Evening World* in December,
1930, "who are giving a too eager ear to wild rumors and
spiteful gossip tending to destroy confidence and create an
atmosphere of general distrust. The victims of vague fear, on
the street and in the market place, are a menace to the community. . . . They are the feeders of that mob psychology which
creates the spirit of panic."

"Mob psychology"! There had been mob psychology in the

days of the Big Bull Market, too. Action and reaction—the picture was now complete.

Two years earlier, when Mr. Hoover had discussed the abolition of poverty, he had prudently added the words "with God's help." It must have seemed to him now that God had prepared for him a cruelly ironic jest. Mr. Hoover was hardly more responsible for the downfall of the business hopes of the nineteen-twenties than for the invasion of Belgium; yet he who had won renown by administering relief to the Belgians had now been called upon to administer relief to the Americans, lest the poverty of which he had once spoken so lightly make tragic inroads among them. He was an able economist and an able leader of men in public crises; yet his attempts to lead business out of depression had come to conspicuous failure. Other business men of wide experience had been as unconvinced as he that the deflation would have to be prolonged and painful; yet when business was on the road to ruin, these men forgot their own former optimism and blamed the President for lack of foresight, lack of leadership, lack of even elementary common sense. They had not been forced to put themselves unforgettably on record; he had. They were not expected to reintroduce prosperity; he was. By the spring of 1931 the President's reputation had declined along with prices and profits to a new low level, and the Democrats, cheered by striking gains in the November elections, were casting a hopeful eye toward 1932. Observing the plight of Mr. Hoover, Calvin Coolidge, syndicating two hundred daily words of mingled hard sense and soft soap from his secure haven at Northampton, must have thanked Heaven that he had not been chosen to run for President in 1928; and Governor Smith must have felt like the man who just missed the train which went off the end of the open drawbridge. Doubtless the Administration's campaign of optimism had been overzealous, but Mr. Hoover's greatest mistake had been in getting himself elected for the 1928-32 term.

The truth was that what had taken place since the Big Bull Market was more than a cyclical drop in prices and production; it was a major change in the national economy. There were encouraging signs even when things were at their worst: the absence of serious conflict between capital and labor, for instance, and the ability of the Federal Reserve

System to prevent a money panic even when banks were toppling. Doubtless prosperity was due ultimately to return in full
flood. But it could not be the same sort of prosperity as in the
nineteen-twenties: inevitably it would rest on different bases,
favor different industries, and arouse different forms of enthusiasm and hysteria. The panic had written finis to a chapter
of American economic history.

[2]

There were other signs of change, too, as the nineteen-thirties began. Some of them had begun long before the panic;
others developed some time after it; but taken together they
revealed striking alterations in the national temper and the
ways of American life.

One could hardly walk a block in any American city or town
without noticing some of them. The women's clothes, for
instance. The skirt length had come down with stock prices.
Dresses for daytime wear were longer, if only by a few inches;
evening dresses swept the ground. Defenders of the knee-
length skirt had split the air with their protests, but the new
styles had won out. Bobbed hair was progressively losing favor.
Frills, ruffles, and flounces were coming in again, and the
corset manufacturers were once more learning to smile. A
measure of formality was gradually returning: witness the
long white gloves, the masculine silk hats and swallow-tail
coats. Nor did these changes follow any mere whim of manufacturers and stylists. Manufacturers and stylists may issue
decrees, but not unless the public is willing to follow does the
fashion actually change. Did not the clothing business try to
bring back the long skirt early in the nineteen-twenties, but
without success? The long skirts and draperies and white
gloves of 1930 and 1931 were the outward signs of a subtle
change in the relations between the sexes. No longer was it the
American woman's dearest ambition to simulate a flat-
breasted, spindle-legged, carefree, knowing adolescent in a
long-waisted child's frock. The red-hot baby had gone out of
style. Fashion advertisements in 1930 and 1931 depicted a
different type, more graceful, more piquant, more subtly alluring; decorum and romance began to come once more within
the range of possibilities.

What the fashions suggested was borne out by a variety of other evidence. The revolution in manners and morals had at least reached an armistice.

Not that there was any general return to the old conventions which had been overthrown in the nineteen-twenties. The freedom so desperately won by the flappers of the now graying "younger generation" had not been lost, and it was difficult to detect much real change in the uses to which this freedom was put. What had departed was the excited sense that taboos were going to smash, that morals were being made over or annihilated, and that the whole code of behavior was in flux. The wages of sin had become stabilized at a lower level. Gone, too, at least in some degree, was that hysterical preoccupation with sex which had characterized the Post-war Decade. Books about sex and conversation about sex were among the commodities suffering from overproduction. Robert Benchley expressed a widely prevalent opinion when he wrote in his dramatic page in the *New Yorker*, late in 1930, "I am now definitely ready to announce that Sex, as a theatrical property, is as tiresome as the Old Mortgage, and that I don't want to hear it mentioned ever again. . . . I am sick of rebellious youth and I am sick of Victorian parents and I don't care if all the little girls in all sections of the United States get ruined or want to get ruined or keep from getting ruined. All I ask is: don't write plays about it and ask me to sit through them."

Apparently a great many playgoers and readers were beginning to feel as Mr. Benchley did. George Jean Nathan noted the arrival on Broadway of a new crop of romantic and poetic playwrights, and reported that "the hard-boiled school of drama and literature . . . is all too evidently on the wane." Henry Seidel Canby, writing in the *Saturday Review of Literature*, came to the same conclusion. Reticence had returned from exile; indeed, even before the Post-war Decade closed, "Journey's End," which managed to make war real without the wholesale introduction of profanity or prostitutes, had been applauded with something like relief. The contrast between "Journey's End" and "What Price Glory?" was suggestive of the change in the popular temper. The success of such novels as *The Good Companions, Angel Pavement,* and *The Water-Gypsies* was perhaps a further indication of the change. There were enough exceptions to the rule to remind one that easy generalizations are dangerous, but two conclusions seemed almost inescapable: sex was no longer front-page news, and glamour was coming into its own again.

Nor, for that matter, were people quite so positive now that every manifestation of Victorianism and of the eighteen-nineties was to be laughed at uproariously by "moderns." Collectors were beginning to look with less scornful eyes upon Victorian furniture, and people who had read *The Mauve Decade* and the debunking biographies with an air of condescension toward pre-war conventions found themselves looking with wistful eyes, only a few years later, at William Gillette's revival of "Sherlock Holmes" and at the sentimentalization of the 'nineties in "Sweet Adeline."

The young people of the early nineteen-thirties presumably knew just as much about life as those of the early and middle twenties, but they were less conspicuously and self-consciously intent upon showing the world what advanced young devils they were. LaMar Warrick, who taught at a large Middle Western university, reported in *Harper's* in the autumn of 1930 that the biological novels of Aldous Huxley, the biological psychology of John B. Watson, and the biological philosophies of Bertrand Russell were "fast becoming . . . out of date" among the students in her classes. She found the new younger generation tiring of what one of these students called "a modernism which leaves you washed out and cynical at thirty." A staff reporter for the *Des Moines Sunday Register* queried professors and undergraduates at three colleges in Iowa as to the validity of Mrs. Warrick's contentions, and an impressive majority of those with whom he talked told him that what he had said held true in Iowa as well as in Illinois. One young Iowan remarked that at his college there was not now a single "Flaming Mamie" who could be compared with "the girls who five years ago were wearing leopard-skin coats, driving expensive roadsters, and generally raising hell." That hell-raising was actually on the decline seemed almost too much to expect of inflammable human nature; but at least the burden of testimony suggested that ostentatious hell-raising was not quite so certain a way to social renown as in the heyday of flapperism.

The revolt of the highbrows had spent its force. The voice of H. L. Mencken no longer shook the country from Provincetown to Hollywood, and people who were always denouncing George F. Babbitt and the dangers of standardization were beginning to seem a little tiresome. Many of the once distraught intellectuals were now wondering if life was such a ghastly farce as they had supposed. The philosophical and literary theme of futility had been almost played out. Even Hemingway, whom the young *emigrés* to Montparnasse in 1926 or thereabouts had hailed as a major prophet of the emptiness of everything, struck a new note, almost a romantic note, in his *Farewell to Arms*, published late in 1929; this novel told the story not of a series of shallow and fleeting passions, but of a great love which possessed the very values of whose future Joseph Wood Krutch had despaired. Lewis Mumford declared in 1931 that Mr. Krutch should have realized that civilization had merely been molting a dead skin, not going into dissolution; speaking for the young intellectuals of the nineteen-thirties, Mr. Mumford announced that "the mood of defeat is dead. We have not yet hauled down our flag, because, like Whitman's Little Captain, we can still say collectively, *We have not yet begun to fight*." Here again, easy generalizations are dangerous; yet one doubts if any representative of the intelligentsia could have spoken of fighting in 1925 and felt that he was representing the opinion of his up-to-date contemporaries. The fashionable posture in 1925 had not been belligerent; it had been the posture of graceful acquiescence in defeat. Now the mood of intellectual disillusionment was passing; the garment of hopeless resignation began to look a little worn at the elbows.

Whether religion was regaining any of its lost prestige was doubtful. The net gain in membership of all the churches in the United States was only a trifle over one-tenth of one per cent in 1930—the smallest gain since Dr. H. K. Carroll began his annual compilation in 1890. But at least the religious scene had changed. The Fundamentalists and Modernists were tiring of their battle. Dayton had become ancient history. The voice of science no longer seemed to deny so loudly and authoritatively the existence of spiritual values in the universe; and when readers of Eddington and Jeans concluded that there was a crack in the air-tight system of scientific materialism after all, and the modernist clergy hastened to report that the crack was wide enough to admit God, their assertion attracted less excited rebuttal than formerly, if only because the new scientific philosophies were too hard to understand and the argument had been going on for so many weary years. The voice of psychology, once so deafening and bewildering, had especially lost authority; it was evident that neither Freud nor Watson had infallible answers for all the problems of humanity, and that the psychologists were no more united than the Democrats. Those who watched the religious life of the colleges as the nineteen-twenties gave way to the nineteen-thirties doubted if the ranks of the agnostics were decreasing, but found, nevertheless, a change in the general attitude: fewer young men and women bristled with hostility toward any and all religion, and there was a more widespread desire, even among the doubters, to find some ground for a positive and fruitful interpretation of life. What was true of the colleges was presumably true of the country as a whole: although the churches were hardly gaining ground, neither, perhaps, was religion losing it. Like manners and morals, religion showed signs of stabilization on a different basis. Whether the change was more than temporary remained to be seen.

The great American public was just as susceptible to fads as ever. Since the panicky autumn of 1929, millions of radios had resounded every evening at seven o'clock with the voices of Freeman F. Gosden and Charles J. Correll, better known as Amos 'n' Andy; "I'se regusted" and "Check and double check" had made their way into the common speech, and Andy's troubles with the lunchroom and Madam Queen had become only less real to the national mind than the vicissitudes of business and the stock market. In September, 1930, the Department of Commerce had found at least one thoroughly prosperous business statistic to announce: there were almost 30,000 miniature golf courses in operation, representing an investment of $125,000,000, and many of them were earning 300 per cent a month. If the American people were buying nothing else in the summer of 1930, they were at least buying the right to putt a golf ball over a surface of crushed cottonseed and through a tin pipe.

Yet the noble art of ballyhoo, which had flourished so successfully in the nineteen-twenties, had lost something of its vigor. Admiral Byrd's flight to the South Pole made him a hero second only to Lindbergh in the eyes of the country at large, but in the larger centers of population there was manifest a slight tendency to yawn: his exploit had been over-publicized, and heroism, however gallant, lost something of its spontaneous charm when it was subjected to scientific management and syndicated in daily dispatches. A few months after Byrd reached the South Pole, Coste and Bellonte made the first completely successful non-stop westward flight across the Atlantic; yet at the end of 1930 it was probable that fewer Americans could have identified the names of Coste and Bellonte than the name of Ruth Elder. Heroism in the air was commonplace by this time. Endurance flyers still circled about day after day in quest of new records, but they were finding the crowds more sparse and the profits in headlines and in cash less impressive. As for Shipwreck Kelly, premier flagpole sitter of the nineteen-twenties, he was reported to have descended from the summit of the Paramount Building in 1930 because no one seemed to be watching. Bathing-beauty contests? Something had happened to them, too. Atlantic City had given up its annual beauty pageant in 1927. And in all 1930 there was not one first-class murder trial of nation-wide interest, not one first-class prize-fight, not one great new sporting hero crowned.

Indeed, a sporting era was passing. Rickard, who had known how to surround two heavyweight fighters with a two-million-and-a-half-dollar crowd, was dead; pugilism had fallen again into shady repute. Dempsey was in retirement. Tunney was reading Shakespeare. Ruth still hammered out home runs, but Jones and Tilden had both turned professional, and Knute Rockne, the greatest football coach of the nineteen-twenties, had been killed in an airplane accident, to the official regret of the President of the United States. With the passing of Grover Whalen to the aisles of Wanamaker's, New York City, the fountain-head of ballyhoo, had lost some of its lavish taste for welcoming heroes to the Western Hemisphere; the precipitation of ticker tape and torn-up telephone books in lower Broadway in 1930 was the smallest in years. Perhaps hard times were responsible for the decline of the hero racket. But perhaps there was more to it than that. The ballyhoo technic possessed no longer the freshness of youth. Times had changed.

The post-war apathy toward politics and everything political continued apparently undiminished. In the autumn of 1929, when Ramsay MacDonald came to America with a message of peace and good will strikingly reminiscent of the preachments of Woodrow Wilson, he was received with astonishing enthusiasm, and for a time it seemed as if idealism were about to manifest itself once more as in the days before the coming of complacent normalcy. The mood persisted long enough for the London Treaty for renewed limitation of naval armaments to pass the Senate with flying colors, much to the credit of President Hoover and Secretary Stimson; otherwise, however, cynicism and hopelessness still prevailed. Chicago threw out the notorious Thompson and the Tammany scandals in New York City aroused some resentment; but the general attitude as the summer of 1931 approached still seemed to be "What's the use of trying to do anything about it?" and the racketeer still flourished like a hardy weed, as did the bootlegger, the rum-runner, and the prohibition issue.

But if the country still expected as little as ever of politics and politicians, and still submitted to the rule of the gangster, at least it was somewhat less satisfied with *laissez-faire* for business than in the days of Calvin Coolidge. The public attitude during the depression of 1930-31 presented an instructive contrast with that during previous depressions. The radical on the soap-box was far less terrifying than in the days of the Big Red Scare. Communist propaganda made amazingly little headway, all things considered, and attracted amazingly little attention; for one reason, perhaps, because many of the largest employers met the crisis with far-sighted intelligence, maintaining the wage-rate wherever possible and reducing hours rather than throwing off employees; for another reason, because during the Big Bull Market innumerable potential radicals had received from the stock-market page a conservative financial education. Naturally, however, there was a general sense that something had gone wrong with individualistic capitalism and must be set right—how could it be otherwise, with the existing system dragging millions of families down toward hunger and want?

There was a new interest in the Russian experiment, not unmixed with sober fear. Maurice Hindus's *Humanity Uprooted*, which had come out during the month of the panic and had sold very slowly at first, became a best seller during the gloomy autumn of 1930. In the summer of 1929 Russia had seemed as remote as China; in 1931, with bread-lines on the streets, the Russian Five-Year Plan became a topic of anxious American interest. The longer the paralysis of industry lasted—and how it lasted!—the more urgent became the demand for some measure of American economic planning which might prevent such disasters from recurring, without handing over undue power to an incompetent or venal bureaucracy.

With the return of full prosperity this demand would doubtless weaken; nevertheless the inevitable slow drift toward collectivism, interrupted during the bumptiously successful nineteen-twenties, promised to be haltingly resumed once more. Despite the obvious distaste of the country for state socialism or anything suggesting it, there was no denying that the economic system had proved itself too complex, and machine production too powerful, to continue unbridled. The chief difficulty, perhaps, was to find any persons or groups wise enough to know how to apply the bridle and persuasive enough to be allowed to keep their grip upon it. The experience of the past few years had given no very convincing evidence of the ability of financiers or economists to diagnose the condition of the country's business, or of the emotional public to respond to treatment. Yet there stood the problem, a problem hardly dreamed of by most Americans when Coolidge Prosperity was blooming; and as 1931 dragged along, month after month, without any immediate promise of business revival, no other problem seemed to the country half so vital or so pressing.

[3]

Many of these specific signs of change were of uncertain significance; possibly some of them were illusory. Yet the United States of 1931 was a different place from the United States of the Post-war Decade; there was no denying that. An old order was giving place to new.

Soon the mists of distance would soften the outlines of the nineteen-twenties, and men and women, looking over the pages of a book such as this, would smile at the memory of those charming, crazy days when the radio was a thrilling novelty, and girls wore bobbed hair and knee-length skirts, and a transatlantic flyer became a god overnight, and common stocks were about to bring us all to a lavish Utopia. They would forget, perhaps, the frustrated hopes that followed the war, the aching disillusionment of the hard-boiled era, its oily scandals, its spiritual paralysis, the harshness of its gaiety; they would talk about the good old days. . . .

What was to come in the nineteen-thirties?

Only one thing could one be sure of. It would not be repetition. The stream of time often doubles on its course, but always it makes for itself a new channel.

APPENDIX

Sources and Obligations

I am under an immense debt to certain writers upon whose books I have drawn extensively in this chronicle. Naturally I have made frequent use, not only in Chapter Five, but elsewhere, of the extraordinarily varied and precise information collected in *Middletown*, that remarkable sociological study of an American city by Robert S. Lynd and Helen Merrell Lynd; I do not see how any conscientious historian of the Post-war Decade could afford to neglect this mine of material. The concluding chapters of *The Rise of American Civilization*, by Charles A. Beard and Mary R. Beard, have been helpful at many points, particularly in the preparation of my short account of the Washington Conference and the situation which led up to it. William Allen White's biography of Woodrow Wilson and his extended portraits of Warren G. Harding and Calvin Coolidge in *Masks in a Pageant* have been especially useful not only for the specific information which they contain, but also for their suggestive interpretations of these three Presidents. To Charles Merz I am indebted for many facts and conclusions about the prohibition experiment, which I have drawn from *The Dry Decade*, his admirably impartial account of the first ten years of prohibition; and also for other facts assembled by him in his other books, *And Then Came Ford* and *The Great American Bandwagon*. Finally, I have made constant use of the *World Almanac*, which is responsible for many of the statistics embodied in this volume; of the *New York Times Index;* and above all of the files of the *New York Times* itself in the New York Public Library. A book of this sort must inevitably rely very largely on contemporary newspaper and magazine sources; the newspapers are invaluable not only for their news accounts of important events, but also for the light which their advertising columns and picture sections throw upon the fashions, ideas, and general atmosphere of the period.

The account of the beginnings of radio broadcasting in Chapters One and Four is based partly upon an address given on April 21, 1928, by H. P. Davis, vice-president of the Westinghouse Electric and Manufacturing Company, before the Harvard Business School.

In the preparation of Chapter Two ("Back to Normalcy"), I found Ray Stannard Baker's *Woodrow Wilson and World Settlement* especially valuable for its exhaustive account of Wilson's part in the Peace Conference. Mr. Baker's findings have of course been compared with those of Colonel House, Secretary Lansing, and others. Lodge's secret memorandum to Henry White was disclosed in Allan Nevins's biography of White. The description of Woodrow Wilson in the last days of his life is based on a personal visit to him in November, 1923.

In Chapter Three ("The Big Red Scare"), I owe many of the facts about the Palmer raids to the account in Zechariah Chafee's *Freedom of Speech*. Senator Husting's pledge was quoted on the cover of the *New Republic* at the time of the coal strike of 1919. Much of the material about the superpatriots is derived from a series of articles contributed to the *New Republic* in 1924 by Sidney Howard. The account of the Chicago race-riot is based on the careful study embodied in Charles S. Johnson's *The Negro in Chicago;* and the account of the Wall Street explosion contains many facts from an article by Sidney Sutherland in *Liberty* for April 26, 1930.

In Chapter Four ("America Convalescent") the facts cited about the Sacco-Vanzetti propaganda came largely from a series of contemporary news stories in the *New York World*.

Chapter Five ("The Revolution in Manners and Morals")

draws freely upon *Middletown,* as previously stated; upon Professor Paul H. Nystrom's *Economics of Fashion;* and upon Walter Lippmann's *A Preface to Morals* and Joseph Wood Krutch's *The Modern Temper.*

In writing Chapter Six ("Harding and the Scandals") I have made much use of White's *Masks in a Pageant* and Beard's *The Rise of American Civilization,* as stated above; of M. E. Ravage's *The Story of Teapot Dome,* a lively account of the progress of the oil cases up to 1924; and of Bruce Bliven's series of articles on the Ohio Gang in the *New Republic.* The quotation from Harry M. Daugherty which appears at the beginning of the chapter is printed as arranged and repunctuated by Mr. Bliven in one of his *New Republic* articles. George G. Chandler of the Philadelphia law firm of Montgomery & Mac-Cracken gave me valuable help in connection with the account of the oil scandals.

Chapter Seven ("Coolidge Prosperity") is based in considerable degree upon the facts and generalizations in Stuart Chase's concise book, *Prosperity, Fact or Myth,* and also cites numerous figures drawn from *Recent Economic Changes.* The sections on the supersalesmen and on religion and business embody a quantity of material set forth by that able student of the ways of business men, Jesse Rainsford Sprague, in various articles in *Harper's Magazine.* Some of the data about the service clubs I owe to Charles W. Ferguson, who gathered them in the preparation of his forthcoming book, *The Joiners;* some of the facts about business courses and business methods in the universities come from Abraham Flexner's *Universities: American, English, German.*

The basic idea of Chapter Eight ("The Ballyhoo Years") is Silas Bent's, as any reader of his book, *Ballyhoo,* will be aware. I have taken many facts from that book. The statistical data on the status of religion during the decade are drawn from the Preliminary Report on Organized Religion for the President's Study of Social Trends, by C. Luther Fry, to which Robert S. Lynd was good enough to give me access. The account of the Dayton trial makes considerable use of Arthur Garfield Hays's narrative in *Let Freedom Ring.* Richard F. Simon, of Simon & Schuster, provided me with much material about the cross-word-puzzle craze, and W. B. Miller, formerly of the *Louis-*

ville Courier-Journal, told me at first hand the story of the Floyd Collins episode.

I am under special obligation both to Walter Lippmann's *A Preface to Morals* and to Joseph Wood Krutch's *The Modern Temper* for their remarkable analyses of disillusionment in the nineteen-twenties; the discussion of disillusion in Chapter Nine ("The Revolt of the Highbrows") could never have been written without the aid of Mr. Krutch's penetrating book.

Chapter Ten ("Alcohol and Al Capone") makes especially lavish use of four sources: Charles Merz's *The Dry Decade*, the Wickersham Report, Fred D. Pasley's fascinating *Al Capone*, and *It's a Racket*, by Gordon L. Hostetter and Thomas Quinn Beesley.

Many figures and incidents and the quotation from Walter C. Hill in Chapter Eleven ("Home, Sweet Florida") are from two articles by Homer B. Vanderblue in the *Journal of Land and Public Utility Economics*, Volume 3. Among other sources, Gertrude Mathews Shelby's "Florida Frenzy" in *Harper's Magazine* for January, 1926, was especially valuable. The data about rentals of New York City office space were given me by the real-estate officer of a large local financial institution.

In Chapter Thirteen ("Crash!") I have cited a number of facts set forth by Richard Whitney in an address on "The Work of the New York Stock Exchange in the Panic of 1929," given before the Boston Association of Stock Exchange Firms on June 10, 1930.

The optimistic statements by leaders of the Hoover Administration, cited in the last chapter ("Aftermath"), were collected in an article by James Truslow Adams ("Presidential Prosperity") in *Harper's Magazine* for August, 1930.

These are only a few of the innumerable sources drawn upon in the book; I single them out for mention only because they are not cited in the text or because my debt to them is especially large.

I am exceedingly grateful to numerous friends who have been kind enough either to hunt up material for me or to take the time to read and criticize parts of the manuscript; particularly to Rollin Alger Sawyer of the New York Public Library, Arthur Besse, John G. MacKenty, Earle Bailie, C. Alison

Scully, Myra Richardson, Gordon Aymar, Agnes Rogers Hyde, Stuart Chase, Robert K. Haas, Arthur C. Holden, and Emily Linnard Cobb. I must especially thank Charles Merz for encouraging me, at the outset, to undertake what has proved an endlessly fascinating task. And finally I must record the fact that up to the time of her death, my wife, Dorothy Penrose Allen, helped me more than I can ever acknowledge.

FREDERICK LEWIS ALLEN

Scarsdale, New York
June, 1931

Index